Palgrave Socio-Legal Studies

Series Editor
Dave Cowan
University of Bristol Law School
Bristol, UK

The Palgrave Socio-Legal Studies series is a developing series of monographs and textbooks featuring cutting edge work which, in the best tradition of socio-legal studies, reach out to a wide international audience.

More information about this series at
http://www.palgrave.com/gp/series/14679

Asher Flynn • Arie Freiberg

Plea Negotiations

Pragmatic Justice in an Imperfect World

palgrave
macmillan

Asher Flynn
Monash University
Clayton, VIC, Australia

Arie Freiberg
Monash University
Clayton, VIC, Australia

Palgrave Socio-Legal Studies
ISBN 978-3-030-06475-4 ISBN 978-3-319-92630-8 (eBook)
https://doi.org/10.1007/978-3-319-92630-8

Printed on acid-free paper

This Palgrave Macmillan imprint is published by the registered company Springer Nature Switzerland AG
The registered company address is: Gewerbestrasse 11, 6330 Cham, Switzerland

To Bernard Freiberg 1925–2017
Who would have been quietly proud

Foreword

In many countries today, courtroom observers will see a small number of trials and a much larger number of sentencing hearings consequent upon a guilty plea where the broad outcome has been determined beforehand but with no indication of how the plea arrangement has been reached. In most of this guilty plea group, the outcome has been determined through an "agreement" reached between the prosecution and defence lawyers in a practice variously referred to as "plea negotiation", "plea bargaining" or "state-induced guilty pleas". Although a lot has been written about the desirability, utility and constitutionality of this guilty plea process, the way in which the settlement comes about is heavily under-researched. This excellent study fills a much needed gap in the literature and, through its astute information collection, penetrating analysis and thoughtful reading of data, provides a bench mark for future socio-legal researchers.

As I write, the criminal justice process in the UK is in a crisis of a depth unparalleled in modern history. Late disclosure of prosecution evidence in scheduled trials has destroyed the credibility of key state witnesses. Trials involving allegations of rape and human trafficking have collapsed; hundreds of other serious prosecutions have been abandoned; thousands more are now subject to official review. Prosecution non-disclosure appears to be rife, perhaps more so than at any time before recent "austerity" measures. The Attorney-General, the Metropolitan Police and the Crown Prosecution Service are vying with each other at the head of the queue to offer public apologies. Instead of justice being done and being seen to be done, the public perception is that justice is being done in. All of this is occurring against a background of institutional pressure increasingly placed upon defendants to plead guilty to save the state the time and expense of an adversarial trial.

A window into how legal practitioners respond to such an environment and how they actually negotiate in a guilty plea setting could not, therefore, have come at a better time.

In this book, Asher Flynn and Arie Freiberg provide a detailed account of the plea negotiation process as it operates in Victoria, Australia, where, as in the UK, the rationales of austerity—efficiency, economy and effectiveness—enshroud the courtroom actors. The study focuses on a sample of cases that had evidence of some form of negotiation (a term the respondents generally preferred as against "bargaining" and its underhand connotations) leading to a withdrawal of charges generally accompanied by a reduction in both the number and seriousness of the remaining charges. In addition, substantial interviews have been conducted with the main players, defence and prosecution lawyers and judges. Empirical data has been collected meticulously and presented in a nuanced way. Utilising a mixture of qualitative and quantitative methods, information drawn from de-identified case files is inter-laced with material derived from sensitive interviews with the participants to elucidate the negotiation process.

So what's to be said about plea negotiation that cannot be found in scores of other books and hundreds of learned articles on this process? As it turns out, a great deal! Although the authors offer insightful suggestions for re-framing the official approach to plea negotiation (thereby laying the ground for further debate), the emphasis throughout is on opening up this closed world to give an understanding of the ways in which the actors conduct themselves and make sense of this negotiation environment. It is here that the authors give insights into how decent people do their best under constrained circumstances and explain their thought process, conflicts and choices. Of course, despite the best efforts of the researchers, some shadows remain. Resource constraints prevented involvement of defendants and victims. There are also intriguing hints of puzzles yet to be resolved. Thus, for example, while half the respondents indicated that bail was an element of negotiation, the case files were completely silent as to this. In another instance, a judge said: "I can provide examples, but I won't." But the overall picture is revealing, vivid and entirely convincing.

The forms of plea negotiation (14 are described) in Victoria are more varied, complex and situationally specific than has been commonly understood. Despite the lack of formal regulation, there is a framework of informal rules and procedures known primarily to those within the legal community with some indications of a closed world suspicious of "outsiders".

The files and interviews suggest that negotiations are not simple, ill-considered or precipitate, thereby giving some comfort to those who may be concerned that defence practitioners do not have their clients' best interests in mind when engaging in negotiations. The reader hears in rich detail the authentic voice of the legal actors and learns the strategies and procedures they employ, how they understand and justify their role in a process that, while not lawless, rests in large measure on pragmatism and the stresses and challenges that such a context necessarily brings. It is in these accounts that a major contribution to the literature is made.

There is much to promote further discussion and, hopefully, more research. One concern explicated by the authors, not confined to but arguably exacerbated in an informal setting, is that although negotiations were said to turn on standard criteria (the strength of the evidence, the public interest and the client's interests), the majority of respondents considered that the outcome of negotiations depended upon personality—which prosecutor or defence practitioner (or indeed judge) was involved—and their respective skill sets. Interestingly, as between lower and higher courts, in pointing to the more serious crimes, participants implied that it was necessary to "pay more attention to negotiations" and "negotiate much more thoroughly and much more based on the evidence" in the higher courts which might imply a differential—even idiosyncratic—form of justice well-attested in other jurisdictions. Again, seemingly authoritative court rulings which might inhibit the plea negotiation process turn out to have had a limited effect upon these practitioners. The incentives to negotiate appear strong enough to bypass higher court rulings.

Although the authors come down on the side of reforming the plea negotiation process and pay respect to the dedicated professionals working within a constrained environment, this is not a proselytising account. It is more about gene sequencing: uncovering the roles of prosecution and defence lawyers and judges in a plea negotiation which takes place within an imperfect environment; and it does this very well indeed. Moreover, the study is far from limited to contextualising the process within a changing criminal justice environment. Instead, it locates detailed and insightful empirical findings of one jurisdiction within the broader international jurisprudence keeping a constant and even-handed dialogue with both critics and defenders of plea negotiation.

This perceptive, insightful and stimulating book will accordingly have wide appeal in the international community of scholars and practitioners, even those who are unaccustomed to compromising their views!

Kowloon Tong, Hong Kong
February 2018

Mike McConville

Acknowledgements

This book arose out of a Criminology Research Council-funded project *Negotiated Guilty Pleas: An Empirical Analysis* (CRG51/13–14). We are thankful for the funding contributions and support of the Criminology Research Council (administered through the then Australian Institute of Criminology) and our institution, Monash University, to enable this research to be conducted.

The idea behind the study informing this book arose from research Asher had completed as part of her doctoral thesis, and several projects Arie has been involved with as part of his role as Chair of the Victorian Sentencing Advisory Council. But completing the research would not have been possible without the assistance of a number of people and organisations. First and foremost, we wish to thank all the participants involved in the study for giving up their valuable time to contribute their perspectives and experiences in interviews, group discussions and consultations. Your perspectives provided a rich source of information to shed light on plea negotiations for those outside the legal community. We are grateful for the immense support of Victoria Legal Aid, with a special thanks to Gabriela Pulczynski, Helen Fatouros and Rosy Jolic. We also acknowledge the support of Victoria Police—in particular, Inspector Richard Koo, Acting Senior Sergeant Sherril Handley, and Dr David Ballek—and the assistance and feedback offered from the Office of Public Prosecutions by the former Director of Public Prosecutions, Mr John Champion SC, Vicki Prapas and John Cain. We would also like to thank and acknowledge Monash University Law students, Monica Lee, Jake Collom and Jacob Uren for their assistance in de-identifying the case files. This was a mammoth, sometimes tedious, but incredibly valuable task, and the preliminary work you undertook formed the basis for the unique contribution this research has made to the field.

We had several research assistants across the life of the project, including Sophie Norman, Kate Burns, Mary Iliadis, Peta Murphy and Louise Kyle—thank you all for your involvement. A special thank you also to Madeline Ulbrick, who provided continued, high-quality research assistance throughout the final stages of the project and identified a range of relevant literature for the book.

We thank Professor Mike McConville for contributing the Preface to this book. His pioneering work on the topic of plea negotiations has paved the way for many researchers in the following decades.

We would also like to express our gratitude to the editorial team at Palgrave for their support in developing the book to publication, particularly Josie Taylor. Thank you also to Julia Farrell for her editorial assistance on previous versions of this manuscript.

Finally, we would like to thank our colleagues for their ongoing comradery, and our families and partners for their support, encouragement and patience. In particular, Asher would like to thank her loving partner, Mark, their beautiful son, Henry, and her parents, Pamela and Allen, without whom she could not have dedicated the time to complete this important work. Arie would like to thank his long-suffering partner Monica Pfeffer for her forbearance and understanding of an all too often absent spouse.

Contents

List of Abbreviations

ABI	Acquired brain injury
ABS	Australian Bureau of Statistics
ACT	Australian Capital Territory
AFP	Australian Federal Police
Barbaro	*Barbaro v The Queen; Zirilli v The Queen* [2014] HCA 2
CCO	Community Correction Order
CCTV	Closed-circuit television
CDPP	Commonwealth Department of Public Prosecutions
CISP	Court Integrated Services Program
CMIA	*Crimes (Mental Impairment and Unfitness to Be Tried) Act 1997* (Vic)
CPS	Crown Prosecution Service
CREDIT	Court Referral and Evaluation for Drug Intervention and Treatment
CTH	Commonwealth
DPP	Director of Public Prosecutions
ERAs	Early Resolution Advocates
ERU	Early Resolution Unit
LIV	Law Institute of Victoria
MacNeil-Brown	*R v MacNeil-Brown* [2014] HCA 2 [at 47]
NSW	New South Wales
NT	Northern Territory
ODPP	Office of the Department of Public Prosecutions
OPP	Office of Public Prosecutions
PRAs	Principal Resolution Advocates
QC	Queen's Counsel
QLD	Queensland
RCFV	Royal Commission into Family Violence

S 6AAA	Section 6AAA of the *Sentencing Act 1991* (Vic)
SA	South Australia
SAC	Sentencing Advisory Council
SC	Senior Counsel
TAS	Tasmania
TES	Total effective sentence
UK	United Kingdom
US	United States
VALS	Victorian Aboriginal Legal Service
VIC	Victoria
VLA	Victoria Legal Aid
VLRC	Victorian Law Reform Commission
WA	Western Australia

List of Figures

1
Introduction

An increasing climate of austerity and the growing influence of managerialist ideologies, across the Western world and elsewhere,[1] have contributed to changing government priorities pertaining to the operation of criminal justice systems. As a result, there has been a renewed focus on "timeliness" and "efficiency". Within these "pragmatic" systems of justice, the most common way of resolving a case is through a defendant entering a plea of guilty. Whatever public perceptions may be regarding the centrality of a contested trial in the criminal justice process, the reality is that in many jurisdictions, including Australia, the most frequent method of case finalisation is not one that follows a fiercely fought battle between guilt and innocence, justice and injustice, and state and defendant, but by a plea of guilty. And in the majority of cases, the guilty plea is the result of a process of negotiation between the prosecution and defence, which takes place in the shadow of the trial (Bushway et al. 2014). In this regard, the negotiated guilty plea has become an everyday form of justice and "an accepted element of criminal prosecutions" (Royal Commission 2017a: 322). Indeed, negotiations are now regarded as "a legitimate means of resolving criminal litigation … fundamental to the efficient operation of an under-resourced system … [in which] the prosecution and defence exchange risks and benefits to achieve mutually satisfactory goals" (Leivore 2004, cited in Royal Commission 2017a: 322).

Negotiated guilty pleas,[2] also referred to as "plea negotiations", "charge bargaining", "state-induced guilty pleas" (McConville and Marsh 2014) and "negotiated resolutions", are processes whereby a defendant will plead guilty in exchange for agreed concessions from the prosecution. While commonly labelled "plea bargaining" in the United States (US), Canada and Europe, this

A. Flynn, A. Freiberg, *Plea Negotiations*, Palgrave Socio-Legal Studies,
https://doi.org/10.1007/978-3-319-92630-8_1

term is generally not used and is strongly rejected by those within the Australian, New Zealand and British legal communities, on the basis that it connotes a covert bargain or trade that occurs outside the formalised rules and scrutiny applied at trial. Flynn (2011: 371) defines plea negotiations as:

> A discussion between the prosecutor and the relevant defence practitioner regarding the accused person's likely plea, the possibility of negotiating the charge(s) and/or case facts, and the Crown's possible sentencing submission. The primary aim of discussions is to arrive at a mutually acceptable agreement, according to which the accused pleads guilty.

Plea negotiations have consistently and trenchantly been criticised for potentially undermining fundamental criminal justice principles, including the presumption of innocence and the defendant's right to a contested trial (Johns 2002; McConville and Mirsky 2005; McConville and Marsh 2014; Woolard et al. 2016). As McConville and Marsh (2014: 216, emphasis in original) maintain, "because the process of State-induced guilty pleas is *intended to replace* in whole or part the promise of adversary justice, it challenges the foundations on which the claim of legitimacy of criminal courts has traditionally rested". Concerns relating to plea negotiations have heightened in light of recent, ongoing austerity measures that have seen re-strategising of funding for government or state-funded legal services and a greater focus on increased efficiency and timely finalisations in the courts generally (Flynn and Hodgson 2017a); an outcome which has resulted in a system focused "on the immediate case facts and outcomes, with less time and attention reserved for discussions about rights, or long-term collateral consequences" (Fountain and Woolard 2017: 1). As Russell and Hollander (2017: 309) have argued, "the domestic and international normative frameworks on fairness in criminal justice have failed to keep pace with the growth in the use of trial waivers". Plea negotiations have also been criticised on the ground that victims' rights are not sufficiently considered in a process that focuses primarily on the relationship between the defendant and the prosecution (Johns 2002). Victims may be distressed if they feel that the charges to which the defendant pleads guilty do not reflect the harm done to them (Royal Commission 2017a: 322). In this context, plea negotiations may be seen to offer limited justice to victims and, in turn, the public (Flynn 2012). As Dixon (1996: 7) argues, "the rights of victims are often a forgotten factor in plea bargaining". Accordingly, Clark (1986: 212) maintains that "it would probably be undesirable for plea bargaining to become the practice in all matters".

It has also been argued that negotiated guilty pleas are problematic because they trade the contested trial, with its strict rules of procedure, for an informal method of case resolution, thereby removing the public's access to a transparent process and creating uncertainty and misunderstanding about "justice" outcomes (Buckle and Buckle 1977; Euvrard and Leclerc 2017; JUSTICE 1993; Westling 1976). As Euvrard and Leclerc (2017: 526) observe, "because it takes place behind closed doors and in the absence of the main players (the victim and the defendant), it lacks the openness and transparency promised by the rule of law".

Misapprehensions about plea negotiations can be problematic, particularly in light of the number of vulnerable people who come before the law. Indeed, the outcome of a negotiated guilty plea—in that an agreement is reached between the prosecution and defence, and a trial is avoided—creates a situation where all parties are unlikely to be entirely satisfied. United Kingdom (UK) law reform group, JUSTICE (1993), has argued that plea negotiations can adversely affect defendants by putting pressure on them to plead guilty in exchange for prosecutorial concessions. Utz (1978) and Morris (1977) likewise contend that plea negotiations create power imbalances between the prosecutor and the defendant, particularly where the possible benefits of the plea negotiation may, and generally will, outweigh the risks inherent to proceeding to contest the case. In this regard, it has been argued that defendants may plead guilty because they feel coerced to do so, with pressures arising from the threat of a more severe sentence, from the need to have the matter over and done with, and from the promise of a more certain outcome, compared with that of a trial. A plea of guilty is arguably a more expedient way to finalise one's case, in that it enables the defendant to resolve the process, save money, get back to work and to their family (Redlich et al. 2017: 464). This argument is further strengthened if one considers the degrading process of the legal system as punishment in and of itself (Feeley 1979), whereby the quicker it comes to an end, the less is the punishment experienced by the defendant. But on the other hand, plea negotiations can be seen as a way to penalise those who believe that they are innocent and choose to "fight" their case, because if convicted, they will face a more severe sentence as a result of exercising their right to trial and forfeiting the benefits of a guilty plea.

The persistence and pervasiveness of plea negotiations in many jurisdictions points to an underlying utility and logic to the practice, which prevails over the often well-founded criticisms expressed by its critics. On its face, plea negotiation appears to derogate from the ideals of criminal justice: the presumption of innocence, the right to a fair and speedy trial before a jury of one's peers and the existence of a public and open justice system. Thus one might question on what grounds they can be justified. One of the key explanations for plea negotiations is their potential to increase court efficiency and reduce court backlogs. As McConville (2007: 213) claims, plea negotiations are "defended as an essential weapon in … the quest for cost-effective criminal justice systems". In this regard, Manikis (2012: 411) considers the process "a legitimate and necessary practice for the effective functioning of the criminal justice system". This view is supported by the cost savings of a guilty plea compared to that of a trial. An analysis of the court systems in the Australian state of Victoria in 2008, estimated that the use of the courts in terms of facilities alone equated to $389 per hour in the (summary) Magistrates' Court, $507 per hour in the (intermediate) County Court and $645 per hour in the Supreme Court (PricewaterhouseCoopers 2008: 24). According to Victoria Legal Aid (VLA) (2014b: 15), the average trial and appearance fees for an instructing solicitor can cost the organisation approximately $20,000 in the County Court and $34,000 in the Supreme Court. This amount increases to approximately $55,000 with a Senior Counsel (SC) or Queen's Counsel (QC)[3] in the barrister role and a junior counsel instructing (VLA 2014b: 15). In contrast, when a guilty plea is entered, the total cost to VLA for preparation and attendance at the plea hearing (where relevant material is presented to the judge to inform the sentence) is $1724 in the County Court and $2353 in the Supreme Court (VLA 2014b: 16). The former Director of Public Prosecutions (DPP) in Victoria, Mr John Champion SC (2014: 3), similarly estimated the cost of a trial for the state in funding the prosecution in the higher courts was approximately $20,000 per day. Accordingly, he argued that a "5 per cent shift in completions from trials to [guilty] pleas can reduce the numbers of trials by around 25 per cent, saving around 175 trial court days. … If my maths is correct, that is roughly a saving of $3.5 million" (Champion 2014: 3). It has also been argued that plea negotiation can free up court resources for trials where there is a real contest, possibly improving the quality of justice in those cases (Gazal-Ayal and Tor 2012: 389). The benefits of this were identified in the Canadian case, *R v Anthony-Cook*,[4] where the court stated:

> Guilty pleas save the justice system precious time, resources, and expenses, which can be channelled into other matters. This is no small benefit. To the extent that they avoid trials … [plea negotiations] permit our justice system to function more efficiently. Indeed, I would argue that they permit it to function. Without them, our justice system would be brought to its knees, and eventually collapse under its own weight.

Further to financial motivations, the (near) certainty of a negotiated outcome can make this a highly desirable outcome from the perspective of the prosecutor and the defendant:

> The Crown's case may suffer from flaws, such as an unwilling witness, a witness of dubious worth, or evidence that is potentially inadmissible – problems that can lead to an acquittal. By agreeing to a joint submission in exchange for a guilty plea, the Crown avoids this risk. Second, the accused may have information or testimony to offer the Crown that can prove invaluable to other investigations or prosecutions. But this information may not be forthcoming absent an agreement as to a joint submission.[5]

Dubber (1997: 604) also argues that plea negotiation "strengthens the defendant's position by permitting her [sic] to shape the proceedings that will settle her [sic] fate". This is because the process can provide an individualised style of justice, whereby a defendant can have all the circumstances relating to the offending behaviour taken into consideration in reaching a mutually acceptable and (primarily) certain outcome.

The benefits of plea negotiations to defendants are generally associated with the charge and sentence concessions offered in exchange for their guilty plea, as well as reduced legal costs and speedier resolution of the case (Douglass 1988; Gerstein 1981; Mack and Roach Anleu 1995; Maynard 1984).[6] Redlich et al. (2017: 464) argue that most defendants plead guilty because they are, in fact, guilty, and a plea negotiation that results in a reduced sentence is simply regarded as a good deal. Thus plea negotiations are considered to benefit "the guilty" (Gazal-Ayal and Tor 2012). As McConville and Marsh (2014: 146) observe, "plea negotiations provide an opportunity for defendants who have committed the forbidden act to minimise their culpability and to capitalise on [the prosecutor's] ... desire to avoid a trial". It has also been argued that plea negotiation may reduce the rate of wrongful acquittals on the basis that without them, some guilty defendants who would be forced to go to trial might be wrongly acquitted for a range of reasons (Redlich et al. 2017).

In recent years, the developments of non-adversarial theories of law and processes which incorporate notions such as therapeutic jurisprudence see a new role for lawyers acting on behalf of defendants. The advent of problem-oriented courts including drug courts, mental health courts and Indigenous courts, have redefined what lawyers and defendants may regard as a "successful outcome". Rather than defining success as an acquittal or a less severe sentence, for defendants with substance abuse or mental health problems, a negotiated therapeutic outcome may mean that a defendant agrees to plead guilty in order to obtain a therapeutic disposition or access to the drug court, which will provide them with assistance in recovering from the addiction which likely fuelled their offending in the first place (King et al. 2014: 263). Other negotiable dispositions, both pre-and post-sentence, may include seeking an adjournment, a deferred sentence, bail under the Court Referral and Evaluation for Drug Intervention and Treatment (CREDIT)[7] scheme or referral to a Court Integrated Services Program (CISP)[8] (King et al. 2014: Chapters 10 and 11). In such circumstances, a defence lawyer must not only be prepared and able to take instructions in a different way, he or she must be prepared to take a more active role in seeking therapeutic interventions on behalf of the defendant, while ensuring that they are neither acting paternalistically or coercively with regard to their client (Winick 1999). Properly managed, a non-adversarial, therapeutic approach to plea negotiation, one which affords the defendant with a voice, validation and respect, can both empower them and contribute to their health and welfare in the long term (Winick 1999: 1069).

There are also potential benefits for victims from the use of plea negotiations, especially following the introduction of victims' rights legislation and charters which require that increased consideration be given to victims as part of the prosecutor's official duties, including consultation before a negotiated guilty plea is accepted (Booth and Carrington 2007; Flynn 2012).[9] A plea negotiation means the victim does not have to face the defendant in court or experience potentially distressing cross-examination (Douglass 1988; Johns 2002), the benefits of which were identified by the New South Wales (NSW) Court of Criminal Appeal in *R v Thomson* (Australia)[10]:

> A plea permits the healing process to commence. A victim does not have to endure the uncertainty of not knowing whether he or she will be believed, nor the scepticism sometimes displayed by friends and even family prior to a conviction. A victim will also be spared the personal rumination of the events.

The potentially negative effects of cross-examination have been well documented, particularly in cases involving child and sexual assault victims (McConville 2002; Powell et al. 2013). However, the true benefits of removing the victim's need to testify, in terms of their sense of closure, have been heavily debated (Cook et al. 1999; Flatman and Bagaric 2001; Flynn 2012; Johns 2002). As the Court went on to state in *R v Thomson*,[11] the benefits for victims of not testifying "like the element of remorse, … depends on the specific circumstances of the offence and overlaps to a substantial extent with other aspects of the specific case". In his submission to the Australian Royal

Commission into Institutional Responses to Child Sexual Abuse, the then DPP (Victoria) noted that many victims preferred a criminal trial to a negotiated outcome in the case of sexual offences against children because they "prioritised the experience of giving evidence at a trial above the certainty of a guilty plea, despite the associated trauma and the possibility that the accused will be acquitted" (Royal Commission 2017a: 345). It has been argued however that a negotiated resolution may provide some "comfort" for the victim, as it spares them from the emotional cost of a trial, and the guilty plea may "indicate an accused's acknowledgement of responsibility and may amount to an expression of remorse".[12]

Plea negotiations are a surprisingly little understood activity, largely because there is an absence of data available on the process. In Australia, no official data are available on the occurrence of plea negotiations (Flynn 2012). As Carol et al. (2016: 1146–7) found in their comparative analysis of plea negotiations across five adversarial legal systems, there are not "any relevant statistics in Australia, but … [the legal community believe] the practice is used frequently". This is similar in New Zealand, where the Ministry of Justice has stated they "do not hold any record of instances of 'plea bargaining'. Therefore, there is no quantifiable means to measure [it]" (Buckman et al. 2016: 3.4). In the US, where some data are available, it has been reported that only around three per cent of felony cases proceed to trial, the rest are resolved by plea negotiation (Rakoff 2014). While comparable statistics for individual states in the US are not readily available, Rakoff (2014) claims that it is "a rare state where plea bargains do not similarly account for the resolution of at least 95 per cent of felony cases". Bibas (2012: 150) likewise contends that negotiated pleas "resolve roughly 95 per cent of adjudicated criminal cases" in the US. Krauss (2009: 26) also supports this view, claiming that "plea-bargaining and prosecutorial discretion determine the outcome of the vast majority of criminal cases" (see also Carol et al. 2016).

In Canada, it is estimated that up to 90 per cent of cases are resolved by plea negotiation (Verdun-Jones 2011: 163) and it forms "an integral element of the Canadian criminal process" (Carol et al. 2016: 1147; see also Euvrard and Leclerc 2017). In England and Wales, McConville (2007: 211) has argued that "plea bargaining [is] a widespread institutional practice and not isolated aberrational behaviour on the part of some maverick lawyers". This view is supported by his earlier, ground-breaking work with Baldwin (Baldwin and McConville 1979: 224), where they found that of the 122 defendants they interviewed who pleaded guilty, almost three-quarters said that they did so as a result of a plea negotiation. More recently, Mackenzie et al. (2015: 578) have argued that plea negotiations occur in more than 95 per cent of cases in

Western countries, although studies continue to highlight the absence of reliable data on the frequency of plea negotiations (see, e.g. Carol et al. 2016; Flynn 2016; Fountain and Woolard 2017).

Estimates of the plea negotiation rate are often made based on the assumption that because, on average, over two-thirds of people plead guilty, negotiations must provide some incentive for these pleas. As Wren and Bartels (2014: 375) explain, "guilty pleas are often the result of negotiations between the defence and prosecution". However, even accessing data on guilty plea rates is difficult, with the level of detail provided in official annual reports changing substantially over time. For example, in the Australian state of Victoria, the annual reports of the Magistrates' Court—the court which deals with all summary offences in Victoria—no longer provide data on the number of guilty pleas entered, and they ceased providing data on the number of cases finalised at their early resolution-focused pre-trial hearing, which was introduced as a formalised way to facilitate plea negotiations early in the process, in the 2013–14 financial year. Likewise, the Australian Bureau of Statistics (ABS) yearbooks ceased recording details on the number of guilty pleas entered in the 2005–06 financial year. Instead, it now provides information on the number of guilty outcomes, which include both guilty pleas and guilty verdicts at trial. In Victoria, the most accurate and consistent data on guilty pleas can be found in the Office of Public Prosecutions' (OPP) annual reports,[13] which show that over the past decade (2005–06 to 2015–16), almost 74 per cent of all serious (indictable) matters they have prosecuted resolved by guilty plea.

Since 2005, the OPP reports suggest that the number of guilty pleas being entered in the higher courts in Victoria has risen (in terms of percentages) from the low 60s to the mid to high 70s (see Fig. 1.1). There have been some

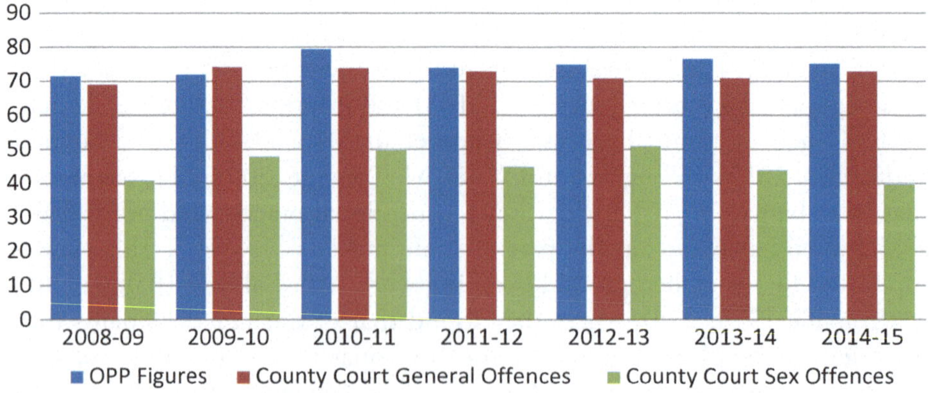

Fig. 1.1 Guilty pleas in Victoria 2008–15

fluctuations in the guilty plea rate, but it has remained consistently above 70 per cent of matters prosecuted by the Victorian OPP since the 2008–09 financial year. These figures are supported by research undertaken by the Sentencing Advisory Council (SAC) (2015: 11) of Victoria, who found that between 1 July 2009 and 30 June 2014, 74.4 per cent of cases in the (intermediate) County Court—the court that handles all indictable offences other than homicide, serious rapes, terrorism and treason—resolved by way of guilty plea. Further to this, the SAC (2015: 11) determined that 72.4 per cent of all guilty outcomes in the Supreme Court—the highest trial court in Victoria—and 84.6 per cent of guilty outcomes in the County Court over this same reference period were the result of a guilty plea. As demonstrated in Fig. 1.1, the only significant statistical difference in relation to guilty plea resolutions in Victoria involves sexual offence matters. This has been a consistent trend since separate data began being recorded on sexual offences in the 2008–09 financial year. This differential is also reflected in national statistics, with the most recent ABS yearbook (2004–05) to contain such information showing that adjudicated defendants with a principal offence of sexual assault and related offences were second only to homicide cases in being least likely to plead guilty nationwide (50 per cent for homicide and 58 per cent for sexual offences).[14]

While it is possible to monitor the rate of guilty pleas, there remains very limited information as to how or why such pleas are entered, and it appears in most jurisdictions that there are no official data available documenting the role of plea negotiations in facilitating guilty pleas. In Australia, there is also very little information available on the processes involved in reaching a negotiated resolution. This is because, across Australian jurisdictions, aside from any confidential prosecution and defence practitioner file notes, no administrative data are recorded on negotiated resolutions. This means that there are no official means to accurately measure the frequency of, or understand the processes involved in, negotiated plea deals. Furthermore, other than the state of NSW and the Australian Capital Territory (ACT),[15] plea negotiations (described in any term) are not recognised or defined in legislation, and there exist only sparse judicial observations of the process.[16] All Australian prosecution offices have issued guidelines in relation to their approach to plea negotiations;[17] however these guidelines are not legally binding, and there has been very little research examining the effects of prosecutorial guidelines on case outcomes (Flynn 2011, 2016). The discretion exercised by prosecutors, including that used for plea negotiations, is central to the legal process but remains largely opaque. As a consequence, criminal matters—including those involving serious misconduct—are resolved with limited external understanding or insight into the process, something that sits in contrast with approaches used in other jurisdictions, such as the US.[18]

Negotiated guilty pleas are neither an alloyed benefit nor a detriment for defendants, victims or the criminal justice system generally. Like all compromises, the perfect gives way to the good, or just the reasonably acceptable. While primarily justified for their pragmatic benefits, plea negotiations are largely misunderstood by those outside the legal community:

> In a world where the vast majority of criminal cases are resolved through some means other than the popularly depicted criminal trial, it is fundamental to a comprehensive understanding of comparative criminal procedure to study and appreciate the different mechanisms for criminal case resolution in different nations. (Carol et al. 2016: 1148–9)

It is this significant gap in knowledge that provides the rationale for this book.

This Book

This book has two primary aims: to investigate the prevalence, nature and effects of negotiated guilty pleas and to examine the processes involved in reaching a negotiated guilty plea using the jurisdiction of Victoria as a case study.[19] To achieve these two aims, the book reports on the empirical findings of the first comprehensive study of plea negotiations in Australia that included access to criminal case files, as well as legal stakeholder interviews and consultations. It draws on this rich primary research to understand the prevalence and effects of plea negotiations, as well as the legal and justice gaps in responding to contemporary challenges to the adversarial system, such as court inefficiency, the shifting nature of discretion and the restructuring of resource allocations. It is the first Australian study to develop a dataset of negotiated guilty pleas through a comprehensive analysis of de-identified case files. The study is also informed by the experiences and perspectives of prosecutors, defence practitioners and judicial officers across six locations in Victoria, obtained through individual interviews, group discussions and consultation. Where relevant, the book engages with international experiences of plea negotiations informed by a comprehensive literature review of plea negotiation research (primary and secondary documents).

Due to budgetary and other resource considerations, this study did not interview defendants and victims, but focused upon those tasked with the daily task of negotiating guilty pleas. In that respect, it is not dissimilar to other studies that were based on interviews with a limited number of parties to, or affected by, the plea negotiation process.[20] While interviews with defendants and victims would have provided an even more comprehensive understanding of the plea negotiation process, their absence does not mean that their perspective could not be obtained from existing empirical studies or through the voices of those interviewed. This approach also reflects those used in other recent examinations of plea negotiations procedures, such as King and Wright's (2016) comprehensive study of judicial participation in plea negotiations, in which they interviewed only judges and attorneys to inform their discussion.

The project had four main goals, namely to:

1. contribute to a highly under-researched area by increasing understanding of plea negotiations;
2. provide an empirical account of plea negotiation processes in the Australian state of Victoria;
3. positively influence legal practice and inform training activities and potential law reform in relation to pre-trial preparation, resource/time allocation and charging practices; and
4. develop new knowledge about plea negotiations with the aim of enhancing community education about the important role they play in the criminal justice system.

A Brief Note on Methodology[21]

The project was informed by a mixed qualitative and quantitative methodology across three phases. Phase One represented one of the most significant contributions of the project: the ability to access and analyse de-identified case files which no Australian-based research has managed to do for this purpose. Approximately 50 files were collated from VLA's indictable and sexual offence divisions for cases finalised between 1 July 2012 and 30 June 2014. Files were randomly selected from VLA cases that had been finalised by a guilty plea within this time period. This task was completed by the research coordinator at VLA. A major advantage of using only VLA de-identified case files over a designated timeframe was that the danger of file corruption or controlled data—whether by intention, self-case selection or because of the researcher effect—was avoided. Additionally, as VLA provides assistance in around 80 per cent of all criminal matters in the jurisdiction (Flynn 2010b;

PricewaterhouseCoopers 2008), it is likely that the case file data are representative of the main body of defendants who come before the courts in the state of Victoria.

The files were analysed using a *Case File Analysis Schedule* prepared in consultation with VLA staff. Each file was assigned a pseudonym comprising three numbers and two letters—for example, 005-BD. They are referred to as such throughout the book.

Phase Two involved conducting 48 in-depth interviews with legal stakeholders representing experience in both summary and indictable cases. This included defence practitioners from VLA (*n* = 12) and private practice (*n* = 13), prosecutors (*n* = 10) and judicial officers (*n* = 13) located in six locations in Victoria—the capital city, Melbourne,[22] and key regional and rural centres, Geelong,[23] Shepparton,[24] Gippsland,[25] Ballarat[26] and Dandenong.[27] These locations were selected to gather a variety of experiences with plea negotiations across city, rural and regional environments to capture the nuances specific to different areas, and identify common approaches and themes across varying prosecution offices and defence practices.

The interviews were conducted between September 2015 and January 2016 with an average duration of 65 minutes. All interviews were audiotaped, transcribed verbatim and verified. The interviews were general in nature and not case specific. Participants were selected according to their location, availability and level of seniority and experience. Each participant was assigned a pseudonym which comprised the occupation (prosecutor, defence, judge), a randomly assigned sequential number based on the number of participants interviewed in their occupational group, the participant's gender (M/F) and whether they were from a rural or regional location (R). For example, a male prosecutor based in Melbourne may be assigned Prosecutor04M. A female magistrate from a rural or regional location may be assigned Judge09FR.

The final phase involved holding a roundtable workshop in May 2016 with key legal and policy stakeholders to discuss the interim research findings from the case file and interview data. The event was attended by 15 stakeholders, 8 of whom had been interview participants. Fifteen key themes that had emerged from the interview and case file data were identified, and participants were asked to respond to specific questions related to these and to identify any flaws or issues of importance that did not appear in the findings—for example, whether the de-identified case files were representative of the types of offences most commonly negotiated. The roundtable provided the opportunity to test the interim findings and to address any inconsistencies in the data.

The roundtable event was audiotaped and transcribed. The transcript was systemically coded to allow for thematic and comparative analysis of the data against the findings from the interview and case file analyses. Similar to the interview participants, the roundtable participants were assigned pseudonyms which included their occupation, a randomly assigned sequential number (based on the number of participants in their occupational group including interview and stakeholder participants) and gender (M/F). For example, a male defence practitioner attending the roundtable may be assigned Defence28M.

Chapter Overview

Chapter 2 begins by presenting an overview of the Victorian legal process and the case study which forms the foundation of this book. Chapter 3 examines the language that has been used to describe negotiated guilty pleas in order to highlight the diversity of victims, perpetrators, outcomes and consequences associated with plea negotiations and the need to adopt an appropriate definition that can adequately reflect this. It also identifies the four most common forms of plea negotiation: withdrawing and substituting charges, rolled-up and representative counts, amendments to the agreed summary of facts and agreements on the prosecutor's sentencing submission to the court.

To date, discussions of plea negotiation have generally focused on three main forms: (1) "charge bargaining", (2) "fact bargaining" and (3) "sentence bargaining". However, based on the case file analysis and interview process, 14 forms of plea negotiation were identified in this study. Chapter 4 presents a detailed overview of these different forms of plea negotiation (excluding the four presented in the previous chapter) to highlight the diversity and extent of outcomes possible from the plea negotiation process.

The negotiation process can be long and sometimes difficult. Chapter 5 examines in close detail how the negotiation process operates, including who is involved, when, how and in relation to what matters. Chapter 6 discusses patterns in the outcomes of negotiations, including identifying offences most commonly negotiated and those offences where negotiations are less likely to occur. In doing so, this chapter builds on the forms of negotiations presented in Chaps. 3 and 4 to provide a unique insight into which types of crimes more commonly feature in negotiations.

Plea negotiations and sentencing are inextricably linked. While it is strongly argued that sentencing is not a part of negotiations in Australian jurisdictions, Chap. 7 examines connections between various sentencing regimes and policies and plea negotiations. An increasing emphasis on economy and efficiency in the criminal justice system fuels one of the major criticisms of plea negotiations, their potential to place undue pressure on defendants to plead guilty. Chapter 8 examines these concerns with a specific focus on unrepresented defendants and defendants presenting with mental health concerns. The criminal justice system aspires to be open, transparent and accountable to the public, something that arguably sits at odds with plea negotiations. Chapter 9 considers how public confidence in the criminal justice system can be developed and maintained when plea negotiations are the favoured form of justice.

Overall, this book argues that plea negotiations are a pragmatic response to an imperfect world in which legal and administrative resources are limited, managerial theories have transformed the criminal justice system and in which good people work in an adverse environment. As Bibas (2003: 1) contends, "we live in a fallen and imperfect world, however, one in which plea bargaining is not going to disappear any time soon". Thus Chap. 10 concludes the book with a number of recommendations as to how the process can be made more transparent and less imperfect.

Notes

1. A survey of 90 countries across six continents showed that 72 per cent allowed for guilty pleas with possibly concomitant increases in plea negotiations (Redlich et al. 2017: 459).
2. In this book, we refer to the process interchangeably as plea negotiations, early resolutions or negotiated guilty pleas.
3. A Senior Counsel (SC) or Queen's Counsel (QC) is the title given to a senior lawyer. The title represents the same level of seniority and expertise, with the difference merely reflecting the timing at which the individual was appointed to the position. Between 2000 and 2014, the state of Victoria changed the title from QC to SC. The title of QC, however, was reinstated in 2015.
4. (2016) SCC 43, [2016] 2 S.C.R. 204 [at 40].
5. Ibid. [at 39].
6. See also *Sentencing Act 1991* (Vic) s 5(e).
7. The CREDIT Bail Support Program is available for defendants with drug addictions to complete their treatment while on bail. The program places defendants into appropriate drug treatment and/or rehabilitation programs with the aim of reducing their long-term involvement in the criminal justice system and addressing the defendant's drug problem (Magistrates' Court 2016).
8. The program provides accused persons with access to services and support to reduce rates of reoffending and promote safer communities by providing short-term assistance before sentencing for accused with health and social

needs, working on the causes of offending through individualised case management, providing priority access to treatment and community support services and reducing the likelihood of reoffending (Magistrates' Court 2018).

9. See also *Victims' Charter Act 2006* (Vic) s 9 which requires the prosecution to give to victims as soon as practicable, information relating to the offences charged against the defendant or, if no charges are laid, the reason for doing so. If charges are laid, information must be provided in relation to the decision to substantially modify them, or not to proceed with some or all of them or to accept a guilty plea to a lesser charge.
10. (2000) 49 NSWLR 383 [at 120].
11. Ibid.
12. *R v Anthony-Cook* (2016) SCC 43, [2016] 2 S.C.R. 204 [at 39].
13. The Victorian OPP is responsible for prosecuting all indictable matters in the state of Victoria. See Chap. 2 for a more detailed discussion on their role.
14. See Chap. 6.
15. See *Crimes (Sentencing Procedure) Act 1999* (NSW) s 35(a) which relates primarily to offences taken into consideration on sentencing and the *Crimes (Sentencing) Act 2005* (ACT) s 35 (2)(c) which instructs the court to take into consideration whether the guilty plea was related to plea negotiations when applying a sentence discount.
16. See, for example, *Talbot v The Queen; Dux v The Queen* [2012] VSCA 118; *Guariglia v The Queen* [2010] VSCA 343; *R v Gas; R v SJK* (2004) 217 CLR 198.
17. See, for example, *Department of Public Prosecutions Director's Guidelines* (Qld); *Department of Public Prosecutions Guidelines Charge Negotiations* (NT); *Department of Public Prosecutions Prosecution Policy* (ACT); *Director's Policy: Resolution* (Vic); *Office of the Department of Public Prosecutions Guideline 6* (NSW); *Office of the Department of Public Prosecutions Prosecution Policy and Guidelines* (Tas); *Prosecution Policy of the Commonwealth* (Cth); *Prosecution Policy Guideline Number Two – Charge Bargaining* (SA); and *Statement of Prosecution Policy and Guidelines* (WA).
18. See, for example, *Federal Rules of Criminal Procedure* (US).
19. Victoria is located in the south-east of Australia. It is the second most populated state in Australia with approximately 6.15 million people. On average, approximately 86,400 people are sentenced in Victoria each year, roughly 97 per cent in the lower court and 3 per cent in the higher courts (SAC 2016a).
20. For example, Baldwin and McConville's renowned study (1977) was based on interviews with defendants only.
21. See Appendix 2 for a comprehensive overview of the research methodology used in this project.
22. Melbourne is the state capital of Victoria and the second most populous city in Australia. It covers an urban area spanning 9992.5 km^2 (3858.1 square miles). As at June 2016, it had a population of 4,725,316.

23. Geelong is a port city located approximately 75 kilometres (47 miles) south-west of Melbourne. It is the second largest Victorian city, with an estimated urban population of 192,393 as at June 2016.
24. Shepparton is a city located near the Goulburn River in northern Victoria, approximately 181 kilometres (112 miles) north-northeast of Melbourne. As at June 2016, the estimated urban population was 50,198.
25. Gippsland is an economic rural region of Victoria, located in the south-eastern part of the state, approximately 322 kilometres (200 miles) from the Melbourne CBD. It covers an area of 41,556 square kilometres (16,045 square miles). As at June 2011, Gippsland had a population of 255,718.
26. Ballarat is a city located in the Central Highlands of Victoria, approximately 116 kilometres (72 miles) from the Melbourne CBD. It is the third largest inland city in Australia with a population of 101,588 as at June 2016.
27. Dandenong is a suburb located approximately 30 kilometres (18.5 miles) south-east of Melbourne. It had a population of 29,906 as at June 2016.

2

Plea Negotiations in Context

Despite the considerable role that plea negotiations play in the criminal justice process, they remain a surprisingly under-researched activity in the Australian context. Indeed, much of the research examining negotiated guilty pleas originates from the US, the UK and Canada, and was conducted from the late 1970s up until the early 2000s (Acker and Brody 2004; Alschuler 1995; Baldwin and McConville 1977; Buckle and Buckle 1977; Cohen and Doob 1989; Douglass 1988; Dubber 1997; Dumont 1987; Fitzgerald 1990; JUSTICE 1993; Pizzi 1999; Solomon 1983; Utz 1978). While this research is significantly more prevalent and extensive than that available in Australia, plea negotiations are still considered an under-researched area across most Western jurisdictions. As Kutateladze et al. (2015: 431) contend, "the majority of cases in the United States are disposed of through plea bargaining; however, this important discretionary point has received relatively little attention from researchers compared with trial and jury proceedings, and other discretionary points such as arrest and sentencing".

The common issues examined in the literature to date include the purpose of plea negotiations (Alschuler 1995; Goldstein 1981; Heumann and Loftin 1995; Moxon 1988; Pizzi 1999); the wide discretionary powers afforded to criminal justice actors involved in negotiations (Atkins and Pogrebin 1982; Breitel 1960; Boyd 1979; Douglass 1988; Fionda 1995; Freidman 1982; Gabbay 1973; Louthan 1985; Stenning 2010); how negotiated guilty pleas influence the sentencing process, particularly in relation to the operation of a "double discount", whereby the defendant receives initial concessions from the prosecution, and then a sentence discount from the court (Frankel 1982; Gerber 2003; Henham 2001; Henry 1992; JUSTICE 1993; Lovegrove 1997;

A. Flynn, A. Freiberg, *Plea Negotiations*, Palgrave Socio-Legal Studies,
https://doi.org/10.1007/978-3-319-92630-8_2

Remington 1993; Sebba 1996); and whether the concessions offered to a defendant may unduly influence them to plead guilty (McConville 1998; McConville and Mirsky 2005; McConville and Marsh 2014). The potential benefits and consequences of legal reforms to the guilty plea process have also featured in US-, Canadian- and UK-based studies, including research proposing improvements to existing processes, such as prohibiting prosecutorial discretion in regard to charging concessions, or introducing more controlled procedures—for example, having negotiations supervised by the court (Blumberg 1967; Canadian Law Reform Commission 1989; Daudistel 1980; Heumann 1978; Heumann and Loftin 1995; JUSTICE 1993; Kerstetter and Heinz 1979; McDonald 1985; Rubenstein and White 1980; UK Office of the Attorney-General 2007; Verdun-Jones and Hatch 1987).

In Australia, negotiated resolutions are significantly under-examined, except in a handful of nationally based studies (Bishop 1989; Mack and Roach Anleu 1995; Standing Committee of Attorneys General 2000), or as part of a sub-topic within a broader study of sentencing discounts and/or indications, or as a response to court delays (Access to Justice Advisory Committee 1994; Brereton and Willis 1990; Chan and Barnes 1995; Coopers and Lybrand 1989; Corns 1997; Freiberg and Willis 2003; Hidden 1990; Hill 1999; Law Reform Commission of Western Australia 1999; Payne 2007; Pegasus Taskforce 1992; Sulan 2000; Victorian Law Reform Commission 2007; SAC 2007; Victorian Shorter Trials Committee 1985; Weatherburn and Baker 2000). The last comprehensive study of Australian plea negotiations was published in 1995, although this analysis was framed around guilty plea procedures more generally (Mack and Roach Anleu 1995). Kathy Mack and Sharon Roach Anleu's (1995) study identified several possible reforms, including the use of sentence indication schemes (which now operate in Victoria and were trialled and discontinued in NSW in the 1990s),[1] and the implementation of prosecutorial guidelines governing negotiated resolutions within internal prosecution departments (which now exist in all Australian jurisdictions).[2] While offering important insights into guilty plea procedures, the evolving emphasis on efficiency and the increasing resource limitations confronting the criminal courts in the 20 or so years following the publication of their research limits the direct applicability of their findings to the contemporary criminal justice context.

In Victoria—the case study jurisdiction of this book—a number of academic articles and studies relating to plea negotiations have focused either on the need for greater transparency of the process, the role of victims in negotiation processes (primarily following the introduction of the *Victims' Charter Act 2006* (Vic)), prosecutorial discretion more broadly or sentence indications as a form of plea negotiation (see, e.g. Clark 1986; Flynn 2009, 2010a, b, 2011, 2012; Flynn and Fitz-Gibbon 2011; Freiberg and Seifman 2001; Seifman 1982). Of these, only a handful have focused on the plea negotiation process in its own right (Flynn 2009, 2011, 2016; Freiberg and Seifman 2001; Seifman 1982), with the majority discussing plea negotiations as part of broader research on sentencing, law reform or procedural justice (Clark 1986; Flynn 2009, 2010b, 2012; Flynn and Fitz-Gibbon 2011; SAC 2007). Much of the more recent research was conducted by Asher Flynn, who undertook several months of observation of OPP staff engaging in negotiations and related processes, and conducted over 60 interviews with legal professionals between 2007 and 2009 to examine the operation of prosecutorial discretion in plea negotiations. While shedding some much-needed light on plea negotiations in Victoria, Flynn's research to date has largely focused on the question of formalisation and increased transparency of plea negotiations, such as through legislative recognition of the process, as opposed to the details, implications or processes involved in negotiating guilty pleas (see e.g. Flynn 2010a, 2012, 2016). There is consequently a significant gap in Australian research about how plea negotiations operate (in terms of frequency and offence type) and how they may affect outcomes of justice in the context of a pragmatically oriented legal system. This is especially important in light of recent research which suggests that already marginalised groups, including Indigenous Australians, women and those from low socioeconomic backgrounds, are more vulnerable to being disadvantaged or pressured in pre-trial decision-making (Flynn 2010b, 2011, 2016; Miller 2005; Stubbs and Tolmie 2008).

This chapter presents an overview of the criminal justice process and the policies pertaining to plea negotiations in Victoria. A discussion of the case file data is then presented, shining light on the characteristics of the types of cases subject to Victoria's plea negotiation process.

The Victorian Prosecution Process

There are three levels of court that hear criminal cases in Victoria—the (summary) Magistrates' Court, the (intermediate) County Court and the Supreme Court. The Magistrates' Court hears summary offences and indictable offences triable summarily. All matters are heard before a single magistrate with no jury. The maximum term of imprisonment that can be imposed for a single offence is two years. The maximum total sentence that can be imposed for multiple offences is five years. The County Court and Supreme Court have concurrent jurisdiction over indictable offences, although the Supreme Court hears the most serious offences such as homicides and serious drug offences. Indictable offences are tried before a judge and jury, unless the defence requests a judge-only trial. Over 90 per cent of criminal cases are finalised in the Magistrates' Court (SAC 2016a). Between June 2006 and June 2016, the Magistrates' Court sentenced 84,438 defendants, on average, per year. In comparison, between them, the Supreme and County Courts sentenced 1950 defendants, on average, each year (SAC 2016a).[3]

All prosecutions in the Magistrates' Court are conducted by Victoria Police prosecutors. Police prosecutors are not required to have a law degree (although some do). However, they are required to undertake an 18-week Prosecutors Training Course (the equivalent to ten subjects in a standard law degree). There are 25 prosecution offices responsible for prosecuting summary offences and indictable offences tried summarily across Victoria. This includes running contested hearings and appearing at all summary pre-trial hearings. The OPP is responsible for prosecuting matters in the indictable stream.[4] Once the police charge a defendant, carriage of the file is transferred to the OPP for the pre-trial process, some of which (as outlined in the next section) takes place in the Magistrates' Court.

The DPP is ultimately responsible for and has oversight over all indictable prosecutions in Victoria, including those at circuit courts.[5] The DPP provides guidance to those tasked with prosecuting indictable offences in order to enable consistency in approaches based on Director's Policies—many of which are available for the public to access online via the OPP website—and Practice Guides, which are located on the internal OPP database accessible only by OPP employees.

At the time of conducting the research, the process within the OPP operated as follows. Each case is assigned to an OPP solicitor, who is a permanent employee of the OPP, and a Crown prosecutor, who is appointed by the DPP but not a direct employee of the OPP. The OPP solicitor is tasked with preparing and running most of the pre-trial hearings (in conjunction with the Crown prosecutor), and preparing the case for plea and/or trial. A Crown prosecutor will generally appear as the DPP's representative on behalf of the state at the trial and/or plea hearing, although they may also appear at some pre-trial hearings, particularly if a contested committal hearing is run. Crown prosecutors also provide guidance to OPP solicitors on options for early resolution, and approval must be sought from a Crown prosecutor (or in cases involving a death, the DPP or the Chief Crown Prosecutor in the DPP's absence) before a guilty plea to lesser charges can be accepted (see *Director's Policy: Resolution*). In March 2016, a new structure was implemented in the OPP which included disbanding the Early Resolution Unit and integrating

Principal Resolution Advocates (formerly known as Early Resolution Advocates (ERAs)) into each new trial section. A breakdown of the OPP's new structure is provided in Appendix 2.

Police prosecutors in the Magistrates' Court operate under the same guidelines that apply to prosecutions conducted by the OPP in terms of exercising discretion, making decisions in the public's interest and conducting prosecutions in an efficient, effective and timely manner. Police prosecutors are not required to obtain approval from the DPP or Crown prosecutors prior to accepting a guilty plea to lesser charges. Instead, they must obtain approval from either a Sergeant or Senior Sergeant of Prosecutions (generally from the prosecuting division involved in the negotiations).

As outlined in Figs. 2.1, 2.2 and 2.3, the pre-trial process in Victoria is lengthy. As Flynn (2010b: 50) observes:

> The primary purpose of Victoria's extensive pre-trial process is to identify the key issues of the case both those in dispute and those that could possibly resolve. The reason for this is twofold: it encourages all relevant issues to be identified at an early stage to prepare counsel for the contested trial; and it allows for the resolution of any non-disputed issues.

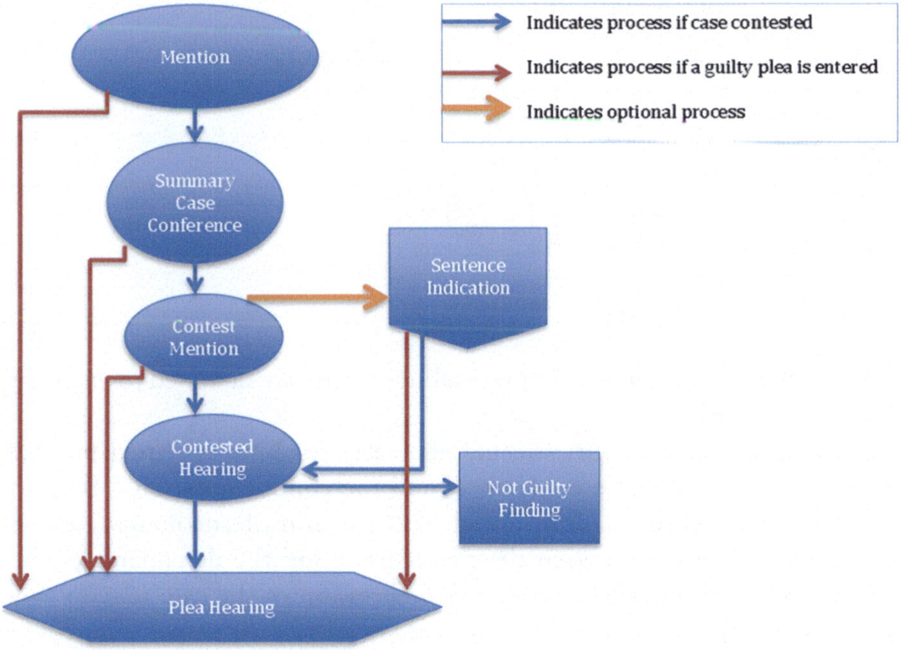

Fig. 2.1 Magistrates' Court process

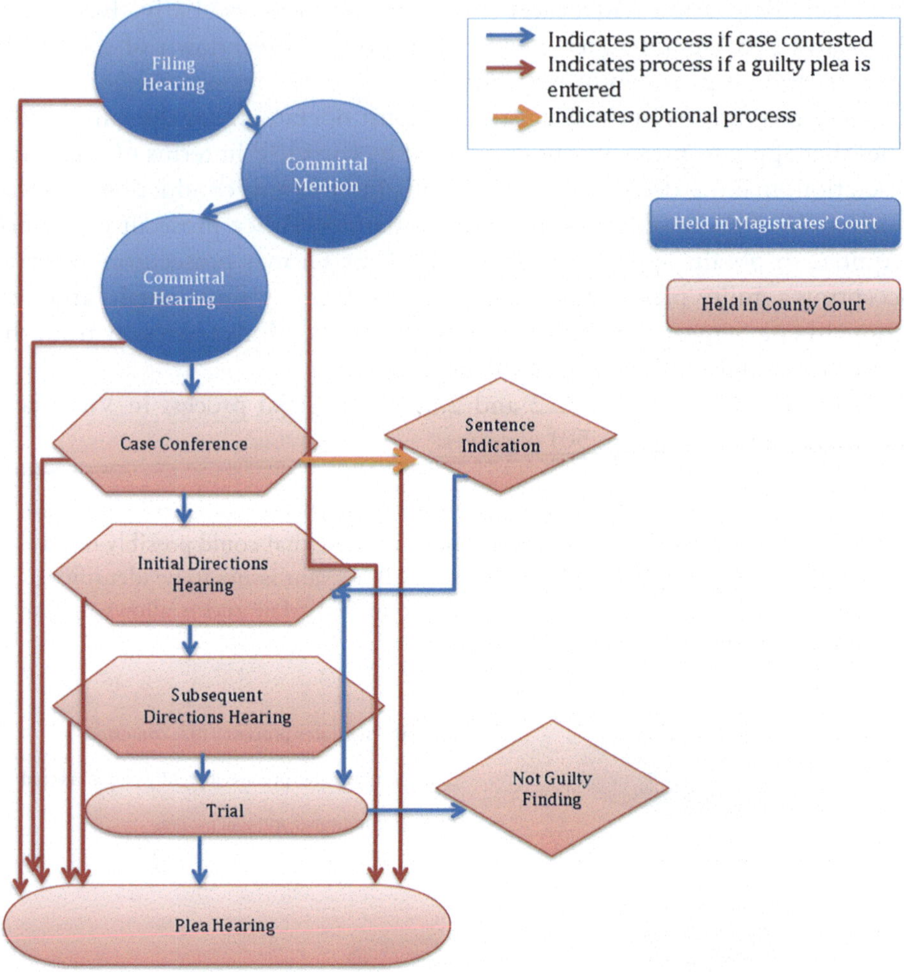

Fig. 2.2 County Court process

Accordingly, there are several pre-trial stages that are designed to encourage plea negotiations.[6]

In the Magistrates' Court stream,[7] the early resolution-focused processes include the summary case conference[8] and the contest mention.[9] The summary case conference was introduced with the aim of encouraging out-of-court communication between the prosecution and the defendant (or their representative) in order to manage the progression of the case (e.g. to avoid unnecessary adjournments or resolve matters at an early stage). The conference is intended to help the defendant understand the evidence available to

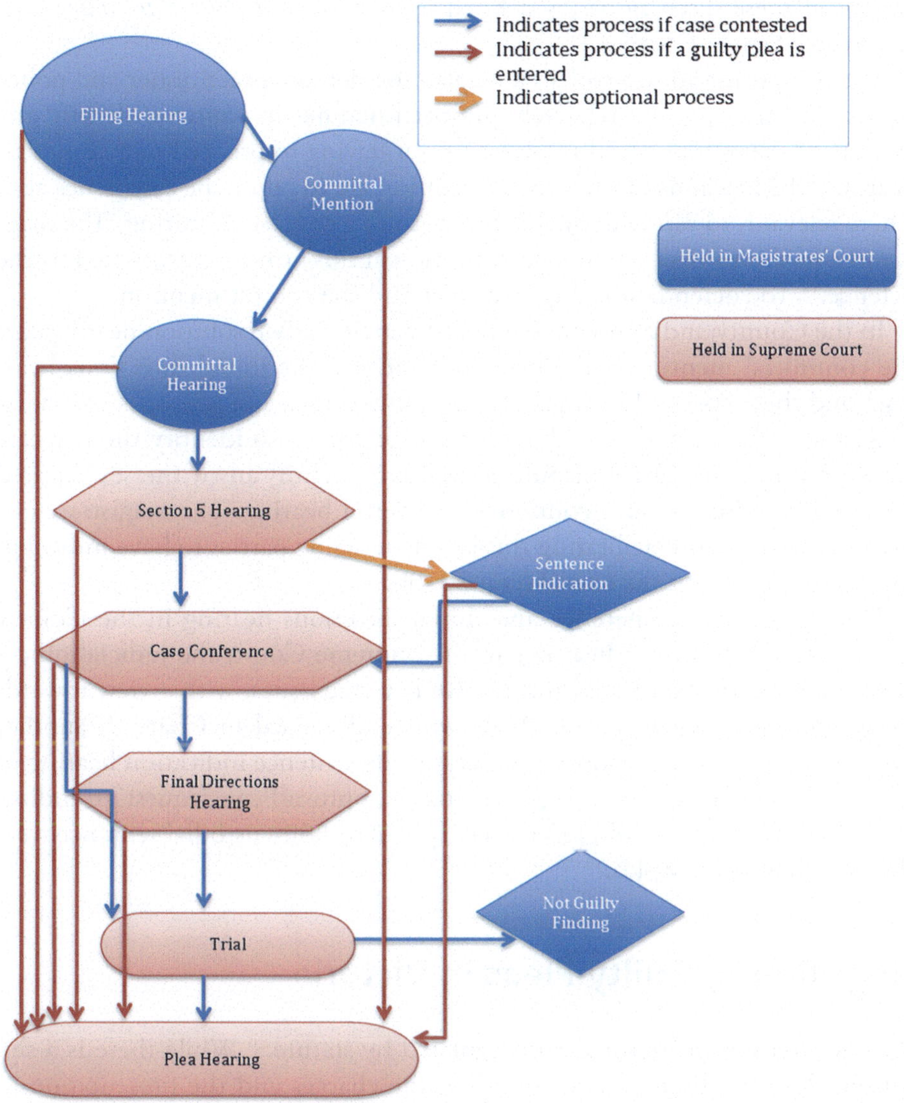

Fig. 2.3 Supreme Court process

the prosecution[10]; enable the parties to identify any issues in dispute[11]; and have the parties identify the steps required to advance the case,[12] which includes the possibility of an early resolution. The conference does not need to occur in the court setting and can take place by email, telephone or face to face. There are summary case conference police prosecutors whose role is to engage in these discussions (as defined by the *Victoria Police Summary Case Conference Service Charter*).[13]

The contest mention involves a magistrate, defence practitioner and police prosecutor meeting in a relatively informal manner in court to identify any matters or issues that could resolve without having to proceed to a contested hearing. The key aims of the contest mention are to refine the case issues and, where relevant, to estimate the likely length of a contested hearing. The magistrate can also provide a sentence indication at this hearing if requested by the defence.[14] The defendant is required to attend the contest mention.

In the County and Supreme Courts, the main early resolution hearings are the committal mention,[15] the case conference,[16] the initial directions hearing[17] and the section 5 hearing.[18] The committal mention is conducted in the Magistrates' Court and provides a forum for parties to identify the key case issues and any issues not in dispute, as well as to identify any witnesses required for cross-examination at a contested committal hearing. The magistrate can play an active role in facilitating this by encouraging parties to have meaningful discussions about the case (Flynn 2010b).

During the case conference and initial directions hearing in the County Court and the section 5 hearings in the Supreme Court, the judicial officer encourages parties to discuss and resolve key case issues, with a view towards early resolution (where possible). As will be discussed in Chap. 7, another early resolution-focused pre-trial process is the sentence indication hearing in which a defendant (subject to prosecutorial approval) can request an indication of whether they would receive a custodial or non-custodial sentence were they to enter a guilty plea.[19]

Negotiating Guilty Pleas in Victoria

Plea negotiation in Victoria is unregulated by statute.[20] While there is a significant level of discretion surrounding the charges and the presentation of those charges, the sentence imposed remains the responsibility of the sentencing judge alone, although the prosecution may limit the sentencing options available by determining the number and seriousness of the charges presented (Freiberg 2014: 107). No agreement between the prosecution and defence as to sentence in Victoria can bind the sentencing judge or any appeal court.[21] Nor can any agreement prevent the DPP acting in the public interest from appealing against a sentence imposed.[22] In *Malvaso*,[23] the High Court of Australia stated that a plea negotiation did not affect:

> the duty of either of the sentencing judge or of the Court of Criminal Appeal ... to impose the sentence which appeared appropriate to the Court in the circumstances. The Court's sentencing discretion is to be exercised in the public interest; it cannot be fettered by a plea-bargaining agreement.

The DPP's policy on the resolution of prosecutions by pleas of guilty in Victoria[24] states that "in all cases, the resolution of a prosecution by a plea of guilty to lesser charges may only be approved if the lesser charges are appropriate charges". "Appropriate charges" is defined to mean charges which:

- adequately reflect the accused's criminality, based on what can be proved beyond reasonable doubt;
- allow for the imposition of a sentence which adequately reflects the accused's criminality; and
- allow for the making of all appropriate ancillary orders.

A sentencing judge may not sentence a defendant on the basis of an offence or offences of which he or she has not been convicted or circumstances of aggravation which would have warranted a conviction for a more serious offence.[25] Yet a judge is rarely able to question the basis upon which a guilty plea has been accepted, as it is for the prosecution to decide which charges to proceed on, unless it is necessary to prevent an abuse of process or to ensure a fair process.[26] Although the DPP does not have:

> ... an absolute and uncontrolled discretion which empowers him to charge an accused person in whatever way he pleases, regardless of the gravity of the conduct of the accused, and then to require the court to give effect to his decision in that regard. ... [T]here are substantial practical limitations upon the power of courts to control the exercise by prosecuting authorities of the wide discretion which they undoubtedly enjoy. ... [I]n practice, the most important sanctions in this regard are likely to be political rather than legal.[27]

In a resource-constrained criminal justice system, a judge's ability to determine the "true" facts will be very limited. Where courts face a situation where prosecution and defence have agreed upon an outcome, but where that outcome may not represent the interests of all those concerned, such as the victim, a court must take special care to ensure that it is being given "accurate, reliable and complete information"[28] with regard to relevant facts in order to ensure that public confidence in the administration of criminal justice is not diminished.[29]

The DPP's policy in relation to the early resolution[30] of cases states that "resolution may only occur if it is in the public interest".[31] In determining whether a proposed resolution is in the public interest, regard must be had to:

(a) whether there is a reasonable prospect of a conviction on each charge. If there is no reasonable prospect of a conviction on a charge, then that charge must not proceed. It is improper for such a charge to proceed to committal with a view to the prospects of conviction being reassessed after the committal;
(b) the strength of the evidence on each charge;
(c) any defences;
(d) the likelihood of an acquittal on any of the charges;
(e) whether the charge or charges to which the accused will plead guilty:
    (i) adequately reflect the accused's criminality
    (ii) allow for the imposition of an appropriate sentence
    (iii) allow for the making of all appropriate ancillary orders;
(f) the views of the victims and the informant;
(g) the need to minimise inconvenience and stress to witnesses, particularly those who may find it onerous to give evidence[32]; and
(h) the likely length of a trial.

It is within this context that plea negotiations take place in Victoria.

The Case Files: An Overview

As flagged in the introductory chapter, Phase One of the study involved analysing 50 de-identified case files from VLA that resolved by guilty plea. Of the 50 cases, three (6 per cent) contained no information about the guilty plea making it impossible to determine whether or not negotiations occurred. A further four (8 per cent) contained no details about negotiations, but resulted in charges being changed. Of the 47 cases that contained some information on how the guilty plea was reached, five (10 per cent) involved the defendant pleading guilty without any apparent negotiation on the charges, and one involved a guilty plea after the prosecution withdrew charges due to a lack of evidence, as opposed to any evident negotiations between the prosecutor and defence.

Overall, 87 per cent of the 47 cases that had sufficient information to determine the charges pre and post the entering of a guilty plea involved some form of negotiation, leading to a withdrawal of charges and usually a reduction in both the number and seriousness of the remaining charges. Of these cases, 89 per cent (n = 42) included charges being withdrawn, which usually resulted in the defendant pleading guilty to fewer, less serious offences than those originally charged. Fifty-one per cent (n = 24) of these cases included specific details of how the case facts (the agreed summary) were negotiated with the prosecutor in order to present a particular version of events; although suggestions that the case facts were amended as part of discussions with the prosecutor were evident in the majority of files, albeit limited specifics were recorded as to what these factual "amendments" entailed.

Overview of Defendants and Victims

Forty-eight per cent of matters involved one defendant (n = 24), with the remaining cases involving two (n = 11; 22 per cent), three (n = 11; 22 per cent) and four or more defendants (n = 4; 8 per cent) (see Fig. 2.4).

The cases overwhelmingly involved male defendants (92 per cent) (see Fig. 2.5).[33]

In the files where age was specified (80 per cent), the majority of defendants were aged between 19 and 30 years (n = 22; 56 per cent), followed by 21 per cent aged 18 years or less (n = 8), 18 per cent aged between 31 and 45 years (n = 7) and 7 per cent aged 46 years and above (n = 2) (see Fig. 2.6).[34]

Indigenous status was only specified in 80 per cent of cases. Of these, the overwhelming majority did not identify as Indigenous or Torres Strait Islander (97 per cent; n = 39) (see Fig. 2.7).[35]

Almost without exception, defendants had a history of one or more problems such as mental illness, intellectual disability, drug and alcohol abuse and

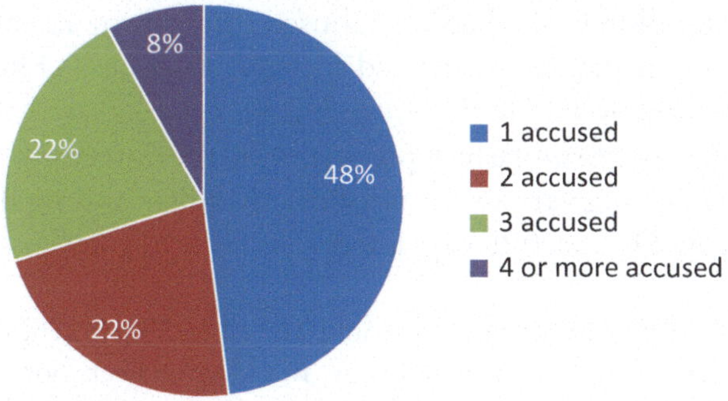

Fig. 2.4 Co-defendants

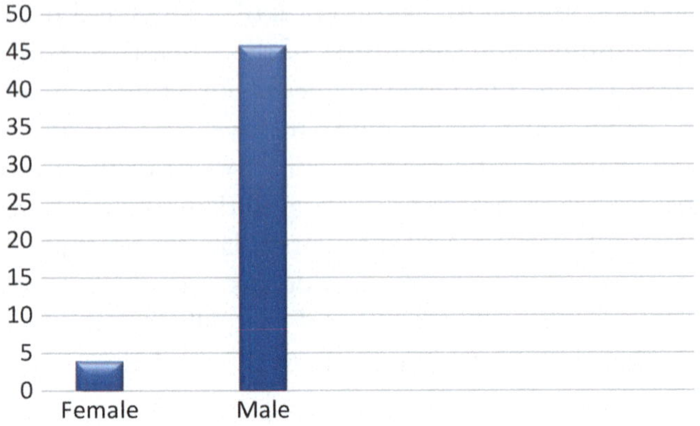

Fig. 2.5 Gender

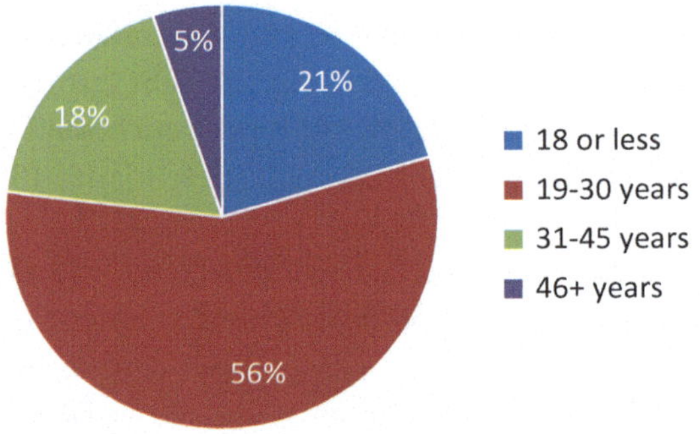

Fig. 2.6 Age

homelessness.[36] For example, the defendant in case 005-BD was intellectually impaired, had drug and alcohol addictions and had suffered sexual and physical abuse as a child. The defendant in case 011-VJ had been the victim of numerous violent relationships and had an acquired brain injury (ABI) and a diagnosed mental illness. She had also abused drugs from an early age. It was not uncommon that the defendant had suffered abuse as a child or was from a difficult or dysfunctional family (see Fig. 2.8).[37]

These findings were similarly represented in the interview data, with all participants recognising various forms of disadvantage among the defendants they deal with. As Defence09F explained:

> A lot of them are poorly educated. I would say 90 to 95 per cent of my legally aided clients have drug issues, whether or not they've been born addicted to drugs because their own parents had drug issues. They come from broken fami-

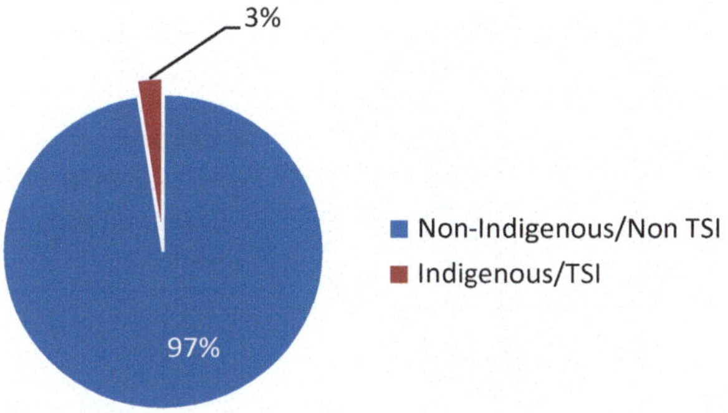

Fig. 2.7 Indigenous status

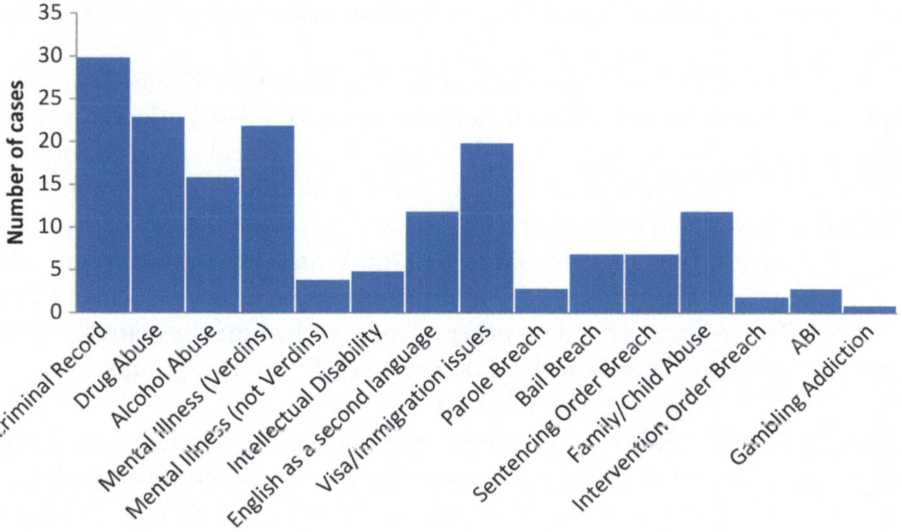

Fig. 2.8 Defendant background

> lies. They have themselves been victims of sexual, physical, emotional abuse. They have very low education. They're socially and economically disadvantaged and mental health is a huge issue.

Judge10F likewise maintained that "there are very few accused who come into this court committing offences at the level that bring them here, that haven't got significant social, drug, lifestyle, family, abuse issues in some form or another".

There were nine foreign nationals among the offending cohort with offences involving drugs, people smuggling and armed robbery. While there were some

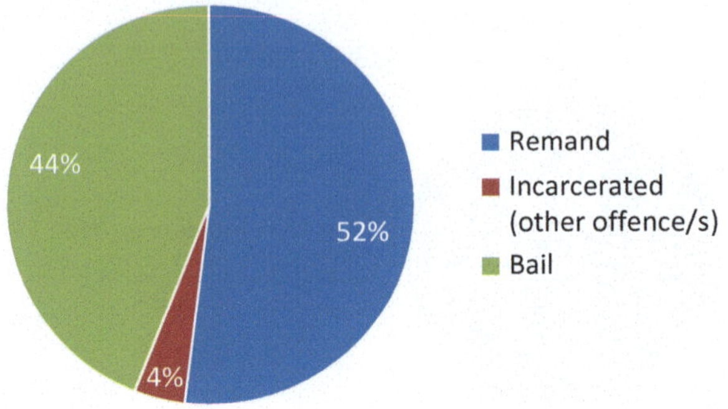

Fig. 2.9 Remand status

defendants for whom this was their first offence, generally the defendant had prior convictions.

There were six younger defendants on bail (aged between 18 and 21 years)—four for violence-related offending and two for drug-related offending. There were only two files where a young defendant was not at liberty pending their sentence. This occurred where a young person was already undergoing a sentence in a youth detention centre.

Fifty-two per cent of defendants were on remand for the offences with which they were charged ($n = 26$), 44 per cent were on bail ($n = 22$), and 4 per cent ($n = 2$) were incarcerated for other offences at the time the matter resolved (see Fig. 2.9). The defendants held on remand fell into two groups: (1) those facing violence offences and (2) foreign nationals.

Due to confidentiality requirements limiting access to the files, much of the information on the victim was redacted. Twenty-six per cent of cases did not specify details about the number of victims. Of those that did, most involved one victim (42 per cent; $n = 21$). Only 8 per cent of cases did not involve a victim ($n = 4$). In cases where gender was specified, most victims were male (63 per cent; $n = 19$). The victim's age was only specified in nine cases, of which the majority were aged between 19 and 30 years ($n = 5$).

Overview of Cases

The cases were prosecuted by the Victorian OPP ($n = 39$; 78 per cent) and the Commonwealth Department of Public Prosecutions (CDPP) ($n = 11$; 22 per cent). The CDPP is responsible for prosecuting all indictable commonwealth offences committed in the state of Victoria. Prior to any negotiations occurring, the majority of cases were scheduled to be heard in the (intermediate)

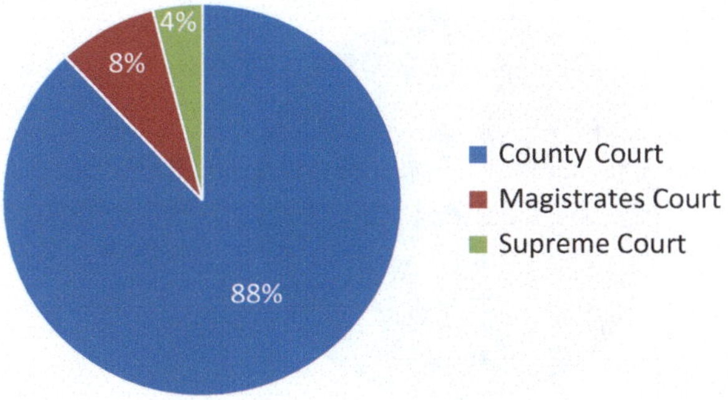

Fig. 2.10 Jurisdiction pre negotiation

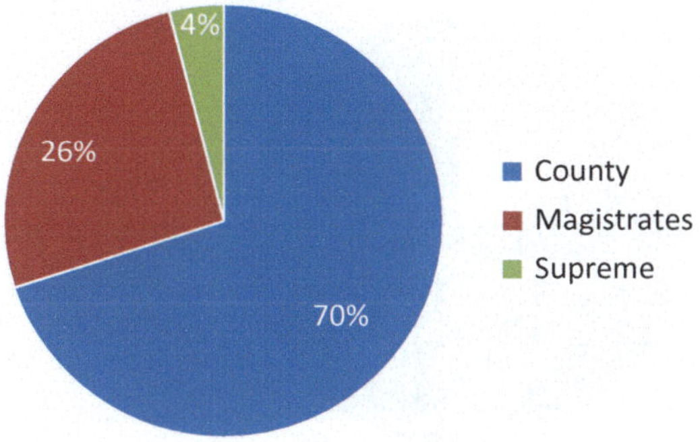

Fig. 2.11 Jurisdiction post negotiation

County Court (88 per cent; *n* = 44). The remainder were heard in the Magistrates' (*n* = 4; 8 per cent) and Supreme Courts (*n* = 2; 4 per cent). Following negotiations, 26 per cent (*n* = 13) of cases were sentenced in the Magistrates' Court. This represents an increase of 18 per cent (or nine cases) that were originally scheduled to be run in the County Court. The number of cases to be run in the Supreme Court remained unchanged (see Figs. 2.10 and 2.11).

Forty-seven of the de-identified case files contained information on the location of the offence. Overwhelmingly, the offences occurred in city locations (81 per cent; *n* = 38), with the majority (60 per cent; *n* = 28) committed in a public setting (see Figs. 2.12 and 2.13).

Sixty-six per cent of cases (*n* = 33) resulted in a period of imprisonment being imposed, with the mean sentence length just under 47 months. The longest period of imprisonment was 240 months, while the shortest was 4 months. The sentence discount applied as a result of s 6AAA of the *Sentencing Act 1991* (Vic) was only recorded in the case files in 22 instances. The dis-

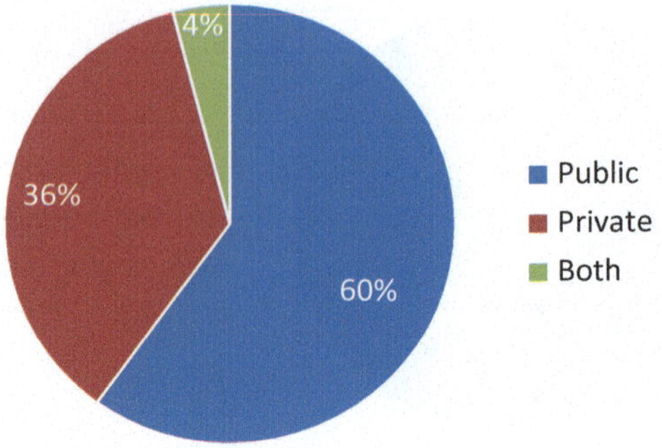

Fig. 2.12 Offence setting

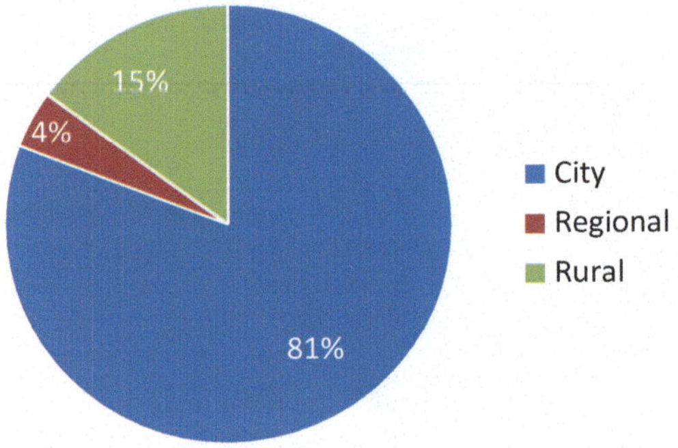

Fig. 2.13 Offence location

counts recorded ranged from between 5 and 72 months.[38] Suspended sentences were imposed in three cases,[39] and Community Correction Orders (CCOs)[40] were imposed in eight cases (16 per cent)—with a mean period of 17.25 months. CCOs were introduced in Victoria primarily as a replacement for Community-Based Orders and suspended sentences, taking effect from January 2012.[41] A CCO can be imposed on its own or in combination with other sentencing orders—for example, a period of imprisonment coupled with a CCO—which is referred to as a combination or combined sentence. In December 2014, the Court of Appeal of the Supreme Court of Victoria handed down a guideline judgment in *Boulton v The Queen*[42] which directed the court when determining whether to sentence a defendant to a CCO to "first assess the objective nature and gravity of the offence and the moral culpability of the offender". Following this, the court should consider whether:

(a) the crime as so assessed is so serious that nothing short of a sentence wholly comprised of an immediate term of imprisonment will suffice to satisfy the requirements of justice punishment; or
(b) a CCO, either alone or in conjunction with a sentence of imprisonment, would satisfy the requirements of just punishment.[43]

Between December 2014 and December 2015 (following this judgment), the SAC (2016b: xii) found that the percentage of combination sentences (imprisonment and CCO) increased from 28.8 to 34.3 per cent in the Magistrates' Court and from 17.7 to 35.3 per cent in the higher courts.

Generally, a CCO will require a defendant to "comply with a range of conditions, such as unpaid community work, treatment and supervision by a community corrections officer". It may also involve "curfews, restrictions on an offender's movements and non-associated conditions" (SAC 2016b: ix). The most common CCO conditions in the de-identified case files included unpaid community work and rehabilitation or treatment.

Notes

1. See, for example, *Criminal Procedure Act 2009* (Vic) ss 60 and 207–209; *Criminal Procedure (Sentence Indication) Amendment Act 1992* (NSW).
2. See, for example, *Department of Public Prosecutions Director's Guidelines* (Qld); *Department of Public Prosecutions Guidelines Charge Negotiations* (NT); *Department of Public Prosecutions Prosecution Policy* (ACT); *Director's Policy: Resolution* (Vic); *Office of the Department of Public Prosecutions Guideline 6* (NSW); *Office of the Department of Public Prosecutions Prosecution Policy and Guidelines* (Tas); *Prosecution Policy of the Commonwealth* (Cth); *Prosecution Policy Guideline Number Two – Charge Bargaining* (SA); and *Statement of Prosecution Policy and Guidelines* (WA).
3. Victorian Sentencing Advisory Council (2016d).
4. This excludes the prosecution of commonwealth offences.
5. This refers to matters that are heard in the County and Supreme Courts in regional and rural locations across Victoria.
6. The other pre-trial hearings include the committal hearing, which can proceed orally or on paper. The committal hearing occurs in the Magistrates' Court. It provides an opportunity to test whether the Crown's evidence is strong enough to support a conviction. If the evidence is considered strong enough, the accused is committed to stand trial (*Criminal Procedure Act 2009* (Vic) s 128-s 144). In the County Court, a subsequent directions hearing aims to clarify and resolve any questions of law or procedure, provide directions

for pre-trial filing, set a trial date and finalise any issues prior to trial that were not previously resolved (*Criminal Procedure Act 2009* (Vic) s 181). In the Supreme Court, the case conference provides an opportunity for the parties to advise the court on witness availability and estimates of trial length. A tentative trial date is also confirmed (*Supreme Court (Criminal Procedure) Rules 1998* (Vic), part 4). The final directions hearing is used to finalise trial arrangements in order to limit the likelihood of an adjournment (*Practice Note 1 of 2004* (Vic)). In the Magistrates' Court, the "trial" is referred to as a contested hearing. All guilty pleas and findings end with a plea hearing in which relevant material is presented to the judge to inform the sentence.

7. It is possible for a matter to proceed directly from the summary case conference to the contested hearing, thereby bypassing the contest mention. This is more common in cases involving unrepresented defendants.
8. Regulated by s 54 of the *Criminal Procedure Act 2009* (Vic).
9. Regulated by s 55 of the *Criminal Procedure Act 2009* (Vic); see Chap. 5 for a detailed discussion of these hearings.
10. *Criminal Procedure Act 2009* (Vic) s 54(1)(a).
11. Ibid. s 54(1)(b).
12. Ibid. s 54(1)(c).
13. See https://www.police.vic.gov.au/retrievemedia.asp?Media_ID=65536
14. See Chap. 7 for a discussion of sentence indications.
15. Regulated by ss 95–126 of the *Criminal Procedure Act 2009* (Vic).
16. Regulated by *Practice Note 1 of 1999* (Vic).
17. Regulated by ss 179–81 of the *Criminal Procedure Act 2009* (Vic).
18. Regulated by *Practice Note 5 of 2006.*
19. *Criminal Procedure Act 2009* (Vic) ss 207–209.
20. *Pun* [2017] VSCA 219 [at 2] (Redlich JA and McLeish JA).
21. *The Queen v JO* [2009] NTCCA 129 [at 105].
22. *Gallagher* (1991) NSWLR 220.
23. [1989] HCA 58 [at 14].
24. Unlike many US jurisdictions, an Australian defendant can only plead guilty or not guilty (other than a plea of not guilty on the grounds of insanity). Australian law does not recognise a *nolo contendere* plea (no contest) or what is termed an *Alford* plea, whereby a guilty plea may be entered but the accused is able to maintain his or her innocence (Redlich et al. 2017: 459).
25. *R v Di Simoni* [1981] HCA 31.
26. *Pun* [2017] VSCA 219 [at 4] (Redlich JA and McLeish JA).
27. *R v Foster Andrew Brown* (1989) 17 NSWLR 472 [at 479–481] (Gleeson CJ, Newman and Loveday JJ).
28. *R v Gallagher* (1991) 23 NSWLR 220 [at 232].
29. However, in a confidential submission to the Royal Commission into Institutional Responses to Child Sexual Abuse, some members of the judiciary expressed their concern that they were required to sentence on the basis

of charges that did not reflect what the accused had actually done (Royal Commission 2017b: 345).

30. Resolution is defined an agreement between the prosecution and the defendant, where the defendant will plead guilty to a particular charge or charges on the condition that the prosecution will withdraw, discontinue or not proceed with a different charge or charges (Policy of the DPP, at iv, See http://www.opp.vic.gov.au/getattachment/b5d48af4-3bef-4650-84fa-6b9befc776e0/DPP-Policy.aspx).
31. For a discussion of the guidelines in other jurisdictions, see Royal Commission (2017a, b: 333ff).
32. The Royal Commission into Institutional Responses to Child Sexual Abuse noted the importance of ensuring that prosecution charging and plea decisions in prosecutions for child sexual abuse offences should ensure that appropriate charges are laid to minimise the risk that they will have be to downgraded or withdrawn at a later date; that the prosecution agencies should recognise the importance to complainants and to the criminal justice system that the charges for which a guilty plea is accepted reflect the true criminality of the abuse that they suffered; and that adequate time be provided to consult victims and policy in relation to any proposal to downgrade or withdraw charges or to accept a negotiated guilty plea (Royal Commission 2017a, b: 62).
33. The effect of gender on guilty plea rates is unclear (Redlich et al. 2017: 461).
34. Age has not been found to be a factor in a decision to plead guilty (Redlich et al. 2017: 459).
35. We note that one reason for the low number of Indigenous and Torres Strait Islander clients may be that the Victorian Aboriginal Legal Service (VALS), which provides representation for the majority of Indigenous defendants, takes most of these Legal Aid cases. In the 2014–15 period, VALS (2015: 10) provided advice, information, case work and duty lawyer work 12,392 times in criminal matters.
36. Defendant background was specified in 48 of the 50 de-identified case files.
37. "Mental Illness (Verdins)" in Fig. 2.8 represents cases in which the *R v Verdins* (2007) 16 VR 269 principles were invoked in sentencing. Ulbrick et al. (2016: 11) explain that the Verdins principles are applicable to the sentencing of defendants who present evidence of mental illness in "at least six ways" where the impaired mental functioning:

    (1) may reduce moral culpability as distinct from legal responsibility; (2) may impact on the type of sentence imposed and the conditions in which it should be served; (3) may moderate or eliminate the need for general deterrence; (4) may moderate or eliminate the need for specific deterrence; (5) "may mean that a given sentence will weigh more heavily on the offender" than a person in normal health ...; and (6) "[w]here there is a

serious risk of imprisonment having a significant adverse effect on the offender's mental health" (*Verdins* [at 32]).

"Mental Illness (Non-Verdins)" represents cases in which mental illness was led in the plea and sentencing hearing but the Verdins principles were not invoked.

38. In essence, the *Sentencing Act 1991* (Vic) s 6AAA requires that, where a court imposes a less severe sentence than it would otherwise have imposed because the defendant pleaded guilty, it must state the sentence that it would have imposed but for the plea of guilty. See Chap. 7 for a discussion of s 6AAA.
39. Suspended sentences refer to "a period of imprisonment that is suspended (i.e. not activated) wholly or in part for a specified period (the 'operational period')" (SAC 2016b: ix). Suspended sentences were abolished by the *Sentencing Amendment (Abolition of Suspended Sentences and Other Matters) Act 2013* (Vic) in the County and Supreme Courts for all offences committed on or after 1 September 2013, and in the Magistrates' Court for all offences committed on or after 1 September 2014.
40. That is, a non-custodial sentence (see *Sentencing Act 1991* (Vic) Part 3A).
41. *Sentencing Amendment (Community Corrections Reform) Act 2011* (Vic).
42. [2014] VSCA 342 (22 December 2014) [at 3].
43. Ibid. [at 4].

3

Defining Plea Negotiations

There are almost as many definitions as there are terms to describe the plea negotiation process. A common theme within most academic definitions of plea negotiations is an agreement between the prosecution and the defendant for some concessions from the former, in exchange for a guilty plea from the latter. The literature refers to "binding promises and agreements between parties" (Manikis 2012: 411) and "state-induced guilty pleas" (McConville and Marsh 2014) which involve "concessions" (Yang 2013: 42), "a degree of clemency" (Bushway et al. 2014: 725), or, as Mackenzie et al. (2015: 580) describe, "the process where the prosecution and defence advocates negotiate or bargain or haggle". This chapter defines plea negotiations as they occur in Victoria including presenting a discussion of the four most common forms of plea negotiation in this jurisdiction.

Plea Negotiations Versus Plea Bargaining?

Referring to the process as a form of bargaining in this study was strongly rejected by the legal participants, who considered this term to have the potential to engender negative and inaccurate perceptions of the process. As Judge11F explained, "bargaining has got a very nasty connotation to it". Likewise, Judge06M claimed, "I hate the term 'plea bargain' because it doesn't represent at all what happens. It's not a marketplace where it's the price to the highest bidder". This view was similarly expressed by Defence20M, who observed that "bargaining implies a sinister interpretation … like somebody is trying to cut an unfair deal".

A. Flynn, A. Freiberg, *Plea Negotiations*, Palgrave Socio-Legal Studies,
https://doi.org/10.1007/978-3-319-92630-8_3

Participants also pointed to phrases like "bargain", "deal" and "plea bargaining" as "having that American connotation" (Prosecutor01F) and creating a view of the process that is not reflective of Victorian practices:

> There's something … a little bit seedy about the word deal or bargain and probably it has connotations of American TV and doesn't really reflect what we do in negotiating pleas. It's not a deal that you strike, it's more complex than that. (Defence03F)

In particular, they pointed to the term plea bargaining as creating a "false perception of pressure" (Judge07M) on defendants, a lack of "consideration of victims" (Prosecutor03M) and "the prosecution inappropriately giving something up" (Prosecutor01F):

> Look, I think in the Australian, Victorian experience … the way that things are negotiated are pretty robust and so that it's not – the fears that we have that result from the American plea negotiation systems are just not here. … But my fear is that people are more seduced by the terminology [plea bargain] and connect it to other experiences, which are not our experiences. So, they say plea negotiations? That must be like that dreadful system where everyone in America pleads guilty because they've got no choice or … deals are done to undersell things because we can't run a trial. That's not our system. (Judge07M)

In contrast to the majority view, some participants described negotiations in more overt terms:

> I call it a deal. (Judge05M)

> Well my preferred terminology's horse trading, I'm serious … that's what it is. (Defence01M)

> I've used the term deal. (Judge09M)

While most expressed a preference for a term like plea negotiations, on the basis that it is more reflective of the process, participants often inadvertently referred to plea negotiations as requiring you to "give up" (Defence14FR) or "give away" (Prosecutor05M), "trade" (Defence01M), "battle" (Defence14FR), "win" (Defence25MR) and "lose" (Defence17F). Participants also referred to the process as "gambling" (Defence19M), something that requires you to have "a bargaining position" (Prosecutor05M), and described the outcome as coming down to who has "the better bargaining chip" (Defence25MR). Another common theme conveyed by the participants was the concept of each side having a "bottom line" (Prosecutor06M). As Prosecutor06M maintained, "there are situations where you put a bottom line to the defence and say, well, look, this is what we'd accept. This is the minimum we'd accept for an early resolution of the matter". At the roundtable, similar comments were also made. Defence30M, for example, referred to plea negotiations as "horse trading, to be crude about it", and Judge15M defined the judge's role in negotiations as "the scoreboard". When asked to expand on this comment, he explained, "it's because you're the result. You determine who wins the negotiation because you determine what the sentence is. You try and look at things impartially obviously, but you're not umpiring, you are the scoreboard".

These phrases, which were all used by the participants when describing their experiences with plea negotiations, as opposed to when they were focused on defining the process, suggest that there is some merit to describing the process as somewhat akin to a bargain:

> Sometimes there are – like in any negotiation, sometimes there are bits you have to give up and you have your wins and your losses in any plea negotiation. (Defence14FR)

Fox and Deltondo (2015) suggest that "the phrase 'plea bargaining' fails to adequately represent the complexity of the processes that may lead representatives of the prosecution and defence … to engage in discussions aimed at the early resolution of a criminal case". This was certainly the view among most of the participants, who considered that terms like "bargaining" fail to capture the many nuances inherent to the negotiated guilty plea process:

> Bargaining is too crude a word but it's a colloquial way of describing what happens. It is a genuine negotiation quite often over time and it's not as crude as bargaining implies. (Judge12M)

> The term negotiation I think is a better term. I don't think we bargain with people. (Prosecutor01F)

> I don't like the word deal or bargain; it's about negotiating the best outcome for your client. (Defence14FR)

> Ninety-nine out of 100 times, the defendant acknowledges that they've done A, B, C and D and the police, as a matter of practice, always charge with every offence that could fit within the factual or the acknowledged evidentiary content of the case, so … finding the right charge to properly represent the culpability, the offending, the behaviour is really what it's all about in 99 out of 100 cases. So that's a settlement rather than any kind of bargaining. (Judge06M)

Ultimately, there was a majority preference among participants for a more all-encompassing umbrella term like "plea negotiations", "early resolutions" or "settlements" to describe what occurs, not only to better capture the process, but also to make sure a "more neutral term" (Judge12M) is applied to put a "more positive shine" (Judge12M) on the process for those outside the legal community. As Defence12FR explained:

> Using the word bargaining or deal implies that it's almost a bit underhanded, or that it's not a fair process or a fair outcome. I think negotiations is a better word to be used for people who aren't in the legal sphere. If they hear about it, they're more likely to trust the process if it's called negotiation.

Most Common Forms of Negotiation

Within both the case file and interview data, there were three forms of plea negotiation most consistently evident: (1) withdrawing and substituting charges, (2) rolling up or creating representative counts, and (3) negotiating the agreed summary of facts.[1] As several defence practitioner participants observed:

> The rolling up of charges, the amendments of summaries, withdrawing alternatives, that sort of stuff's the everyday negotiations. (Defence03F)

> Withdrawing charges, negotiating the summary and alternative charges. ... Those are the bread and butter, every day ones. ... They'd really be the ones we'd be dealing with on a daily basis. (Defence08MR)

> Agreements on the summary of facts and withdrawing or substituting or rolling up counts, that's what we do in most of our matters. (Defence14FR)

> Rolling up, representative agreement ... that's my bread and butter. (Defence17F)

> Withdrawing of charges and substituting of charges. ... That's probably the most regular negotiation point. ... Withdrawing some of the charges happens in almost every case. (Defence18M)

In addition to these three forms, the interview data strongly indicate that an agreement on the prosecution's sentencing submission is a very common form of negotiation, identified as such by 97 per cent of interviewees. Although it was only evident in 10 per cent of the de-identified case files ($n = 5$), the stakeholders at the roundtable also identified this form of negotiation as one of the most common. Thus, based on all the available data, it is contended that the most common forms of plea negotiation in Victoria (in no particular order) are (1) withdrawing and substituting charges, (2) rolled-up charges and representative counts, (3) negotiating the agreed summary of facts and (4) agreements on the prosecution's sentencing submission.

Withdrawing and Substituting Charges

In almost every file examined, the defendant faced multiple charges arising from the one incident, which were either alternative charges (such as armed robbery or robbery, and intentionally causing serious injury or recklessly causing serious injury) or duplicitous, lesser included charges (such as armed robbery and possession of a controlled weapon). In each of these circumstances, the plea offer always included identifying which charge/s the defendant would plead guilty to and which charge/s would be withdrawn. For example, in case 011-VJ:

> The VLA solicitor initially wrote to the prosecutor identifying which charges the defendant would be contesting and why. The defendant was prepared to plead guilty to two counts of intentionally causing injury, but contested the charges of assault police, assault and assault in company. There were several email exchanges recorded back and forth between the VLA solicitor and the prosecutor in an attempt to negotiate these remaining offences. The key argument was whether the evidence made out the charges, and then whether there was a defence at law.

> With regard to the assault police charge, the defendant's solicitor argued that the police actions were improper and the charge could not be made out. The assault and assault in company offence relied on closed-circuit television (CCTV) footage, which the defence solicitor argued was not sufficient to make out the charges laid. In responding to this initial offer, the prosecutor replied that the matter relating to the assault police was made out, as there was a lawful basis for the defendant's arrest, and that the CCTV footage did support the assault and assault in company charges. The prosecutor accepted the guilty plea offers to intentionally causing injury, and said he would accept a guilty plea to affray in exchange for dropping the assault in company and assault charges. No offer on the *assault police was* made.

> The VLA solicitor responded by confirming the defendant would plead guilty to the intentionally causing injury counts, but argued that the brief involving police would be a contest on the basis of whether the arrest was lawful or not, and that a charge of affray was not appropriate for the other contested charge, as the defendant was acting in self-defence. In response, the prosecutor accepted the defendant's account of the fight, and offered to accept a guilty plea to assault in company (instead of affray), but the assault police charge would need to proceed.

The VLA solicitor briefed counsel to appear before the magistrate for pleas to two settled matters (intentionally causing injury and assault in company), and requested that they try to hold a summary case conference with the prosecutor to get the assault police charges withdrawn. These negotiations resulted in a withdrawal of the assault police charge and the defendant pleaded guilty to resisting police.

Another example of the withdrawal of charges can be found in case 035-ST:

The defendant was charged with a number of burglaries and alternative charges of possessing the proceeds of crime. The resolution involved the prosecution withdrawing the burglary charges and the defendant pleaded guilty to possessing the proceeds of crime only.

The decision to withdraw charges was viewed by interview participants as "common" (Judge10F; Judge11F; Judge13F) and "routine" (Judge12M):

> That's routinely done after a discussion, normally after a person has agreed to plead guilty to a particular charge or a group of charges, other charges of a less serious [nature] are withdrawn. Sometimes more serious charges are withdrawn. (Judge12M)

As Prosecutor05M observed, "that is something that I would do on a regular basis". Defence01M went so far as to describe withdrawing charges as "the essence of all plea bargaining". Defence25MR similarly highlighted this as a primary aim of negotiations, noting that "the ultimate goal is to get as few charges as possible". In describing the "pretty common" process, Defence08MR explained that:

> Quite often you'll get, you know, particularly in a sort of assault type situation, you'll be given a number of charges of intentionally causing injury, reckless[ly] cause injury, assault and it's a matter of working out which ones get withdrawn as the alternative.

Defence20M similarly maintained, "usually most withdrawals come in a context of, would you accept a plea of guilty to a lesser charge on the basis that you withdraw the most serious charge?"

Participants identified withdrawing charges as something akin to an administrative task, as a way to "simplify" and "clarify" matters moving forward. As

Prosecutor03F noted, "most cases you would probably withdraw some charges, just purely for simplifying matters in the end". Similarly, Prosecutor01F observed that the criminality of the offending conduct can be represented in fewer counts, or even less serious charges; hence, withdrawing charges is a common practice for prosecutors:

> You don't need ten charges when two of the more serious ones may reflect the criminality. Now, by that I'm not meaning to say, well, we withdraw charges willy-nilly … that's not what happens. … Sometimes when I look at things, if you've got a number of charges, well, do you really need that one? Or technically it might be there, but, sentencing-wise, the person is going to get concurrency for that so it may not ultimately make much of a difference.

In the de-identified case files, it was also very common for the defendant to plead guilty to a substituted charge, whereby the OPP or police prosecutor would accept a guilty plea to an alternative charge, usually one that reduced the severity and aggravation of the original charge/s. For example, in case 019-DD:

> The defendant was charged with burglary with intent to assault, intentionally causing serious injury, intentionally causing injury and recklessly causing serious injury. The defendant offered to plead guilty to recklessly causing serious injury on the basis that there were reliability issues with the victim's evidence and insufficient medical evidence to support the other charges. The OPP initially rejected this offer but eventually accepted the guilty plea, if the defendant would also plead guilty to criminal damage. This was accepted by the defence and guilty pleas were entered to recklessly causing serious injury and criminal damage as a substitute for intentionally causing serious injury and intentionally causing injury. This agreement also resulted in the burglary with intent to assault charge being withdrawn.

In the interviews, participants referred to the substituting of charges as "very common" (Defence19M; Defence22M) and "a matter of course" (Defence02F). In fact, Judge09M described it as "the most common form of plea negotiations", while Defence11M suggested that "you'd be negligent if you didn't pursue it". Defence12FR detailed the following common examples:

> Quite frequently we substitute use of threatening words in a public place, instead of a threat to kill charge, or threats to inflict serious injury, instead of threat to kill, or a dangerous driving, instead of reckless conduct endangering life, that kind of thing.

Defence22M likewise provided the following example of a recent case involving the substitution of charges:

> I acted for a person … and the police were contemplating charges of reckless conduct endangering persons, or serious injury. And we said, we don't think you're going to be able to sustain that charge. … [*outlines reasons why*].[2] And so we said, but we'll plead guilty to a charge of … criminal damage. … [A] much less serious charge. So, we eliminated the reckless conduct charge, which was what he was investigated for … then the person was charged with criminal damage.

While recognising the frequent use of this form of negotiation, the prosecutor participants were quick to point out that accepting a guilty plea to the lesser charge is only done if it "adequately represent[s] the criminality" (Prosecutor06M). As Prosecutor06M went on to explain:

> If you're resolving a matter as a plea of guilty, the lesser charge must encompass the criminality involved in the offending. … There has to be evidence of it, obviously, and again it has to represent the total criminality and that's an important consideration. I mean, if you got to the stage of saying, we would accept a lesser charge, however, that doesn't really represent criminality, then that's not the right decision.

Defence practitioners also pointed to the need for the evidence to support the lesser charge:

> It really does depend on the evidence, whether or not it supports it. Some drug offences are quite straightforward, it's either you have the quantity or the commercial quantity or you don't have the commercial quantity. (Defence02F)

However, in line with the perceptions of McConville and Marsh (2014) and Newman (2013), one of the judicial participants argued that sometimes the "pragmatic benefit" of the negotiated guilty plea may override adequate consideration of the evidence. Drawing on some recent examples, he explained:

> It causes a lot of difficulty, because you may get an offer from the defence to plead to an offence which is less grave than the one they're charged with, and one understands the sense of doing that at a pragmatic level. But you reach a point where the new charge to which the person offers to plead guilty simply doesn't fit the facts, and that's when problems really arise. … I did a plea … involving two [defendants]. … One of them offered to plead guilty to culpable driving causing death. The other … wouldn't plead to that, but would plead only to dangerous driving causing death, which is a lesser penalty carrying a lesser maximum sentence. Their

> conduct was relatively indistinguishable and the Crown accepted the plea [I believe] in order to avoid a trial. That made it quite difficult for me when sentencing the lesser offender to justify, as it were, given that it's objective liability, there wasn't a question of mens rea, it was just both of them acted with a high degree of negligence. That was the basis on which the culpable was put, and of course the lesser offence. I've also had examples where people have imported or dealt with very large quantities of drugs, plainly large commercial quantity or whatever, and have been allowed to plead to just a commercial quantity. Well, again the judge is put in a difficult situation.

In the US context, Brown (2014: 113) argues that the pragmatic benefits of the plea negotiation combined with the caseload pressures experienced in the court system "force[s] courts and prosecutors to find ways to adjudicate more efficiently and to take those efficiency gains in the first form – by increasing the supply of adjudication, or the production of convictions, to meet increased demand". He continues, "the goal of judges and prosecutors who find ways to process cases more quickly is not to handle the same number of cases and allocate the savings elsewhere; the goal (and need) is to process more cases" (Brown 2014: 113).

In Australia, the efficiency pressures facing the courts and prosecutors have been well recognised (Flynn 2011). In his time as Victorian DPP, Mr Jeremy Rapke QC (2010: 46) identified efficiency-driven pressures on prosecutors, noting that the OPP was managing "a higher volume of cases across both traditional and new areas of the criminal law", while also "fac[ing] continuing pressure to contribute to reducing case backlogs". The practical manifestation of these pressures can be seen in the legislation binding prosecutors,[3] which imposes a statutory obligation to ensure prosecutions are conducted in an efficient, economic and effective manner—an outcome erstwhile Victorian DPP John Champion SC (2012: 2) claimed was assisted by plea negotiations: "early plea resolutions in cases have a clear role to play in achieving this". Significantly, the legislation governing the role of government-funded defence lawyers in Victoria[4] is presented in identical terms.[5]

Flynn's (2016: 574) study of plea negotiations and prosecutorial discretion in Victoria found that the "strong focus on efficiency can lead to prosecutors experiencing some pressures to resolve cases through plea-negotiations". While recognising that these pressures were not resulting in prosecutors resolving cases inappropriately where the public interest dictated that a case should proceed to trial, Flynn (2016: 574) argued that they do create an unfortunate "perception that this could occur; that the external and internal pressures placed on prosecutors by the courts, their office, and the legislation to move matters more efficiently, will lead to inappropriate plea-negotiations".

Rolled-Up Charges and Representative Counts

Common in the de-identified case files were agreements to a representative count, or to charges being rolled-up. A rolled-up charge "can comprise a number of separate offences against the same statutory provision, even where they do not amount to a single transaction (e.g. where the acts occurred on different occasions)" (Victorian Government Solicitor's Office 2014). Defence23M described rolled-up counts as follows:

> It might be that there are multiple thefts from the same victim, and rather than them having 21 charges of theft ... when it may be over a very short period of time with the same victim, the prosecution are willing to negotiate to say, for example, that between the first of September and the first of December, that Mr X did steal 'x' number of items owing to 'x', but it [this conduct] is recognised under one charge.

Many participants described rolling up charges as "extremely sensible" (Judge05M). As Judge01M maintained, "rolling up charges is almost just a sensible, a perfectly sensible way of resolving a number of matters". Judge13F identified that the rationale for this form of negotiation is "to avoid having what is often described as an overloaded presentment or an overloaded indictment". She explained:

> You might end up instead of 50 charges you might have five. ... It's more prevalent in sex and fraud cases ... and drugs cases ... where there's lots of different individual transactions or events or incidences of criminal conduct, all of which really are much the same as each other and it can just be dealt with in that fashion.

In this regard, the rolling up of charges was commonly identified as a way to "simplify everything" (Defence07M). Defence07M further stated that "the court likes it. Clients usually gravitate to it and it's sort of a hybrid way of resolving a matter". An example of this form of negotiation from the de-identified case files was case 009-SA:

> The defendant faced almost 30 charges of obtaining financial advantage by deception arising from his fraudulent use of money owned by various investors to conduct trades. The resolution included the prosecution withdrawing charges which were not supported by evidence, and, where there were multiple instances of fraud using money owned by one investor, rolling up these multiple incidents into one charge.

One of the main reasons why participants identified this form of negotiation as "administrative" was because while the number of charges a defendant pleads guilty to is reduced when the counts are rolled-up, the summary of facts presented to the court for sentencing should explain that the charge encompasses a number of distinct offences, so that the sentence takes into account that there has been more than one offence committed. This means that the sentence is likely to be similar to what it would have been were the charges not rolled-up, regardless of the fact that the defendant is pleading guilty to fewer charges and will have fewer convictions recorded. For this reason, participants tended to identify this form of negotiation as a "tool" (Prosecutor08M) and "technique" (Judge08M) used by prosecutors in acquiring guilty pleas, which may not have the same level of benefit for defendants. As Prosecutor08M maintained:

> That's quite often a tool that is used ... because for the accused, all of a sudden they're only facing ten charges rather than 120, but from our behalf we're still prosecuting them on all of the offences with the same summary. So that's a big tool that we use.

Judge08M similarly observed that "rolling up counts is a technique used in plea negotiations ... in some respects it's a little bit of a sweetener to the defendant, to [help] get the plea resolution over the line". When asked to clarify what was meant by the use of the term "sweetener" in this context, Judge08M maintained that:

> The prosecution really doesn't lose a lot by it because, ultimately, whether it's a rolled-up charge or individual charges, the defendant will still be sentenced for the very same conduct. In other words, one's not actually withdrawing any conduct, wrongful conduct, off the table; just the number of charges is less. Instead of sentencing the person for multiple, less serious charges, the judge is sentencing the person probably more realistically for a handful of between dates charges.

This outcome was also identified by Judge05M, who claimed that:

> Realistically, you know if you get a rolled-up charge of ten indecent acts against children or one, the difference is going to be minimal ... [in terms of] the actual sentence. It makes everybody feel better, but the actual difference in the sentence isn't going to be that great.

While such an outcome "makes everyone feel better", according to Judge05M, this view may not be shared by victims who have their victimisation experiences "rolled-up" into one charge. As Flynn (2012: 86) observes, plea negotiations "will often require a negotiation between the interests of the victims involved and a satisfactory outcome in terms of the broader public's interests". In addition, the benefits may not be fully shared by the defendant, especially in cases where they are unaware that their guilty plea to fewer charges will likely not affect the sentence imposed.

Like rolled-up counts, representative counts are used to reduce the number of charges to which a defendant will plead guilty, purportedly without reducing the criminality of their conduct. Judge09M described representative counts as "another technique which is used in plea negotiations … to simplify", while Judge08M observed that "if we didn't have representative counts we'd have indictments with hundreds of charges on them which we couldn't deal with". Representative counts are thus used as a way of representing a course of conduct—so the defendant may plead guilty to one count of rape that is representative of several charges of rape against the same individual (Freiberg 2014: 153). For example, in case 029-ZM, the defendant offered to plead guilty to one charge of indecent assault to cover two relevant acts (touching the victim's breast and rubbing his penis against the victim). Participants suggested that representative counts are "most commonly used in sexual offence cases" (Defence10FR; see also Defence 18M, Defence20Ml, Judge07M, Judge11F). As Defence 09F explained:

> My experience has certainly been that representative counts are most often found in sex cases. Again, you might have a number of different charges to begin with and the matter will generally resolve as a plea to a representative count, being representative of a number of different occasions, but the client feels more comfortable pleading to one charge (even though it's classed as a representative charge), rather than, say, three different charges.

In particular, participants observed that historical sexual offences are commonly made into representative counts, usually because it can be difficult for the victim to identify exact dates and times, making the prosecution more complex. Prosecutor05M identified these difficulties, noting that "often you have statements that say he did this to me once a week, or something, but we don't have exact dates and so it may be appropriate to have a representative count on that basis". In such circumstances, the defendant should still be sentenced on a history of misconduct "on the basis that this is not an isolated event" (Prosecutor05M). Defence04M similarly maintained:

> The explanation in relation to sex cases is probably because you have a complainant who will say, I can remember that it happened on my birthday. I can remember that it happened on the last day of school. They can pick out particu-

lar dates where they have a specific memory, but then they will go on to say, but it was happening on a regular basis. And so the counts that you actually plead to are seen as representative of what is invariably an ongoing … [illegal] sexual activity.

Defence03F used a recent case she had dealt with in the County Court to demonstrate the evidentiary difficulties in historical sexual offence prosecutions:

It was a historical sex matter [with] two complainants, ended up with one charge of carnal knowledge of a girl between ten and 16 for both of them and that was representative for one complainant of a three-year period and involved conduct of penetration, touching, it encompassed a lot of different conduct. And the other one was over a 12-month period for the other complainant. So, I think that's probably something we commonly see with historical sex matters, particularly because it's so hard to pinpoint times and dates, so for them [the prosecutor] to come up with individual counts can be quite difficult. And especially given the passage of time, it becomes a lot easier for the prosecution to accept a representative count than to try and prosecute numerous counts.

As in the case of rolled-up charges, the fact that the offence is representative should be specified in the summary of facts presented to the court for sentencing to ensure that the penalty acknowledges that this is a course of conduct, not simply a one-off offence. However, unlike rolled-up counts, in relation to which participants suggested that it "doesn't make a lot of difference [to the sentence]" (Judge05M), representative counts were identified as both a "tool to minimise the number of charges on the indictment" and a way to generate a "lesser sentencing outcome than if you have specified charges for each of the alleged forms of behaviour" (Judge08M). While Defence02F stated that in the case of a representative charge "the sentence itself does not actually change; the client is still being sentenced on, for example, a ten-year period of offending"; in contrast, most judicial participants argued that the sentence would be lower, because "there's a particular way the court looks at representative counts and it generally would result in a lesser sentencing outcome" (Judge08M). Judge09M similarly outlined the different manner in which a judge must approach sentencing in representative versus rolled-up cases:

One's got to be very careful with a representative charge that the representative charge adequately and properly reflects the overall offending … unlike a rolled-up charge. … With a rolled-up charge, the judge must punish the person for everything that falls within the ambit of the rolled-up charge in sentencing the defendant. With a representative charge, the rules are different. With a represen-

> tative charge, technically the judge can only punish the person for the charge. … He's [sic] punishing the defendant with respect to that individual charge, but within that wider context. … It's not isolated, that's the true basis of it. But he [sic] can't actually punish him [sic] directly for the other acts.

For these reasons, Defence05M identified representative counts as "more advantageous to an accused than a rolled-up count, because it will get rid of a number of different offences that would be used for accumulation, so we would try and look at representative conduct counts to avoid what otherwise might be accumulation".

Taking Offences into Account

Under s 100 of the *Sentencing Act 1991* (Vic), when sentencing a defendant, the court may take into account other pending charges that have been filed with the court and that the defendant admits to having committed (Freiberg 2014: 148–52). Known as "taking offences into consideration", this procedure is similar to that surrounding representative counts in that it allows offences in relation to which the defendant has not been formally convicted to be taken into account in sentencing while barring any further proceedings in respect of these offences. Additionally, the admission is not regarded as a conviction. This means that these offences are formally accounted for, or cleared, and obviates the need for further investigation. While the offences taken into account will generally augment the sentence for the principal offence, the increase is likely to be less than that which would have been the case had the charges been separately prosecuted (Freiberg 2014: 150).

Although this procedure has been available for decades, it was almost unknown to participants and, according to those who were aware of the procedure, rarely, if ever, used. When the subject was raised in the interviews, some respondents had to resort to the legislation to ascertain what the procedure involved.

Judicial participants knew of the procedure, but hardly ever employed it. One judge expressed his dislike for it on the ground that it is not transparent, analogising it to aggregate or global sentences where individual sentences for individual charges are subsumed under one total sentence (Judge 09M). Prosecutors varied in their views. Most agreed that it was rarely used, and was solely a means by which a defendant could get rid of some charges (Prosecutor 07M). However, one prosecutor stated that the procedure was used frequently and is useful because it allows a number of matters to be dealt with at once, while enabling the court to understand the totality of the person's offending (Prosecutor03F). The defence practitioner participants rarely invoked it, with the majority unaware of the provision. When it was identified by defence practitioners, it was mostly in relation to sex offences. Of the defence practitioners who knew of the procedure, Defence21M noted that it happens occasionally as "part of a cleaning up of a mess situation rather than anything else. It's just mopping up so that there's finality and that is sensible". Defence22M likewise noted the pragmatic rationale for the procedure:

> We always do it and, generally speaking, it benefits our client. … If you've got an armed robbery and you're going to go to jail for three to five years and you've got five burglaries, you might get some small level of accumulation. … But, if you deal with them individually, you're much more likely to get [a discount for bulk].

It was surprising that these longstanding legislative provisions are so little known and used. They have been the subject of appellate guidance and, in some Australian jurisdictions, specific comment in prosecution guidelines.[6] If the procedure is now considered irrelevant or impractical, it should possibly be repealed, but if it still serves a purpose, its existence and usefulness might be drawn to the attention of prosecutors and defence practitioners through continuing education programs or other means as another form of plea negotiation, similar to representative counts.

Negotiating the Facts

There were 24 de-identified case files where the negotiated outcome included a specific agreement on the entirety or part of the facts to be put before the court on the plea. For example, in case 023-LM:

> The offer made by the defence acknowledged that the defendant had committed an armed robbery with a weapon, but contended that the charge of recklessly causing injury (and the charged alternatives of assault and assault with a weapon) could not be made out because the victim's hand was cut by accident. The prosecution accepted this argument, and those charges were withdrawn. The fact that the victim's hand was cut did not remain in the agreed summary of facts as relevant to the narrative of the incident.

Among the 24 files, the agreement about the facts related either to the facts that supported the elements of the offence to which the plea was to be entered, or the facts that were to be led as "context" (and could be used in aggravation or mitigation) but were not seen as directly relevant to whether the offence was made out. An example of a negotiated agreement on the facts supporting an element of the offence was evident in case 016-AF:

> The defendant hit and injured a pedestrian with his car. Both the prosecution and defence agreed that the appropriate charge was recklessly causing serious injury. The issue in dispute was the facts upon which the element of recklessness was based. The negotiation around the facts was conducted to avoid a contested fact hearing on the plea.

The following are examples of files where the factual negotiation was not integral to the proof of the offence (or an element of the offence), but was instead focused on which facts would be led as context and were deemed relevant to either mitigation or aggravation:

> The defendant conceded that he cultivated a commercial quantity of cannabis. However, the facts negotiated were how he came to be involved, what he *actually did, and* whether he was paid (case 008-VT).

> The defendant was charged with armed robbery on the basis that he was armed with both an imitation firearm and a knife. The defence offered to plead guilty to armed robbery if the reference to the knife was removed from the summary of facts. This was agreed to by the prosecution (case 010-CD).

Even in the absence of specific details of the revised summary of facts, the de-identified case files revealed that the facts were almost always discussed during plea negotiations as part of the process, whereby one or both parties contended that certain charges were supported (or not) by the evidence. All interview participants likewise identified the agreed summary as a key element of negotiations. As Judge02MR observed, "that happens in every case. That there is a form of agreement, there is always some form of negotiation, particularly when you've got an offence against the person and in terms of words perhaps spoken, or actions pre or post the offence". Judge13F maintained that "the settled summary is very significant and it's a very major part of whether a case resolves or not". Defence14FR similarly claimed that:

> We negotiate bits out of summaries on a very regular basis; even when there are not charges being withdrawn. … It occurs often. Sometimes with big changes and sometimes with relatively minor ones that just make a big difference to the way the client feels about what they're pleading guilty to. … Sometimes it's just about, we'll plead to an assault but the client says he didn't kick her. Certainly he pushed her over but he denies the kick. The kick comes out, the client pleads. Everybody's relatively happy.

Prosecutor08M commented on the prevalence of this form of negotiation, describing it as "the most regular resolution tool I use. … Quite often it's beneficial to resolve it to that because you've still got the same charges, it's just a less aggravating summary". When discussing this form of negotiation at the roundtable, Defence28M likewise observed:

> I'd be very reluctant to go anywhere near a plea without having the broad facts outlined. … When your client pleads, with the facts, we've got to establish as much as possible that it's in the lower end or it's in the middle end [of culpability]. I've found that prosecutors are open to that, not to drafting line-by-line openings, but a sequence of events that are critical.

Defence03F provided the following example of a negotiated summary of facts from one of her recent plea negotiations involving sexual offences against two persons:

> [In this matter], some of the allegations included anal penetration and also the use of various objects. And that was something that, as part of those negotiations, we had any reference to objects or anal penetration removed. … This matter also involved a co-accused. … We didn't accept anything that they alleged against her. They said that she knew [the victims] were having sex with him and that she was giving them alcohol to encourage them to do that. Now, our client completely denied that and part of the resolution was that there not be any reference to her, other than that she is the co-accused and has committal proceedings pending. And then I get the summary and it's littered with all of this stuff [implicating the co-defendant]. … So, that was just a process then of me writing back to them and saying, no we don't accept that, them coming back with another version without that in it and we pleaded [guilty].

The only participants who considered negotiations on the agreed summary of facts as a less common outcome were two prosecutors in the indictable stream. Prosecutor01F, for example, claimed:

> Why should I change the facts unless they're wrong? … I refuse to change the facts … just to soften it for the defence. … I might give instructions to whoever is coming to see me: okay, we'll accept the plea to that, but we're not changing the facts at all. The facts stay as they are. … So often that's the twin side of the negotiating process. We might agree to a lesser charge, but no, not to [altering] the facts.

Prosecutor05M similarly observed that "there would be a lot of cases where there is no fact bargaining. … I would have thought that a vast majority of pleas, there's not actually really that much discussion about the facts". However, in putting forward these views, both Prosecutor01F and Prosecutor05M then went on to provide personal examples involving this type of negotiation, with Prosecutor05M later describing it as "not uncommon", and Prosecutor01F listing a number of exceptions to her refusal to "change the facts":

> The facts stay as they are, except, and this, again, gets a bit tricky, except where if you've completely withdrawn a charge then you sometimes can't allege the facts. It sort of just depends … so yes, it does happen. (Prosecutor01F)

Prosecutor05M did stipulate that, in his experience, such negotiations generally relate "to peripheral matters, matters on the edge". He went on:

> The decision is often, well, is this really necessary? Do we really want to run a trial just to establish this particular fact? … It's often important to the accused, and the question becomes, how important is it to the prosecution? If it's important, then you'll say no, if it's not important; then you might agree to removing that particular fact. I mean, it may be that it's simply something that there is no evidence about, but somehow has found its way into the [summary] … so then you're happy to give it away.

The stipulations expressed by these two prosecutors may be due to the sense of unease that arises from the idea that facts can be altered or amended to support a lesser charge—a "process that does not 'mislead the court', rather it just avoids telling it the entire story" (Flynn 2012: 83). Altering the agreed summary of facts has numerous implications particularly in relation to the sentence imposed, and, as participants explained, it is the summary that "informs the punishment, even more so than the charges listed" (Defence22M). Such concerns about negotiations on the agreed summary have also been expressed internationally. In England and Wales, for example, McConville and Marsh (2014: 144) have observed:

> Many instances in which the CPS [Crown Prosecution Service] has misrepresented the facts, failed to check the factual basis of the plea, failed to assess intelligently the defendant's factual claims, or engaged in extensive bargaining over facts of which it had no clear knowledge.

This unease was evident in several participants' descriptions of this form of negotiation—as "interference with the summary" (Judge02MR) and a "misrepresentation by both the defence and the Crown, but accepted for matters expedient" (Defence01M). Defence25MR similarly spoke of this process as a way "to water it down as much as you can really, make it [the offence] sound a bit better for the accused". Some participants went so far as to suggest that this form of negotiation can result in a very different set of circumstances being presented to the court that borders on being "fictitious" (Judge01M), which may explain the hesitation of some prosecutor participants to acknowledge the frequency with which this process is used. As Judge10F maintained, "sometimes it is difficult to reconcile having read the dispositions with the police summary that is ultimately presented. One would think one was reading a different case". Similarly, Judge01M observed:

> We had one recently where the Crown accepted a plea to murder, but on a 3A basis,[7] rather than express malice. … 3A is the old felony murder, and it would normally carry a much lower penalty.[8] But the evidence was overwhelming that this was an intentional killing. Now, they did it [I believe] to get rid of the case and to save a trial and presumably thinking there isn't much difference between a 3A plea and an express murder. … But the judge is told that it's done on the basis of 3A and then you put the judge in an impossible situation. What does the judge say? … You're creating a fictitious set of facts upon which to sentence. … I feel that's wrong.

The concerns expressed by Judge01M have since been addressed in *DPP v Perry; Perry v The Queen*,[9] where the Court provided approval for a sentencing judge to depart from the agreed summary of facts in s 3A cases, if the evidence supports an intention to commit murder. The Court stated:

> [E]ven if the parties are agreed as to how the presence or absence of intent should be approached, if the admitted facts would support an inference of murderous intent, the sentencing judge is not precluded from drawing that inference and treating it as an aggravating factor.[10]

The Court went on:

> Thus, if in a future case the prosecution agreed not to allege murderous intent, the judge would not be bound by the parties' agreement if he/she considered that the undisputed evidence supported an inference of intent. And, if the admitted evidence supported no other conclusion, the judge could not sentence upon facts that were plainly wrong. To do so would impede the course of justice. In any such case, of course, procedural fairness would require that the judge inform the parties of his or her provisional view, in order that they may be given a sufficient opportunity to make submissions.[11]

Accordingly, there is now scope in these cases for the judge to sentence according to the evidence presented, as opposed to only the agreed summary of facts.

Many participants identified the process of negotiating the agreed summary of facts as often being about "tweaking" (Defence09F) the facts for the defendant, usually in the form of minor revisions to some wording at which they have taken offence. Defence12FR claimed:

> Sometimes it's just a good way, if your client's really stuck on the point, like it was a slap instead of a punch, even though that's still an assault, an unlawful assault, then the prosecutor, I'll put to them that if you could change it to a slap then we'll accept the summary.

Defence09F similarly explained:

> It comes down more to certain clients. It's funny, even if they're pleading to the same charge as they start out with, sometimes clients tend to be a lot more amenable to pleading if the summary is to be amended. In those circumstances, it's a matter of going to the prosecution and saying, without prejudice this is the aspect of the summary my client takes issue with and every client is different, they all have particular things that really bother them. I had a client recently who was pleading in relation to charges of sexual penetration of a child under 16 and the complainant in question was someone who is loosely related to him. … He wasn't charged with incest or anything like that, but there was reference to the fact that she was [related to him] and he took real exception to the fact that, notwithstanding the fact he was pleading to sexual penetration of a child under 16, that there was any suggestion that she might be related to him. So when the Crown agreed to remove those aspects of the summary, and some of them were aggravating circumstances of the offending conduct, he was quite content to plead on that basis. So each client gets quite principled about certain things, regardless of the charge they're actually pleading to.

In addition, Judge05M noted that when you:

> Read the depositions and you then see an agreed summary and there'll be things missing from it that you think are quite crucial, and you think, hang on a minute, ... [but really] the court knows nothing about the background of it. ... You don't know how bad the witness was ... so then you've got to think, well, if that had gone to trial, they may have lost the whole thing because the witness might be terrible, or something like that.

Judge07M also maintained that "judges will sentence people on the broad 'what they did', not the finest details of the facts", thus downplaying some of the effect these negotiations have on the sentence imposed. Despite this claim, the importance of the agreed summary was identified by participants because it should be the basis on which the defendant is sentenced, and it is where the culpability of the defendant can be substantially reduced, thereby affecting the likely sentence imposed. As Defence23M explained:

> You shouldn't really be agreeing that a guilty plea is going to be entered until there is an agreement as to what you're pleading guilty to. And that's not just the charge, that's how the charge is made out [in the agreed summary]. So there's a difference between saying you're agreeing to a theft, which is, I went into the shop and I took the item with the intention of keeping it forever, or agreeing to a theft where it's on the basis that you've subsumed the rights of another, but that there's an intention to return it at a later stage. They're both thefts, but it could obviously have a big difference in terms of your culpability in terms of what you're agreeing to, even though they both might be made out on the face of the charge.

Defence11M went so far as to label this form of negotiation as "the biggest one, often more important than the charge itself". He claimed that "that's where you can have real gains even if you don't get substitutions or lesser alternatives, but on the narrative of events because that's what you get sentenced on ultimately, not the charge" (Defence11M).

Agreements on the Prosecutor's Sentencing Submission

In contrast to jurisdictions like the US, prosecutors in Victoria cannot agree to specific punishments, either quantum or type, in exchange for a guilty plea. Instead, the sentencing decision is at the judge's discretion. A firm reminder of this occurred in *R v Williams*.[12] In this case, a plea negotiation had been undertaken between the prosecution and the defence with the defendant's son, notorious underworld figure Carl Williams, which included an agreement that the prosecutor would recommend a wholly suspended sentence in the defendant's (unrelated) case (George Williams). This agreement was made in light of George Williams's ill health and as recognition of the resource savings for the public, the courts and the OPP resulting from Carl Williams's guilty pleas to murder and conspiracy to commit murder. In reflecting on this sentencing submission, King J observed:

> There is no doubt that it is important that the court uphold, if possible, any concessions or so called 'deals' that are made between the Crown and the defence, if they are proper and appropriate concessions. Here there is no doubt that the Crown were extremely anxious to conclude the potentially lengthy and costly series of trials that were being conducted in respect of these underworld murders, and there is no doubt that those involved in the prosecution of those matters determined that it was appropriate to make the concession.[13]

However, King J went on to state that:

> [I]t is ultimately for the court to determine what sentence is appropriate. The Court is not bound, in any way, by the negotiations between counsel as to the appropriateness or otherwise of a sentence. That is clearly the role and function of the court …[14]
>
> For reasons that I shall set out shortly, I do not agree with the Crown and defence submission that a wholly suspended term of imprisonment would be appropriate in this case.[15]

George Williams was sentenced to four and a half years' imprisonment, with a minimum non-parole period of 20 months.

The separation of responsibilities identified by King J in relation to the plea negotiation process became case law following the decision of the High Court in *Barbaro*,[16] in which the Court stated:

> It is for the prosecution, alone, to decide what charges are to be preferred against an accused person. Second, it is for the accused person, alone, to decide whether to plead guilty to the charges preferred. … Third … it is for the sentencing judge, alone, to decide what sentence will be imposed. … [The defendant's] decision cannot be made with any foreknowledge of what sentence will be imposed. Neither the prosecution, nor the offender's advisers, can do anything more than proffer an opinion as to what might reasonably be expected to happen.

There is a very clear consensus among the legal community and the existing literature—both primary and secondary sources—that plea negotiations in all Australian jurisdictions do not involve discussions on sentencing. Accordingly, this study sought to identify whether this is in fact the case, and if there are any forms of negotiation that exist in relation to sentence outcomes, particularly both pre and post the High Court's decision in *Barbaro*.

In brief, *Barbaro* reversed the Victorian Court of Appeal's decision in *R v MacNeil-Brown* (*MacNeil-Brown*)[17] which required prosecutors to make a submission on sentencing range if:

> (a) the court requests such assistance; or (b) even though no such request has been made, the prosecutor perceives a significant risk that the court will fall into error regarding the applicable range unless such a submission is made.[18]

In *Barbaro*, the Court stated that:

> Contrary to the view of the majority in *MacNeil-Brown*, the prosecution's conclusion about the bounds of the available range of sentences is an irrelevant statement of opinion, not a submission of law …[19]
>
> To the extent to which *MacNeil-Brown* stands as authority supporting the practice of counsel for the prosecution providing a submission about the bounds of the available range of sentences, the decision should be overruled. The practice to which *MacNeil-Brown* has given rise should cease. The practice is wrong in principle.[20]

Despite claims to the contrary, the case file data and interviews suggest that prosecution sentence recommendations are a common discussion point in the plea negotiation process, even post *Barbaro*, although they are evidently less specific as a result of the High Court's decision in that case.

Following the decision in *MacNeil-Brown*, sentence ranges became a key element of negotiations in Victoria. Reflecting on this period (2008–14), Defence11M explained the process as follows:

> Well it's quite straightforward. We'd say, we plead guilty if you agree on a range of X and Y and pre *Barbaro* they'd come back and say, yeah okay or no, and you'd either continue negotiating the range or, alternatively, just plea to have a discrepancy on the range.

Participants with prosecutorial experience likewise acknowledged that sentence range recommendations did form part of the negotiation process for a period of time:

> When I was at the Crown [pre *Barbaro*] we gave range all the time. It's the thing that the defence were always looking for – in the more serious indictable offences –whether or not the Crown will concede, for example, when suspended sentences were in, that a period of imprisonment is open. That was a big green light for an accused to plead. (Judge02MR)

Prosecutor05M similarly maintained:

> The very early stages after *MacNeil-Brown*, there were occasions when plea ranges were used as part of the negotiation process. ... There were occasions when defence would say, if we plead, what would you say as to range?

This type of negotiation was identified by many defence practitioner participants as offering a strong incentive for their clients to plead guilty, as Defence03F noted:

> [It] gave clients some comfort if you could get an agreement out of the prosecution about what they would give as a range ... [because] you knew if you had some agreement on range, unless you were before [*names particular judge*] who had no regard for ranges whatsoever, that you'd probably fall somewhere nicely within it and you could assure your client of that.

Likewise, Defence09F maintained that this type of negotiation was beneficial to clients as one could explain to them that "the Crown have indicated that if you pleaded this is the range that they would provide, that they would submit that you've done enough time or they would submit that you only have to do X much more and the sentencing judge is likely to go along with that". In other words, many defence practitioners argued that it provided additional certainty in negotiations, which is considered a benefit for defendants in plea negotiations.[21]

An example of this type of agreement was evident in case 012-XC:

> The defence offered to plead guilty to aiding and abetting the importation of some of the drugs which he was charged with importing. The OPP rejected the offer on the basis that it did not encompass the criminality of the case, but noted it would accept a guilty plea to either attempting to import or attempting to possess the entire amount of drugs charged. The defence lawyer responded by asking for the likely *MacNeil-Brown* range if the guilty plea was accepted. The OPP responded with an indicative range, and the defendant agreed to plead guilty to attempting to possess the entire amount of drugs charged on the basis that this range was presented to the court.

While the majority of defence practitioner participants openly acknowledged that range was discussed as part of plea negotiations during the entirety of the *MacNeil-Brown* reign, the prosecutor participants claimed that this only happened for a short period of time as it quickly became frowned upon by the DPP, and prosecutors were advised not to engage in this type of discussion. As Prosecutor05M explained, "at a very early stage we decided that – well the Director decided – that was inappropriate and so that stopped. So in terms of giving indications as to what the Crown said in terms of range, that was in the main done after the plea was entered". Likewise, Prosecutor03F said, "certainly now, but even sometime before [*Barbaro*], we don't provide a range … we would probably not have an agreement with defence about that even to that limited extent". As noted, this comment contrasts with the views of defence practitioners, who commonly identified discussions on range as a major part of negotiations up until *Barbaro*, when it became less relevant as prosecutors were no longer asked by the court to provide a range. Defence03F maintained, "that discussion happened a lot until [*Barbaro*]". When asked to clarify this comment, Defence03F said "Yes [those negotiations happened], right up until the landscape changed, with sentencing ranges now out". The case file data indicated at least five examples where the plea negotiation included an agreement on the prosecutor's sentencing range (it was not possible to state when these cases occurred, other than to say that they took place prior to *Barbaro*, so these may have been prior to the DPP's notification).

A minority of participants suggested that, even post *Barbaro*, range can still form part of negotiations:

> Well, the prosecution can still tell us what they think, and they might not give us a range, but actually sometimes they will. It really depends on your relationship with the prosecutor. (Defence16F)

Defence17F similarly maintained, "I mean the prosecution do still talk about sentencing range". When asked how often this occurs or what the benefit of the discussion is given the prosecutor is no longer able to submit a range to the court, Defence17F claimed:

> Look, I still do have prosecutors that will say, we will submit [to the court] even though we know we shouldn't, that the appropriate sentencing range is X, in order to put pressure on me to agree to what they propose.

At the roundtable, Defence30M likewise declared that:

> *MacNeil*[*-Brown*]'s drifting back in because we want to know what's within the range, custodial, non-custodial, upper end, sentencing in terms of years. And whether or not *Barbaro* is supposed to have eliminated that, the fact of the matter is, it's drifting back in, particularly for non-custodial [sentences]. So it does still form a part of the guilty plea and the negotiations.

This view was supported by Defence28M:

> We have a fantastic resolution rate at the County Court because we have these plea negotiation discussions. The prosecutors will say, I'm making submissions and we'll accept that non-custodial is within range.

Also at the roundtable, Judge16F confirmed that "*MacNeil-Brown* is sneaking back in", but only in relation to "combination sentences [CCO and imprisonment], because, whilst prosecutors aren't allowed to pitch on range anymore, they're freely pitching on combination sentences".[22] Judge15M similarly noted at the roundtable that:

> You'll frequently get prosecutors who say, we don't take issue with what's going to be said and sit down again. That's not giving a range, it just means that the defence barrister can then confidently assert this is what we want and you as a judge or a magistrate know, well, if I do this, if I think it's right, then that's the end of it.

This view was similarly reflected in the interviews, where participants expressed the view that the negotiations around sentencing and penalties have shifted away from specific range discussions, to focus instead on whether the Crown may recommend to the court that a non-custodial penalty or a CCO is within range—an outcome several defence practitioners identified as negatively affecting negotiations:

> Yeah, after *Barbaro* it's a little bit up in the air. Certainly prosecutors don't go into the specifics that they did pre *Barbaro*. It's kind of gone back to the old days where they submit either jail that's appropriate or it's not appropriate. Unfortunately, it doesn't, now that *Barbaro* is where it's at, it doesn't really assist in resolving matters because we can't say to a client that we'll submit this and the prosecutors will confirm it. (Defence07M)

Defence09F similarly noted:

> I was at the court at first when it happened and I think the initial reaction was, well, this is going to stop pleas. It is going to create a barrier, because you can't talk about range and it stops us being able to have that agreement and knowing that you can then go to a judge, because now the figure is just completely plucked [out of the air].

Despite identifying these potential limitations, most participants acknowledged that the prosecutor's submission still forms an integral part of negotiations and is a common discussion point during negotiations: "there will sometimes be an agreement about saying a non-custodial is within range or all sentencing options are open" (Judge11F). Defence11M maintained that "it used to be that you'd make your offers contingent upon a sentencing range being given, [but] the OPP have disavowed that process so it's not as effective anymore … post *Barbaro* you just leave the ranges out of it". Significantly, some participants claimed that this part of the agreement influences whether a defendant will accept the resolution and plead guilty. As Defence03F explained, "often agreement about a non-custodial disposition can also form a really important part of those negotiations". Likewise, Prosecutor03F noted, "if we weren't going to persist with an immediate custodial submission, then that might make a difference to whether a matter is going to settle or not". In this vein, Prosecutor06M observed:

> We don't negotiate range but we do in terms of – the defence will say, as part of the negotiations, what disposition are you looking at? And when I say that, they're obviously asking, are you submitting that it's an immediate custodial sentence or as a non-custodial sentence? … So there are some cases that you can go and see a Crown prosecutor and say, look, this is the case. They're pleading up to those charges. Would we submit that it warrants an immediate custodial sentence? There's a number of ways we can put that. We can say that a non-custodial sentence is 'within range' and that's where the range comes in, but we can't say what the range of the actual custodial sentence is. So we can say the non-custodial sentence is 'in the range' or we would have to submit that an immediate custodial was appropriate. Then you get back to the defence and it's up to them whether they want to resolve or not.

Defence19M also identified this practice, noting that "you struggle with that a little bit [post *Barbaro*], but sometimes [you say], we'll plead guilty on this basis if you don't submit for imprisonment. That does happen". An example of this type of negotiation was recalled by Defence09F in relation to a child sexual abuse case:

> I had a case not so long ago. … We sought the Crown's view as to whether or not they would be submitting that an immediate custodial disposition was the only appropriate one in the circumstances. … They indicated that they would get instructions and come back and indicated that they wouldn't seek an immediate custodial disposition. Obviously there's no real way of determining what will happen because as you know, the judge can decide whether or not to accept the Crown's view, but we knew at least the Crown wouldn't appeal if we got that particular [non-custodial] disposition and that is what the client needed to push him over the line towards pleading.

Commonly, defence practitioners identified these types of discussions occurring post *Barbaro* in relation to CCOs, in a similar way to how discussions about suspended sentences used to run pre *MacNeil-Brown*:

> Look, we do [have those discussions], it's less so now [post *Barbaro*], but we do. So we will try and see if they'll have anything to say or any objection for us to say a CCO is within the range. (Defence05M)

Defence02F similarly explained:

> What you're negotiating on primarily … with the OPP in relation to the sentence is whether or not they're going to oppose a CCO and that hasn't changed. … I guess post *Barbaro* it's just a matter of whether or not they're conceding a term of imprisonment or a term of imprisonment combined with a CCO or whether they're conceding a CCO.

Defence15M also noted that "there are still concessions on the appropriateness of, say, a CCO versus imprisonment and that type of thing. … And those arguments come up a lot". In this regard, Prosecutor05M identified the CCO discussion as a relatively common part of the negotiation process:

> When defence come and say, we're thinking of pleading. We've got to talk to our client, are you going to accept that the CCO's within the range? If you do that, then when I talk to my client it will make it easier. Again, as I said earlier, if it's obvious [that a CCO is appropriate] then … [we'd say] yes, you've given us your material, we've looked at it. When it comes to the plea, we're likely to say that a Community Correction Order is within the range, if that helps you.

The importance of this agreement to the negotiation process was acknowledged by Defence16F, who maintained that:

> I go back to the client and say, well, look. If it resolves in this way, the prosecution won't be seeking jail. That can be a big factor. Or it might be that the prosecution comes to us and says, look, if we can resolve this … all options are open. Or they might even go so far as to say a CCO, for example, would be within range. … Sometimes that is the difference between resolving and not resolving.

At the roundtable, a similar view was expressed by Prosecutor13F, who highlighted the "importance" of these discussions. She explained, "if that's what will assist a resolution then … you can then take it back to a Crown prosecutor to talk about whether we would concede that a non-custodial sentence was within the range, it helps".

While the plea negotiation process in Victoria in no way resembles that of a system where prosecutors can offer specific sentences in exchange for a guilty plea, it appears that, in the wake of *MacNeil-Brown*, discussions ventured into this area for a period of time, at least until (if not beyond, according to a few defence practitioner participants) the DPP prohibited this type of discussion by OPP solicitors. Thus, if given the opportunity, it is likely plea negotiations in Victoria would expand into this territory. While specific sentence ranges appear not to form part of plea negotiations, the data suggest that discussions on sentencing particularly in relation to CCOs, non-custodial or time served do play a major role in Victorian plea negotiations—the fourth most common, according to the interview data—despite many participants adamantly declaring that "sentencing isn't part of plea negotiations" (Prosecutor13F) and much research making similar claims (Flynn 2011, 2016; Mack and Roach Anleu 1995; Seifman 1982).

Notes

1. The case file data included documented evidence of negotiating the agreed summary of facts in 51 per cent of cases, and such evidence was inferred or referred to but not documented in almost all cases, aligning with the interview data, in which *all* participants identified this as a form of negotiation.
2. Details pertaining to the reasons have been removed to avoid possible identification of the defendant.
3. See *Public Prosecutions Act 1994* (Vic) ss 41(a), 23(b).
4. *Legal Aid Act 1978* (Vic) s 4(a).
5. See McConville and Marsh (2014) for an in-depth analysis of the role that prosecutors, judges and defence practitioners can play in state-induced guilty pleas.

6. See, for example, *Office of Director of Public Prosecutions* (NSW), *Prosecution Guidelines, Guideline 20, Charge Negotiation and Agreement: Agreed Statement of Facts: Form 1*; see also Freiberg et al. 2015: 35.
7. Judge01M is referring here to the offence of unintentional killing in the course or furtherance of a crime of violence, which is regulated by s 3A of the *Crimes Act 1958* (Vic). This offence is defined as:

    (1) A person who unintentionally causes the death of another person by an act of violence done in the course or furtherance of a crime the necessary elements of which include violence for which a person upon first conviction may, under or by virtue of any enactment, be sentenced to level 1 imprisonment (life) or to imprisonment for a term of ten years or more shall be liable to be convicted of murder as though he had killed that person intentionally.

8. Clarification has been provided to the sentencing of defendants in relation to s 3A offences by the Supreme Court of Victoria Court of Appeal since the interview was conducted with Judge01M. In *DPP v Perry; Perry v The Queen* [2016] VSCA 152 (1 July 2016) the court stated that:

    A number of sentencing decisions in this State have proceeded on the erroneous basis that the offence of statutory murder [s 3A] is a less serious form of murder than common law murder and should therefore attract sentences of a lesser order … [at 8]

    [T]he mere fact that the offence is a s 3A murder, rather than common law murder, has no bearing on sentence … [at 81]

    Statutory murder is not to be viewed as inherently less serious than common law murder, or as having a lower 'starting point' for sentencing. Both intentional murder and s 3A murder carry the same maximum penalty, that of life imprisonment. The sentencing guidance which the maximum penalty provides is therefore the same for both offences [at 83].

9. [2016] VSCA 152 (1 July 2016).
10. Ibid. [at 90].
11. Ibid. [at 92].
12. [2007] VSC 490 (15 November 2007).
13. Ibid. [at 4].
14. Ibid. [at 6].
15. Ibid. [at 8].
16. [2014] HCA 2 [at 47].
17. [2008] VSCA 190.
18. Ibid. [at 3].

19. [2014] HCA 2 [at 48].
20. Ibid. [at 23].
21. *R v Anthony Cook* (2016) SCC 43, [2016] 2 S.C.R. 204.
22. As discussed in Chap. 7, combination sentences refer to a sentencing order that includes a period of imprisonment and a CCO.

4

Other Forms of Negotiations

As detailed in Chap. 3, discussions of plea negotiation to date have generally focused on three main forms: (1) "charge bargaining" (Manikis 2012: 411), which incorporates withdrawing charges and substituting charges (Flynn 2016; Fox and Deltondo 2015; Johns 2002; Mackenzie et al. 2015; Wren and Bartels 2014; Yang 2013); (2) "fact bargaining" (Manikis 2012: 411), which incorporates discussions on which facts will form the basis of the agreed summary presented to the court from which the defendant is sentenced (Flynn 2016; Johns 2002; Mackenzie et al. 2015); and (3) "sentence bargaining" (Manikis 2012: 411), which incorporates discussions on the prosecutor's sentencing submission, agreements as to what stage in proceedings the defendant indicated an intention to plead guilty and in which jurisdiction the offence should be heard (Flynn 2016; Fox and Deltondo 2015; Mackenzie et al. 2015). However, in this study, 14 forms of plea negotiation were identified in the interview and case file data, 8 of which (marked with an asterisk below) were identified as common "everyday" outcomes arising from negotiations. This represents a significant expansion on previous discussions of the differing forms of plea negotiation. The 14 forms identified, in no particular order, include:

1. Withdrawing charges*—evident in 44 files and identified by 95 per cent of participants.
2. Substituting charges (a less serious charge)*—evident in 20 files and identified by 95 per cent of participants.
3. Rolling up counts (combining like offences into one charge or fewer charges)*—evident in 14 files and identified by 100 per cent of participants.

A. Flynn, A. Freiberg, *Plea Negotiations*, Palgrave Socio-Legal Studies,
https://doi.org/10.1007/978-3-319-92630-8_4

4. Representative counts (representing a course of conduct)*—evident in 10 files and identified by 95 per cent of participants.
5. Agreement on the summary of facts (fact bargaining)*—evident in 24 files and identified by 100 per cent of participants.
6. Agreement as to what the prosecutor will submit as part of their sentencing submission (e.g. whether a non-custodial sentence is within range or a CCO)*—evident in 5 files and identified by 97 per cent of participants.
7. Agreement to change jurisdiction—evident in 9 files and identified by 92 per cent of participants.
8. Defendant to provide information on another matter (which may also involve the defendant acting as a prosecution witness and/or confidential police informant)—evident in 4 files and identified by 89 per cent of participants.
9. Agreement for the police/prosecution not to pursue charges/investigation into other offences involving another person known to the defendant—identified by 44 per cent of participants.
10. Agreement not to pursue charges/investigation into other offences involving the defendant—identified by 47 per cent of participants.
11. Agreement to provide some form of protection or financial support to the defendant and/or their family (e.g. payment of school fees or relocation fees)—identified by 29 per cent of participants.
12. Bail as a point of negotiation—identified by 49 per cent of participants.
13. Diversionary programs/options*—evident in 6 files and identified by 76 per cent of participants.
14. Agreement on costs (e.g. an outcome that includes an agreement not to apply for costs against the opposing party)*—identified by 67 per cent of participants.

This chapter presents a detailed overview of these different forms of plea negotiation (excluding the four discussed in the previous chapter) to highlight the diversity and breadth of outcomes possible from the plea negotiation process.

Agreement to Change Jurisdiction

Agreeing to have a matter heard in a lower jurisdiction as part of the resolution was identified as a relatively common form of plea negotiation (evident in nine files and identified by 92 per cent of participants), more so in relation to (intermediate) County Court matters being heard in the (summary)

Magistrates' Court, although a couple of the indictable stream prosecutors also spoke of Supreme Court matters being shifted to the County Court. Participants identified two main reasons for moving the jurisdiction to the summary stream. The first is that it reduces the severity of the penalty that can be imposed on the defendant (Judge08M).[1] As Judge13F maintained:

> That is quite common in the Magistrates' Court, particularly where the matter might have been going to go to the County Court because if it is kept in the lower jurisdiction costs are lower and the penalty range is lesser.

The second main "big carrot" (Judge02MR) is the appeal de novo available in the Magistrates' Court, which entitles a defendant to a right of appeal without a requirement to obtain leave from the court.[2] As Judge09M observed:

> You've got the one advantage in the Magistrates' Court, which you don't have in the County Court, and that is if you're on the cusp of going to jail, and a magistrate sentences you to jail, then you've got a right to an appeal de novo. … So the appeal process is easier to overturn … whereas, of course, if you get sentenced [in the County Court], you need to demonstrate error [to appeal], and it's not easy. … You buy yourself an extra bite at the cherry if you're dealt with by a magistrate. I've got no doubt that drives some people to accept that type of agreement.

Interestingly, several participants with a defence background suggested that the potential benefit of receiving a lesser penalty in the Magistrates' Court was not necessarily reflective of practice. As Judge07M maintained:

> If you negotiated it and want it heard in the Magistrates' Court, it might be the most serious case that the magistrate hears for a month, whereas it's just a very small beer in the County Court. … [When practising as a defence barrister,] I didn't rush for the Magistrates' Court on every occasion and sometimes where the police [prosecutor] said 'you must go up to the County Court', as if that's where the harsh sentences come from, I said 'fine' and we got a much better deal and they were as angry as anything. And they would have got a much harsher outcome in a Magistrates' Court.

Defence07M similarly claimed that:

> Sometimes it's – even though a matter can be dealt with in the Magistrates' Court – sometimes it's better to deal with it in the County Court because often the more serious charges following a resolution in the Magistrates' Court aren't viewed anywhere near as seriously in the County Court and there's a much

greater opportunity in the County Court to develop a plea [in] mitigation than there is in the Magistrates' Court. So, contrary to the view that it's better in the Magistrates' Court because the powers to sentence are more limited, there are occasions where it's better to go off to the County Court, but that's always subject to whether your client's in custody or not because you can deal with it quicker in the Magistrates' Court.

A main benefit of having the matter heard summarily was said to be that "it's over and done with more quickly" (Judge13F). Prosecutor05M provided the following overview of the decision-making process in these types of resolution:

> Say, for example, it's an aggravated burglary involving an assault. It goes to the County Court, and a [police evidence] brief comes in, and it's apparent that the person had permission to go into the house. One of the elements of the charge is not there, and what's left is a minor assault. Then in all the ordinary course of event, the instructions would be given for that minor assault to be dealt with in the Magistrates' Court. I'd be asking two things: (1) do we proceed with the aggravated burglary charge? That question would come from whoever was appearing in the committal, for example, or the committal mention. A solicitor from this office who had been instructing, they'd come along and say we've got this charge of aggravated burglary, but it turns out we can't prove this particular element. I would then, going back to the first point, if I agreed with that, I'd give instructions to withdraw the charge, and then the next question would be: (2) do we deal with this as an indictable charge in the County Court or do we deal with it in the Magistrates' Court? Now if the charge involves splitting someone's head open with a tomahawk, it would probably go forward [in the County Court]; but if it involves a bruise to the cheek, it would probably stay in the Magistrates' Court, and obviously there's a whole range of circumstances between those two. Sometimes the decision is easy to make and sometimes it's a bit borderline.

Drawing on her recent experiences, Defence09F provided the following example of this form of plea negotiation:

> It was an armed robbery matter that was booked in for trial. We had made an offer some time ago to plead to robbery charges which hadn't been laid in the alternative, and part of the resolution that we reached with the Crown was that the matter would resolve as a plea to a charge of robbery with a consent to the matter being remitted to the Magistrates' Court, and the Crown didn't take any issue with that at all.

Defence03F also provided an example:

> I had a clandestine laboratory matter that I did that was charged in the committal mention [indictable] stream. We resolved it on the day [of the pre-trial hearing] with the agreement that the prosecution wouldn't oppose summary jurisdiction. … This was a guy that had some boxed-up materials, so beakers and things, and there were some precursors spread around his house, but it wasn't actually a lab set up in his house. And so that was something that really did form part of the negotiations that we had, that yes, we will resolve this today, but on the provision that you don't oppose summary jurisdiction. And that's often one of our strongest tools I think in committal things, when you've got something that can be heard summarily, trying to negotiate a resolution that includes the prosecutor not being opposed in terms of summary jurisdiction.

Defendant to Provide Information on Another Matter

Eighty-nine per cent of participants identified the provision of information on another matter as a form of plea negotiation. The criminal law encourages defendants to inform on each other and to assist law enforcement agencies and the legislature,[3] and the courts support this policy by taking it into consideration cooperating with the authorities as a mitigating factor in sentencing, which may be in addition to any reduction in sentence on account of a guilty plea (Freiberg 2014: 395). Judge03M maintained that this form of negotiation occurs "frequently. … I mean, how else do you get the bad guys to talk? You've got to give them something and what they want is either a reduced sentence or no charge at all". Similarly, Judge06M claimed "that does happen regularly and it's a very powerful component of a plea if someone's prepared to stick their neck out and assist the cops". Overall, our judicial participants described this as a "very common part of a plea negotiation" (Judge09M), particularly in relation to drug offences (Judge01M); and most provided examples of taking the level of cooperation shown by the defendant into consideration in sentencing.

The prosecutor and defence practitioners recognised this as a form of negotiation, but did not consider it to be commonplace—"look it does [occur], but it doesn't happen very often" (Defence08MR). Only around half of the prosecutor and defence practitioner participants had direct experience with this form of negotiation. The remainder spoke of other practitioners they knew being involved in this form of negotiation. As Defence17F maintained:

> Personally, I cannot recall ever having been involved in a matter with that. I mean, some of my colleagues have. I've witnessed it happen in court. You know, indications of it, but I myself have never been part of that.

Defence16F similarly claimed, "if it was available, if it was relevant, yeah absolutely. … I don't know that's arisen for me, but certainly if it arose, I would. I'd do whatever I thought was necessary". Defence17F gave a hypothetical example of one of the ways in which this type of negotiation can play out:

> Say you might have a simple driving matter where they've got false plates on their car. They [the defendant] might say, they're not mine, they belong to X and I'll go back to that to the prosecutor and they might say, cough up the name of X and I'll withdraw the charges against your client. Unless we get a name, we're pursuing the charges against your client. … So, the indication is, you give us the name and we'll drop the charges against the client.

Prosecutor01F reflected on her direct experiences with this form of negotiation, recognising it as a very useful way to resolve a case:

> In those instances, I will often do all I can to resolve the matter, i.e., if a solicitor or a barrister comes to me and says, well, look we've got this case I've got, say, three accused, one is making waves. He might, as we say, 'roll over'. … He may be talking about making a statement against the others and I pretty much usually say, well, I think that's a really good idea and you should make it clear to his barrister, or her barrister, whoever it is, that we will make it very clear on appropriate [sentencing] submissions if he or she provides a statement that assists, but it has to be one that assists. … And they have to give evidence and so on.

As outlined by Prosecutor01F, often such an agreement requires the defendant to give evidence in a related or another matter. For this reason, several defence practitioners expressed concern about the potentially negative outcomes this could have for their client, and identified this as a reason why they might not always seek out this option as part of a resolution. Defence11M explained:

> It's not my practice to … actively encourage such a process, though it would also be negligent of me to completely disregard that process. If the OPP or Victoria Police – it will only ever be the OPP – put that to me, I will, as a matter of course and obligation, put that to my client and I will supplement that in terms of my advice to the client with the sentencing benefit that goes with it. Will I automatically, where there are co-accused, put that to my client? I will again

> apprise him of the ability to do that but I won't take it much further than arming my client with the information.

Defence20M expanded on this view:

> I've been involved in that and it's a very long and difficult process. It's a very difficult position for accused persons to be in. Very often they expose themselves to danger when they provide information in relation to other people's illegal activities. And it's a very long process to make sure that you, I suppose, get the best result for your client, given the value of the information that they're going to provide. The people who provide information are almost always down the lower end of the scale of culpability, so they're usually people who might or might not go to custody … and where it will be relevant, if they can give up people that are higher up in the hierarchy then they may receive a bargain that makes it less likely to actually go to jail.

Likewise, Defence22M maintained:

> Well, I'm apprehensive now. I'm really apprehensive – particularly in drugs stuff – of getting people to provide information. … There's this sort of confusion about how we recognise cooperation. Do we do it in closed court? How do we stop other people extraneous to the proceedings being alerted to the fact? Because they know it's a closed court, they suspect something's going on. … They get suspicious, it's clumsy, it's really clumsy, and so we're still identifying, we still talk about it and we still – in appropriate cases where we think our client's not going to be at risk, he's not part of that entrepreneurial drug culture where you really are at the greatest risk. … Lower down, we still talk about it, we still do it, but higher up, I'm apprehensive to do it.

Participants identified the two formal ways in which this type of agreement is recognised in the court. The first is through a "letter of comfort" in the summary jurisdiction; the second is a "can say statement" in the indictable stream (see also Freiberg 2014: 401). The "letter of comfort" was defined by Defence23M as "a sealed letter that goes to the judge or the magistrate to detail the level of assistance that they've provided". Prosecutor04M described this process as follows:

> It's usually a confidential letter that's handed up to the magistrate in private. It's handed up without comment with the prior history and the magistrate reads it, and there's no indication to the public what's happened.

Judge01M described the "can say statement" used in the indictable stream as follows:

> This is when somebody's either charged or about to be charged with an offence and they want an indemnity or they want some sort of reduction in penalty. … It is an unsigned statement outlining what evidence [the defendant] would be able to give in relation to either this offence or other offences. It was always done in what was called a 'can say'. So you get a bit of paper which is unsigned and the DPP would look at that and might discuss whether that's adequate, whether that's all that can be said. … If the deal is then done, the 'can say' is converted into a statement and he's [the defendant's] called to give evidence.

Defence09F provided the following examples of negotiations involving a "can say statement":

> I had one recently, my client was originally charged with [drug-related offences]. … Ultimately, the Crown agreed to resolve it on the basis of a trafficking simpliciter charge with a condition that our client provide information or a statement in respect of the remaining co-accused, and he did agree to that. … I had another matter where my client provided a lot of information to the AFP [Australian Federal Police]. He provided a 'can say statement' and obviously the CDPP then went away and got instructions as to any discount he should be afforded.

Agreement Not to Pursue Charges Against Another Person Known to the Defendant

An agreement not to pursue charges against another person known to the defendant was identified as a form of plea negotiation by 44 per cent of participants, although it was considered less common than other forms and something that happened "more often in the past" (Judge05M). This form of negotiation was not present in the de-identified case files. There was some concern raised about the ethicality of this form of negotiation, with participants identifying it as "a bit edgy" (Judge05M), "dubious" (Judge12MR) and "a tricky issue" (Judge09M). In most instances, participants stated that this form of negotiation occurs in relation to intimate partners, such as husbands and wives, in drug offence cases, given the circumstances in which drugs are grown and cultivated:

> I think we all know that that happens, most often in relation to drugs, where drugs are found at premises. It's often quite clear that, given that the drugs are, for example, all over the house, that all those living there were probably privy to some kind of offending, but sometimes it's the case that – and generally it's the male that seems to be charged and the female walks away. (Judge10F)

Judge09M similarly observed:

> It's almost always when we're talking about partners, husbands and wives, girlfriends/boyfriends. … Because it's, the house has been raided, and they're both implicated, the wife's or the partner's been drawn along in it, watered the [marijuana] plants or whatever, and they're both charged.

Judge13F likewise maintained that "sometimes husbands are put on the spot where the police say, look, we won't charge your wife if you confess and take responsibility. And sometimes even beyond that stage there can be those sorts of circumstances". The participants also recognised this occurring in relation to other family members, whereby a defendant "will put their hand up to protect their family members" (Judge05M). Defence09F expanded on this, noting:

> I certainly have clients who are charged alongside family members, friends, girlfriends, that sort of thing, and a lot of the time they say, well if I plead will they agree to withdraw the charges against this person? I have got a current matter and it's sort of one where they've agreed to give information about a co-accused and resolve their matter on the basis that his partner, the charges against her are dropped, and that's ultimately been agreed to.

Prosecutor participants stressed that such decisions are always made on the basis of the evidence, where there is "a complete inequality of the evidence against the two people charged" (Prosecutor05M). Prosecutor05M explained:

> There might be virtually no case against one [defendant], and a strong case against the other … so you're not weighing one off against the other, you're just saying one case is so weak that you can't – and sometimes people ask, I'll cop this one, but leave my wife alone? But usually the decision is made on the strength of the evidence in relation to the wife, for example, rather than – and sometimes that is the case, that there is, the police charge both. But there's no evidence against one or there's minimal evidence against one, and so that inequality is what usually solves it.

Defence03F provided the following example of this type of negotiation:

> I had an intention to cause serious injury [charge]. … And on the days leading up to his [the defendant's] trial, because he'd denied it all along, his partner was alleged to have gone around to the complainant's [victim's] house and left a note with her phone number and tried to talk to him, to try and get him to change

> his story. Now the police wanted to investigate her and charge her with attempting to pervert the course of justice. And we ended up resolving his matter to intentionally causing injury and we had a sort of unspoken agreement, no-one explicitly said, and by the by, you won't pursue these things, but that was just what was understood as part of his plea, that the partner would just be left alone. And that's what happened and that was really important for him in terms of the resolution, because the idea for him that the missus was going to get prosecuted on top of him going to jail was just too much.

Agreement Not to Pursue Other Charges/Investigations into the Defendant

In a similar vein to agreeing not to pursue charges against someone known to the defendant, an agreement not to pursue other charges or investigations into the defendant was recognised as a form of plea negotiation (47 per cent of participants; not present in the de-identified case files), but one that participants felt was "very sensitive" (Judge08M) and not one that you would "let on about in the open" (Judge01M). As Judge08M explained, "I can provide examples, but I won't". Similarly, Judge05M noted, "we used to do it all the time … like we'll put our hand over this [plead guilty] if it just stops here … but it always made me edgy doing that". Defence11M likewise claimed, "yes, it happens on occasion, but they're [the OPP] never going to sign a document to that effect, but I've never seen them abscond [sic] from any in-principle agreement that's been reached". He went on to stipulate, however, that such circumstances are "rare" because "it's not that common to have something on the horizon that hasn't currently been charged if the OPP are aware of it" (Defence11M). Instead, Defence11M suggested that a more common outcome is where there are two separate proceedings against the defendant "and you want to reach an arrangement either wholesale on the two and … that is we'll have a compromised charge on both sets of charges and they'll take a pragmatic view, or alternatively yes, you offer them one on the condition that they discontinue against another" (Defence11M). Prosecutor03F also identified this as "something that could happen", but more so in relation to minor charges associated with the offending conduct. She explained:

> There may have been some minor charges associated with it that we might have been going to pursue that we wouldn't once he [sic] pleaded guilty. … But we wouldn't, I mean where the criminality needs to be addressed, we wouldn't ignore criminal offending where it needed to be charged. But there might be cases where the substantive charges are in agreement, then other matters that are

> affiliated. For example, if there's some admissions as to drug-taking or something like that and they were going to plead guilty to a major charge, then the admissions about taking drugs may not be charged because it wouldn't be the substantive, most important charges.

Defence17F reflected on her experiences with this form of negotiation, noting that "it doesn't happen very often but …":

> I had an accused charged with – they were driving offences I believe – and part of the brief of evidence he'd provided was a sworn statement. … He gave a sworn statement to the police officer, which in the context of the instructions that he was giving me indicated that the original statement was false, and the police officer said, if he pleads to the driving charges, I won't pursue the perjury charge. If he doesn't settle on the basis of these driving matters, I'll be considering a perjury charge. I put those instructions and advice to the client and he decided to settle.

Prosecutor07M similarly observed that this form of negotiation "happens from time to time", but recognised the independent nature of the OPP and Victoria Police in this regard. He explained:

> We don't intrude too much on what the police do. I mean, obviously we're not a charging agency and if the police have got other charges sitting in the background and they're unrelated to the case that we're actually running up here, I would have thought there would not be too many occasions when we would be binding the police and they would seek to be binding us on that sort of issue. … I mean if the police come to [us] and say, look, because of this, we've made agreements with the accused that we're not going to investigate, I think that's a difficult area because you never know quite where an investigation is going to take you and what the degree of responsibility is. You might actually be stopping an investigation of a very serious matter. … I don't say it doesn't happen, but maybe [it's] not that common.

Defence09F maintained that her experiences with this form of negotiation often involved an "unspoken agreement" that other charges and investigations will not be pursued. She gave the following example:

> I had another [client] who had provided this 'can say statement' and the charge he was pleading to was importation of cocaine. He was effectively making admissions in the course of that 'can say statement' to having done that on six more occasions but obviously in circumstances where he was providing that to assist the AFP with broader investigations, there was an unspoken agreement effectively that he wouldn't be prosecuted for that. And he wasn't.

Defence16F also provided an example of this form of negotiation:

> I had a really interesting WorkSafe prosecution where I was defending, and it was listed for I think ten or 20 days in the Magistrates' Court. It was going to be incredibly complicated, and it was a huge brief, of course very well prepared by the prosecution, and it was overwhelming. And what I was concerned about was that in the course of defending this, earlier behaviour would come out, particularly if the client gave evidence, which it seemed to me was about his only chance of defending it. … So part of the negotiations in that case were that the prosecution would not refer to any previous behaviour, which they can't really anyway, but also that they would agree not to prosecute [the previous behaviour], because it looked to me that it was well open to them. … And so that was an agreement that was part of the resolution of the matter.

Providing the Defendant and/or Their Family with Protection and/or Financial Support

Providing protection or some form of financial support to a defendant in exchange for them pleading guilty and providing information on other matters was recognised by just 29 per cent of participants as something that occurs (not present in the de-identified case files), and very few had had any direct involvement in this type of negotiation. As Judge11F noted, "they're obviously the high-level, high-risk informer cases and we've set up a protocol here so that there are only a couple of judges who, by and large, deal with those". Defence24M similarly observed, "it does happen from time to time, but I've not been involved in that sort of case". Many participants pointed to the now infamous Carl Williams plea agreement which was reported in the media to include the payment of school fees for Williams's child as an example of this form of negotiation (ABC 2010). Most prosecutor participants, however, stressed that this was "a one-off" (Prosecutor05M, Prosecutor07M) and was "not something we would normally have as part of our negotiating process" (Prosecutor07M). Instead, they pointed to financial support as "being a matter for the police, as informers sometimes pay [for information]" (Prosecutor07M). The only examples provided by participants related specifically to witness protection for the defendant and/or their family. For example, Defence13FR recalled a case:

> I had an agreement with the OPP, my client provided some information, and I discussed, he had a child and I discussed with them what sorts of measure would

need to possibly be put in place in relation to the child for protection. … He was also in protective custody, and then when he was on bail, he was put into witness protection from that point.

Bail as a Point of Negotiation

Approximately 31 per cent of Victoria's prison population is comprised of alleged defendants who have been refused bail (Corrections Victoria 2017). The average time served on remand by prisoners tried in the higher courts is around nine months, and for those tried in the Magistrates' Court, it is just over two months (SAC 2016c: 48–49). Loss of freedom, even if temporary, represents a significant intrusion into a person's life. It has been argued that remand in custody can constitute "structural coercion" which places pressure on a defendant and which may induce them to plead guilty (Euvrard and Leclerc 2017; Chen 2013). Unsentenced prisoners in custody may be induced or encouraged to plead guilty for a number of reasons. They may wish to be transferred to a custodial facility that offers them better facilities than those on remand. They may lose hope that their case can be successful or they may believe that by pleading guilty that may receive a non-custodial sentence or one that takes into account time served, so that the sooner they are sentenced the sooner they may be released from custody (Euvrard and Leclerc 2017: 527). Some may just want to resolve their case as quickly as possible in order to reduce the stress of being in custody. There is also evidence that in some jurisdictions, prosecutors are less likely to withdraw charges against a person remanded in custody than one on bail (Kellough and Wortley 2002; Gazal-Ayal and Tor 2012: 401).

Bail was identified as an element of negotiation by just under 50 per cent of participants (but was not present in the de-identified case files). Judge12M described bail as "a place for negotiation routinely", usually as an added basis to encourage the defendant to plead guilty, whereby the prosecution would not oppose bail while awaiting the plea hearing. As Judge01M explained, "yeah it happens. The defence says, we'll plead guilty but we don't want you to oppose bail at this stage". Judge11F similarly maintained that "the Crown will sometimes say they don't oppose somebody remaining on bail after the plea has started and before sentence. They say, it's been agreed this person should stay out on bail". Defence11M provided the following example: "a client was charged with armed robbery and was on remand, and I knew there was going to be a four-month delay to the plea. I said, 'we'll plead guilty subject to you not opposing bail being entered'." Defence16F likewise had a case where the negotiation included bail. She explained, "I said, look, let's enter the plea now and start it, but give him bail to go on the CREDIT[4] program ... otherwise this will be defended". Defence09F also provided an example from her negotiations with the CDPP:

> I had the young man who was charged with the importation of cocaine. He'd made full admissions in his record of interview, but the CDPP's position and the AFP's position was, we'll agree to bail because we want him out ... so he can assist us with our investigations. So that was a bit of a sweetener [for the defendant] in terms of saying, if you agree to assist us, we'll agree to bail, because otherwise he would've been in a very different position [held on remand until the plea hearing].

While recognising this form of negotiation, several defence practitioners felt that it did not offer a highly desirable resolution, viewing it either as "not my greatest bargaining chip, I prefer to extract something better for a client than bail" (Defence11M) or as somewhat unethical. As Defence14FR maintained a "if he pleads to this, we won't oppose bail [statement] has come up before ... but I try and keep bail out of my discussions about pleading. That feels a bit dirty. But it's certainly come up in the past".

Agreement to Recommend a Diversion

Diversions were considered a common outcome of plea negotiations where the circumstances permit, and were evident in six de-identified case files and identified by 76 per cent of participants. As Defence05M maintained, "where we get a low-end offence we definitely, as part of the negotiations, look at diversion first, and it's a common thing. It's got to be an appropriate case fitting the criteria, but we definitely negotiate for diversion outcomes". Defence08MR similarly claimed, we "always negotiate on diversion". As Defence25MR noted, "my goal is to minimise everything as much as possible and if that means my client can have no record, well that's a win".

In Victoria, a defendant is eligible for a diversion if (1) the offence is heard in the Magistrates' Court, (2) there are no set minimum or fixed sentences or penalties for the offence and (3) the defendant acknowledges responsibility for the offence. A diversion recommendation must be given by the police informant or prosecutor. As a general rule, a diversion is only permitted if it is the defendant's first offence and the offence is not considered too serious. If the magistrate supports this option, they "may adjourn the proceedings for a period not exceeding 12 months to enable the defendant to participate in and complete"[5] a diversion program.[6] If the defendant completes the diversion program to the satisfaction of the court, the court must "discharge the accused without any finding of guilt".[7] In describing the diversion option, Defence04M explained that it usually involves "someone [who] has got no prior convictions, someone who's usually relatively young, the offence itself is generally not of a serious nature and the other aspect has to be that the person is prepared to concede their involvement".

There is a significant benefit to the defendant in having the matter heard by diversion. In addition to resulting in no conviction or record, it has rehabilitative benefits (SAC 2008). As a result, some participants saw this outcome as only beneficial to the defendant—as Defence22M observed, "we jokingly say in the office, if the prosecution thinks they've got a weak case, they'll offer us a diversion, but we take it".

Participants provided several examples of negotiations involving diversions:

> I had one case last year that was scheduled for trial and my client was charged with two charges of armed robbery and two charges of aggravated burglary and we resolved it on the first day of the trial to a plea in respect of a charge of trespass. It was remitted to the Magistrates' Court, she had no priors. It was a good resolution and she would've been crazy not to take it, but part of the resolution was, we'll agree to resolve it on the basis of a trespass charge and we want the informant to recommend diversion and they did. (Defence09F)

> I had a guy who had a – he was 60-odd – a completely clean driving record. He had a total brain fade in some fog and caused an accident. There was an agreement, he'll plead to a careless [driving charge] rather than a dangerous [driving], but I think it's a diversion-worthy matter and the prosecutor agreed. So that was how the matter proceeded at that time. (Defence14FR)

Many of the examples provided included comments like "watered down the summary" (Defence25MR) and "somehow managed to get a diversion" (Defence03F), suggesting that the matters did not necessarily fit the typical diversion criteria. For example, two defence practitioners observed:

> I just got back from court for a diversion for a kid, it was a self-defence argument; a late-night violence out in [*names suburb*] and he wanted to run the self-defence argument and I thought it was a good one. The prosecution eventually decided not to run it because they didn't want to I suppose, and so as part of the negotiation we both made a recommendation for diversion and watered down the summary and the charges such that it was possible. (Defence25MR)

> I got a double diversion out at [*names suburb*]. It involved a woman who … had a son that she raised on her own, had never been in any trouble before and had a … relationship breakdown, so she had gone a little bit off the rails. One matter

> was graffiti … and then the other one was some drug possession … and we managed to get diversion for both of those things. … Another was for a sex offence case involving an elderly man who had grabbed his genitals and made lewd kissing noises at a woman and her child at a children's playground and we got diversion for that. I mean he was in his 70s and had never been in trouble, barely spoke any English, but somehow, I managed to get diversion for that. (Defence03F)

This suggests that, despite the criteria outlined in statute, there may be "room to move" (Defence03F) as part of the negotiation process when considering diversion. And much of this will relate to how the prosecutor and defence negotiate the agreed summary of facts presented to the court.

Agreement Not to Seek Costs

The costs agreement as a form of negotiation was identified as specific only to the Magistrates' Court, and applied only in cases where the police prosecutor intended to withdraw all charges (67 per cent of participants, not present in the de-identified case files). Such an agreement was described as somewhat of an unusual outcome of negotiations, as it does not involve the defendant agreeing to plead guilty; rather, it involves them simply agreeing not to pursue costs on the basis that charges are no longer being proceeded with. The magistrate has the discretion to award costs (usually covering any legal fees paid by the defendant) to a defendant if the case against them is dismissed or withdrawn.[8] Participants working in the summary jurisdiction identified this as something that is "routine" (Defence23M) and "happens all the time" (Defence03M, Defence12FR, Prosecutor08M). Indeed, Defence03F found it hard to pinpoint an example "because it happens all the time, weekly that that is the agreement". As Prosecutor08M maintained:

> I've found when you're withdrawing a matter that's going down contest mention in advance of the hearing date, quite often it's a discussion I'll have. [I'll] say, if I withdraw this, you know, is there going to be an application for costs? And so it's quite often an agreement you come to there with [the] defence.

Defence18M similarly explained:

> That happens almost invariably when police are withdrawing charges, almost finvariably they'll say, well, we'll withdraw as long as you don't seek costs. Because their position is, oh well, we'll just run it anyway if you're going to seek costs and we'll see how we go.

Defence practitioner participants identified this practice as putting some pressure on the defendant, on the basis that it only occurs in cases where the prosecution realise they have a weak case and the defendant would probably be able to fight it at a contested hearing and win. As Defence10FR explained:

> Often we will, for the sake of getting that resolution sorted or getting that matter withdrawn, we'll agree to there being no application for costs. But it is frustrating because it tends to arise in the context of either an earlier plea offer that's been refused or us saying all along, how are you going to run this case? There's no merit. This is a really weak prosecution case. And them saying, no, no, no, no, no. And being really insistent on running it and then, you know, at the eleventh hour, oh, we'll pull it if you don't apply for costs.

In this vein, Defence25MR noted that when a prosecutor says they will withdraw the charges if no costs are sought, then he will "talk to my client about it and usually recommend to them they don't seek costs because it's better to lose the money than have the [criminal] record, in my view. But it's more an issue for privately funded clients". Defence23M likewise identified this form of negotiation as more difficult for privately funded clients, who have to cover the costs of their defence themselves, as opposed to those funded by VLA. He explained:

> The answer at the end of the day is we have to act in the best interests of the client, and that is, if the charges are going to go away, we'll wear the cost. … It is a bit different in the private practice where the client is going to have to wear those costs themselves. So if a client was paying privately and they might be forking out $5000, $10,000, $20,000 and the charge might be of a more minor nature, it might be that that's an informed decision they would make to run the risk of conviction, depending on how strong they think their case is. But it's a big call to run the risk of conviction.

As this and the previous chapter have revealed, the forms of plea negotiation in Victoria are more varied, complex and situationally specific than has been commonly understood. The experiences of participants in relation to any of these forms varied according to their practice and experience; however, taken overall, it is clear that there are many aspects of the criminal justice process that are amenable to some form of negotiation and compromise, to the advantage of one and/or other of the parties.

Notes

1. In the Magistrates' Court, the maximum term of imprisonment that can be imposed for a single offence is two years. The maximum total sentence that can be imposed for multiple offences is five years. A magistrate invited to deal with an indictable offence triable summarily in the Magistrates' Court may decline to deal with the matter summarily if he or she if of the opinion that the lower maximum penalty specified for the indictable offence would not be adequate to reflect the seriousness of the crime: *Criminal Procedure Act 2009* (Vic) s 29.
2. Under s 16K(4)(a) of the *Magistrates' Court Act 1989* (Vic) (formerly s 83 of the *Magistrates' Court Act 1989*) and s 254 of the *Criminal Procedure Act 2009* (Vic), the defendant has a right of appeal to the County Court on sentence, or on both conviction and sentence.
3. See, for example, *Sentencing Act 1991* (Vic) ss 5(2AB) and (2AC); *Crimes Act 1914* (Cth) s 16A(2)(h).
4. The CREDIT Bail Support Program is available for defendants with drug addictions to complete their treatment while on bail. The program places defendants into appropriate drug treatment and/or rehabilitation programs with the aim of reducing their long-term involvement in the criminal justice system and addressing the defendant's drug problem (Magistrates' Court 2016).
5. *Criminal Procedure Act 2009* (Vic) s 59(2).
6. The conditions of a diversion program may include the defendant making an apology, making a donation or compensation to the victim, undertaking voluntary work, participating in an anger management course, a defensive driving or drug and alcohol awareness course, counselling or treatment programs or other conditions relating to the offender's behaviour.
7. *Criminal Procedure Act 2009* (Vic) s (4)(b).
8. *Magistrates' Court Act 1989* (Vic) s 131.

5

The Negotiation Process

The negotiation process can be long and sometimes difficult. Although it is conducted out of the sight of the public and in the shadow of the trial, the research conducted as part of this study indicates that there is a framework of informal rules and procedures relating to the negotiation process known to those within the legal community. This chapter examines in close detail how the negotiation process operates, including who is involved, when, how and in relation to what matters.

Initiating Negotiations

Of the 35 de-identified case files where it was clear who started negotiations, 91 per cent ($n = 32$) were initiated by the defence and 9 per cent ($n = 3$) by the prosecution (see Fig. 5.1). It was unclear in 20 per cent ($n = 9$) of the 44 cases involving negotiations who initiated discussions.

This breakdown was likewise reflected in the interview data, although participants acknowledged that the early resolution culture developing within the OPP (discussed in more detail below) meant that it was becoming more common for prosecutors to initiate discussions and put forward an offer to the defence, and this seems to be a trend more generally in Australia (Flynn 2016; Stubbs and Tolmie 2008). Overall, however, participants pointed to defence practitioners as "usually being the ones to break the ice" (Defence19M).

Discussions were undertaken via phone and email (or letter), and often a combination of both. In 35 de-identified case files where specific details of how the negotiations first commenced were available, email was the most

A. Flynn, A. Freiberg, *Plea Negotiations*, Palgrave Socio-Legal Studies,
https://doi.org/10.1007/978-3-319-92630-8_5

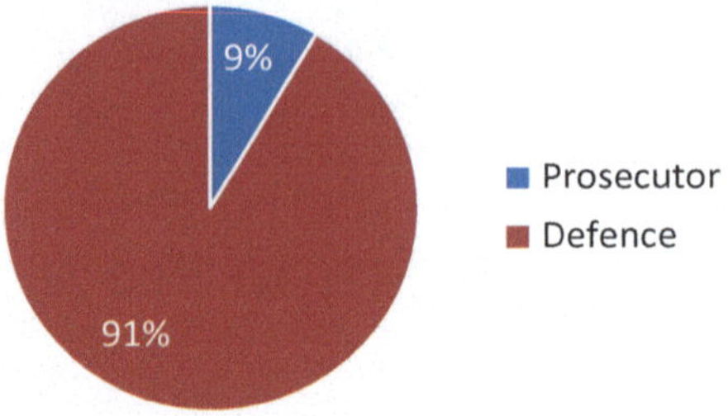

Fig. 5.1 Who initiated negotiations

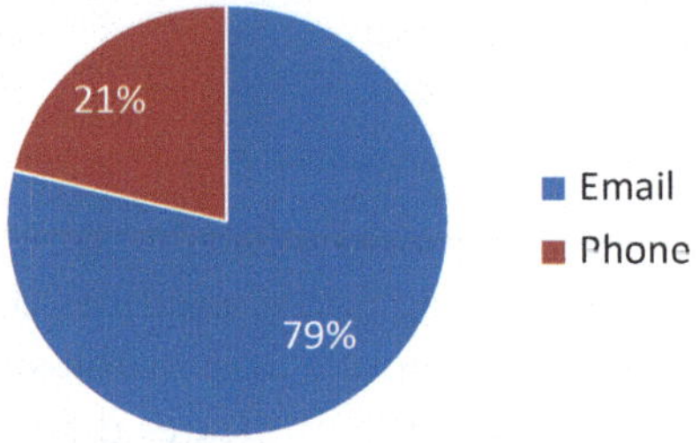

Fig. 5.2 How negotiations initiated

common form (*n* = 16; 74 per cent), followed by phone (*n* = 7; 20 per cent) (see Fig. 5.2). On limited occasions, it appeared that the first discussions took place at court (during a pre-trial hearing).

From the de-identified case files, it was difficult to determine the exact nature and content of some of the conversations that formed part of negotiations. For example, even where the file notes recorded that a phone conversation occurred, it was not always possible to tell from the file whether a call was made in order to:

- propose an offer—for example, in case 019-DD, there was a phone conversation preceding a written plea offer, but the contents of the call were not documented;
- respond to an offer—for example, in case 026-IH, the notes of the phone conversation indicate that the police called VLA "re plea offer", but they do not specify whether the police prosecutor was making or responding to an offer; or
- discuss in general how the matter was likely to proceed and the ensuing discussion identified a potential settlement—for example, in case 020-JD, the first phone conversation from the VLA solicitor to the OPP seems to

have involved a discussion about what might be a possible resolution, as opposed to the defence making a concrete plea offer.

Written offers were made in emails, posted letters, or on the Form 32 where the defence would include an indication of the charge to which the defendant would plead guilty. The Form 32, also known as a case direction notice, must be signed by both parties and filed with the court prior to the committal mention hearing (in indictable cases). The defendant (or their lawyer) and the informant (represented by the OPP) are required to certify on the Form 32 that they have read the brief of evidence. The parties must also indicate how the matter will proceed at the committal mention. If the matter has resolved, this requires stating which charges the defendant will be pleading guilty to and whether there is to be a summary jurisdiction application. If the matter has not resolved, this requires stating which witnesses the defendant seeks leave to cross-examine at a committal hearing and whether the informant opposes this leave. The Form is completed by the defence and sent to the OPP, who then fill in any relevant boxes (indicating, for example, whether they consent to or oppose a witness being called at a committal hearing), sign the Form, file it with the court and send a copy to the defence. The Form 32 essentially represents a "formalised encouragement" (Defence21M) of plea negotiations, although this is not officially noted on the Form.

Timing of Negotiations

The timing of negotiations is of particular interest in light of the benefits of early guilty pleas to the system and the various incentives that have been introduced to address court inefficiency.[1] Research suggests that late guilty pleas constitute one of the main contributors to court delays (Payne 2007; Pedley 1998; Rahman et al. 2017; SAC 2007). Late guilty pleas generally refer to pleas that are entered on the day of or up to two days prior to the commencement of a trial (Ashworth 1994). These pleas waste preparation time and resources and disrupt court schedules. In Australia, late guilty pleas have been a focus of investigation since the 1980s, with numerous commissions, reports and reviews recommending ways to prevent such pleas (Chan and Barnes 1995; Corns 1997; Payne 2007; Standing Committee of Attorneys-General 1999, 2000; Sulan 2000; Victorian Shorter Trials Committee 1985; Rahman et al. 2017). Importantly, in the context of this study, plea negotiations—including a delay in their commencement or a delay in the prosecutor's decision to accept a guilty plea—have consistently been identified as one of the main reasons behind late guilty pleas (Payne 2007; Weatherburn and Baker 2000; Rahman et al. 2017).

Despite the persistence of late guilty pleas, over the past decade in Victoria, there has been a "statistically significant increase in the proportion of early guilty pleas" (SAC 2015: 11), which may be due to the cultural changes in the OPP's approach to plea negotiations and early resolutions.[2] In its analysis of guilty plea rates, the SAC (2015: 21) found that "the proportion of cases resolving as a guilty plea during the [pre-trial] committal stage has been steadily increasing (with the biggest jump between 2008–09 and 2009–10)". This increase in early guilty pleas can also be seen in the resolution rates identified in the OPP annual reports, which show that, between 30 June 2010 and 30 July 2014, approximately 73 per cent of guilty pleas were achieved before trial.

In the dataset of this study, the initiation stage of negotiations was recorded in 37 cases. Of these, all occurred prior to the trial, with the majority—81 per cent (n = 30)—occurring prior to the committal hearing.[3] It was clear from the files that both the prosecution and defence were actively engaging in plea negotiations and resolved matters to a plea of guilty at the earliest opportunity. Predominantly, the first approach was made by the VLA solicitor to the OPP solicitor prior to the committal mention hearing (25 files).[4] There were only two cases where the first approach was made by the OPP solicitor prior to the committal mention hearing. A further six cases were resolved prior to the committal mention, but it was not possible to identify from the files which party initiated discussions. In four cases, a plea of guilty was indicated on the Form 32 (meaning that the matter resolved prior to the committal mention), seemingly without any prior negotiation occurring between the parties.

Of those cases where the matter did not resolve prior to the committal mention, there was one where the first approach was made by the defence practitioner at court during the committal mention hearing (case 003-JC), and one where the prosecution approached the defence after the committal mention hearing, but before the committal hearing (case 022-FI). In three instances, the matters ultimately resolved at court on the day on which the committal hearing was scheduled (cases 033-HM, 003-JC and 004-NO).

There were only five cases where plea negotiations commenced after the defendant had been committed to stand trial. In three of these cases, the files indicate that the initial approach was made by the OPP. No file included the matter being listed for trial and settled at court on the first day or during the trial. All matters were settled by the final directions hearing.

Frequency of Negotiations

Due to the absence of any official record of negotiated guilty pleas (outside confidential prosecutor and defence practitioner case file notes), it has been nearly impossible to accurately determine or even confidently estimate how often plea negotiations occur or to what extent they influence the entering of a guilty plea. As Flynn (2016: 568) explains, "the only snapshot of information available in Victoria is a brief, ambiguous statement located in the OPP Annual Report that since 2007, 63 per cent of the 3,500 cases assigned to the Early Resolution Advocate division have resolved by guilty plea". While previous research in Victoria has proposed what was anecdotally believed to be true—that plea negotiations are a very common criminal justice process, occurring "very regularly in Victoria's superior and lower courts" (Flynn 2012: 80; see also Flynn 2011; Freiberg and Seifman 2001; Seifman 1982)—until now, this has been based solely on empirical estimates and the views of those involved in discussions.

The case file dataset in this study suggests that 87 per cent of guilty pleas involve some form of negotiation. The interview data shed further light on the frequency of negotiations, extending beyond this initial estimate to suggest that it occurs in between 90 and 100 per cent of cases. As Judge02MR explained, "every day … every case is negotiated". Similarly, Defence02F claimed that negotiations occurred in "almost every file. I don't think there's a file that you wouldn't negotiate on." This was a very common view among our defence practitioner participants:

> I would say almost all, unless you've got a very simple set of charges with no alternatives. … There's always room for a discussion in any case. (Defence15M)

> Every single day. There's barely a day goes by that you're not either engaging in discussions with the client about it or at the other end with the prosecution. (Defence03F)

> In every case. (Defence18M)

> I would say it would be 100 [per cent]. … There's not a case that I don't speak to the prosecution beforehand or the investigators. … I couldn't conceive any case where we don't have some … meaningful discussions. (Defence22M)

> Occurs in every single case – 9.5 out of 10. (Defence11M)

> Almost in every case … I can't think of any situation where you can't really engage in negotiations. (Defence12FR)

Drawing on his experience over the previous 12 months, Defence07M observed that negotiations occurred in "most of my cases in the County Court – I would say this year I would have … been briefed in 12 trials. I've done five. The others settled". In fact, all the defence practitioner and judicial participants suggested that some discussion occurs in every case. As Defence05M explained:

> The vast majority of plea of guilty cases result from negotiations, even higher than that, but in terms of my own experience, almost every case that I do involves a form of negotiation, not always successful but almost every case, I don't think that there's a [guilty plea] case where we don't negotiate something about it.

The only group to suggest a lower negotiation rate were prosecutors of serious indictable matters, who estimated that negotiations occur in "at least 50 per cent of cases maybe" (Prosecutor08M). This difference in perspective may be due to defence practitioners being the most likely to initiate discussions (see Fig. 5.1), or due to the types of matters the prosecutors in the study were used to dealing with, which, due to their seriousness, may limit the feasibility of negotiations.[5]

Aside from these prosecutors, the common view among participants was that most, if not all, guilty pleas are entered as a result of some form of negotiation. As Judge07M observed, "the vast majority of cases have some element of negotiation. … With [guilty] pleas, negotiations would almost be 100 per cent. … It would be rare cases where it's entered [the guilty plea] when there's no talking" (Judge07M). Defence09F similarly noted, "every indictable matter … that is dealt with in the committal stream. … I'm yet to deal with a matter, particularly these days, where you don't have at least some form of even informal two-minute phone conversation". This view was also held by Judge01M, who said that "very rarely will you see a defendant come in and plead guilty to everything. It just won't happen. Charges are withdrawn all the time … so there has to be a negotiation at some point".

The Negotiation

One of the key themes to emerge from the case file data was that there is often a long period of back and forth communication between prosecutors and defence practitioners prior to a resolution being reached. In the cases where the plea offer was not immediately accepted, the prosecution response generally addressed the defence arguments and outlined the reasons why the offer was rejected. In addition, the majority of these responses included the OPP proposing a counter-offer (see discussion of case 013-DC below). It was rare for the prosecution to simply dismiss a plea offer out of hand without explanation, although this did occur in at least three cases.

The defence offered by phone to plead guilty to cultivate cannabis (not commercial quantity) if the other charges on the indictment were withdrawn. This offer was made on the basis that there was no forensic evidence that the defendant entered the relevant rooms, that he only moved into one room, and turned a hose on to assist his co-defendant. The defence also argued that the defendant's involvement was around 7–9 days in total.

The OPP asked for the offer in writing and said it would be taken to a Crown prosecutor. The defence did this the next day. The OPP initially said the offer was under consideration, but when VLA followed up two weeks later, the OPP rejected the offer. They made a counter-offer that they would accept a guilty plea to cultivate a commercial quantity in exchange for withdrawing the other charges.

At the committal mention, the magistrate granted a two-day adjournment for the parties to get instructions. VLA requested further particulars from the OPP as to how it would prove knowledge of all plants under cultivation. The OPP responded by saying that the presence of the defendant in two rooms of the house would be relied upon. The OPP also said they planned to make a forensic procedure application for the defendant (indicating they were seeking more evidence of his involvement in cultivation).

The OPP provided a "sketch" of the house to VLA, and after going over it with their client, the defendant decided to plead guilty to cultivate a commercial quantity. VLA advised the OPP that the defendant would plead guilty to cultivate a commercial quantity but that his involvement would be limited to 7–9 days. The final agreement was a guilty plea to cultivate a commercial quantity of cannabis, in exchange for the other charges being withdrawn. The agreed summary of facts was also negotiated to limit activities inside the house and not to articles in the garage, and to 9 days' involvement (case 013-DC).

The evidence of such back and forth communication processes contained in many of the de-identified case files provides a unique insight into the intricacies and nuances inherent to plea negotiations, particularly in the indictable stream. Contrary to some criticisms of plea negotiations, the case file data suggest negotiations involving indictable offences are not simple, flippant or hastily completed. Case 009-SA provides another excellent example of this back and forth process:

> VLA sent the CDPP a letter setting out the charges that the defendant would plead guilty to, including charges the defence sought to have "rolled up" (and would plead guilty to). The letter also stated that the guilty plea would be on the basis that the rest of the charges were withdrawn. The CDPP prosecutor phoned the VLA solicitor to explain that she did not have instructions to accept the offer and would have to reject it. However, she said the prosecution were prepared to roll up some charges (leaving 26 charges). This call was followed up by a letter setting out the same details.

> Following that rejection and counter-offer, the committal mention was adjourned for further negotiations. The CDPP then rang VLA and VLA said the defendant would not plead guilty to the charges where there were no witness statements. The CDPP rang back within the hour and said that if VLA would make an offer to plead guilty to all counts where there are witness statements, they would consider accepting the plea, which would amount to over $1.5 million worth of fraud.

> The defence then made a second written offer, repeating their previous offer in addition to offering to plead to seven more charges (one charge on the basis that two existing charges were rolled up). In relation to the additional charges, VLA put the offer on a specific factual basis that would say the money was paid back.

> The CDPP solicitor responded with a phone call indicating "without prejudice" that the matter should resolve; however there may be some dispute as to the factual basis put (e.g. that money was paid back), and that would be relevant to the way the matter was put in the prosecution opening. On the same day, the CDPP sent a detailed letter via email, setting out the charges it would accept a guilty plea to, the charges which would be withdrawn, and its position regarding the amounts traded and amounts returned to investors. The CDPP claimed that this position reflected the evidence in the brief and that any differences between the VLA offer and CDPP counter-offer could be resolved between the parties on the settling of an agreed summary for the plea. The CDPP offer amounted to guilty pleas to charges of obtaining property/financial advantage by deception in excess of $1.5 million and admitting that the story the defendant told in his record of interview was false. The scheduled committal mention was again adjourned pending further discussions of this offer.

VLA emailed after receiving instructions from the defendant that they would concede that the record of interview was false. This was followed by a CDPP email confirming that "the office is content for the matter to be resolved on the basis previously discussed". This included "for charges 1,4,5,8,9,17,24,25,26 to be withdrawn and for your client to enter guilty pleas to the remaining charges ...". The email also set out what would be contained in the Crown's opening statement in dot points, in response to a request from VLA to do so. This included that the defendant has falsely represented the money invested, the defendant's admissions and the defendant's "false stories".

A guilty plea was then entered at the committal hearing to 18 charges (reduced from almost 30 charges). There were some final discussions before the plea hearing settling the nature of the charges (whether they should be financial advantage or property by deception) and finalising the agreed summary of facts (case 009-SA).

These highly detailed negotiations were recorded in a number of files, including that of case 010-CD, which further demonstrates the level of work and depth of negotiation involved in a guilty plea resolution:

The defence approached the OPP offering to plead guilty to five of the eight charges listed on the indictment, if certain changes were also made to the agreed summary facts, such as the defendant only had an imitation firearm, not a knife as alleged. The OPP responded by phone that they were rejecting the offer to plead guilty to charges 1–4 and 7 but would agree to the others. The OPP conceded that count 7 was weak, but they were "still instructed to reject the offer". They made a counter-offer to accept a guilty plea to handle stolen goods for charge 1 and to remove reference to the knife in the agreed summary for the other charges if the defendant pleaded guilty to the rest of the disputed charges. This was followed by an email from the OPP outlining in writing what was discussed.

VLA responded by email that the defendant would plead guilty as per the OPP position, on the basis that charge 7 was withdrawn, as there was no evidence that the defendant attempted to rob the victim. The OPP solicitor said they would take that offer to the Crown prosecutor. This was followed by phone calls where the OPP said it would accept the offer, but it would not delete reference to the knife in charge 3. VLA emailed the OPP confirming that it would settle the matter as per discussions, with the final agreement that the reference to the knife will remain in charge 3, but charge 7 would be withdrawn. The final agreement involved pleading guilty to six of the original eight charges, with one additional charge introduced (handle stolen goods replacing one theft) and two charges dropped (case 010-CD).

These examples might also provide some comfort to those who may be concerned that defence practitioners do not have their clients' best interests in mind when engaging in negotiations.

Involvement of the Defendant

Every file contained notes documenting the discussions between the defence lawyer and the defendant. These discussions were undertaken over the phone, in conferences at VLA premises and during jail visits. VLA solicitors sought instructions from their clients at each stage in regard to plea offers and how to respond to OPP offers. The files also contained "update letters" to the defendant from VLA either confirming instructions or reporting on the outcome of court hearings. In instances where the OPP put an offer or counter-offer to VLA, VLA solicitors relayed this counter-offer to their client, provided advice and sought instructions from the client. Again, this occurred in writing, via phone and/or meetings (at VLA or during jail visits).[6]

Approval Sought

Many of the files contained a file note indicating that the OPP solicitor would seek instructions from a Crown prosecutor on a plea offer, or correspondence indicating that the Crown prosecutor had accepted or rejected an offer. There were 26 files in the committal stream that did not contain a reference to the solicitor seeking approval from a Crown prosecutor. Three points should be noted, however, before inferring that approval was not sought in these cases: (1) these are VLA files, so the absence of such a reference does not mean that approval was not sought within the OPP, (2) there were only 2 (of 11) CDPP files that referred to "taking instructions", and (3) the 26 files included those cases where there was no record of a negotiation occurring.

In discussing what levels of approval exist at the OPP with participants who had a prosecutorial background, it was confirmed that "there's always someone who has to approve" (Prosecutor03F) any negotiation before a resolution is reached. Prosecutor03F explained:

> The Crown prosecutors must approve the resolutions. We [the solicitors] do the groundwork, we form our own view, we get the victim's view, we get the informant's view, study the strength of the case and then we go and discuss it with the Crown prosecutor and the Crown prosecutor then makes that final decision.

Prosecutor06M further maintained that, in some cases, approval is required "not only from the Crown prosecutor, but it requires the Chief Crown Prosecutor or even the Director's approval".

Under the *Director's Policy: Resolution*, it is stipulated that all plea negotiations require approval from a Crown prosecutor or the DPP.[7] While the DPP can provide approval of any resolution, where the OPP solicitor requests it, in the first instance the policy advises solicitors to seek written advice from a Crown prosecutor. In cases involving a death, the policy requires that approval be obtained from the DPP (or the Chief Crown Prosecutor in the DPP's absence). The policy also states that, "in all cases, the resolution of a prosecution by a plea of guilty to lesser charges may only be approved if the lesser charges are appropriate charges". In this regard, plea negotiations appear to be part of a bureaucratic process within the OPP that has its own internal authorising and accountability mechanisms.

Benefits of Negotiations

Much like the existing research on plea negotiations, participants identified a range of benefits that flow from the process as a primary reason for resolving cases by negotiated guilty plea. Judge06M reflected on the process "supporting the very core principles of our justice system which is equal and fair, dispassionate treatment of people in the administration of our community's laws". Defence10FR identified resolutions as providing a check on the prosecution. As she explained, "there's lots of benefit to negotiating resolutions. And it's about keeping the prosecution accountable partly, so that you don't end up pleading guilty to things that there's no evidence to support" (Defence10FR). Judge06M expanded on this view, maintaining that "when the appropriate charges come before the court, then that is very much ensuring fairness for all the parties ... the vast majority of cases are settled properly and effectively and with huge utilitarian benefits to the community". The efficiency benefits of plea negotiations were recognised by numerous participants:

> The system would break down if we didn't have plea negotiations. (Judge01M)

> It's a truism that justice delayed is justice denied. (Judge03M)

> The obvious efficiency benefits are the reasons we need them. (Prosecutor03F)

> The system cannot cope with trials going ahead, all trials going ahead. So, it is essential to have a managed system whereby most things are settled. (Defence22M)

Defence18M expanded on these views, highlighting the potential benefits to all relevant parties to the case from a guilty plea:

> Look, they're vitally important. I mean otherwise you just – the system would just grind to a halt. The negotiation, if done properly and done well, is really the cornerstone of the system. Without plea negotiations, you traumatise the victims over again, you cause an enormous amount of inconvenience for witnesses, that's before you get to issues in terms of court resources. You also take away police resources, they should be out on the streets, and then you drive Legal Aid further into difficulties. They're just a must, they've just got to exist.

Key Considerations

In a justice system that relies upon the negotiated guilty plea, it is important to understand the key considerations of those who engage in the process. In the case file data, there were two main reasons recorded for charges being withdrawn or plea offers being accepted by the prosecutor—legal and factual/evidentiary. The legal reasons centred on three key factors: (1) whether the charges were duplicitous (such as aggravated burglary and going equipped to steal), (2) whether multiple charges could be rolled up into one count and (3) what the elements of the offence entailed. For example, in case 044-CP:

> The defendant faced charges of false imprisonment and armed robbery arising out of four incidents. Negotiations primarily focused on whether as a matter of law, the false imprisonment charges were duplicitous to the armed robberies (the OPP arguing that they were not, as the victims were detained for a time prior to the co-defendant attending and the theft from the victims occurring). In this case, there were three people who were simultaneously the victim of the armed robbery (i.e. three people in the one place, threatened at the one time with the weapon, who had items stolen). As an incentive to the defendant to settle the matter, the OPP solicitor advised VLA that if the matter was to go to trial, the last armed robbery would be charged as three armed robberies on the indictment, as there were three victims. However, it would remain as one charge on a plea indictment. Therefore, if the defendant pleaded guilty, he would be convicted of one offence only (but the sentence imposed would reflect that there were three victims). If found guilty at trial, he would be convicted of three offences. The matter resolved to a guilty plea to armed robbery and the Crown accepted the legal argument VLA proposed and withdrew the other charges (case 044-CP).

In considering factual/evidentiary reasons, the case file data indicated there is a difference between what a defendant is alleged to have done and what the prosecutor can prove. This reflects comments made in the Royal Commission into Institutional Responses to Child Sexual Abuse (2017b: 345) that "the relationship between the adequacy of charges and the strength of the prosecution evidence is a fundamental part of … negotiations". The factual/evidentiary reasons underpinning the plea negotiations present in the de-identified case files focused on identifying what the evidence in the prosecution brief could establish, and whether the evidence was sufficient to support a conviction. These were the most common factors supporting the arguments made by VLA as to why the OPP should resolve the matter in a particular way. For example, in case 021-NH, VLA made detailed written arguments to the CDPP as to why charges of drug importation could not be sustained, based on a combination of evidence which was said to establish the defendant's innocent state of mind and that the chemical make of the imported substance did not fall within the definition of prohibited import.

In relation to deciding whether or not to resolve a matter through plea negotiations, four key criteria emerged from the interview data: (1) the strength of the evidence, (2) the public interest, (3) the client's interests and (4) personalities.

Strength of the Evidence

In the interviews, the strength of the evidence consideration referred to whether the prosecution had a strong case supported by substantive evidence against the defendant. As Prosecutor03F maintained, "the strength of the evidence needs to be taken into consideration". Defence04M similarly noted that he always asked, "what's the evidence in the particular case against your client? … Really the heart of it is the evidence". Defence20M expanded on this, maintaining that "when you are asking the Crown to negotiate a resolution you are almost always talking about the strength of the evidence". This was also noted by Prosecutor07M, who claimed that "there are usually very good reasons why we will give away a major charge. It's usually we can't prove it. It's usually evidentiary".

Public Interest

Public interest considerations were identified by participants with prosecutorial experience as the outcome that would best serve the public—for example, a guaranteed conviction versus running an expensive trial with the possibility of losing. Judge09M provided the following example:

> You might have somebody that's charged with three drug-trafficking charges and when one looks at the evidence, the first two charges, the evidence is strong, but on the third charge [it] is very weak. There's a prosecutable case, but it's weak. … We're talking about quite long, complicated businesses here. They offer to plead guilty to the first two. I would see that as being in the public interest because the first two properly reflect that they were a drug trafficker at a significant level, and they've indeed committed more than one offence. Secondly, the fact that they've committed drug trafficking on two separate occasions is going to provide a judge with sufficient scope for sentencing purposes. Thirdly, the community benefits from this because there is a guaranteed conviction and sentence associated. Fourthly, in truth, one's not losing a lot because the third charge, the evidence was always pretty weak, so the prospects of getting a conviction were never that great. So it's in the public's interests to accept the [defence's] offer.

The *Director's Policy: Prosecutorial Discretion* outlines 21 different factors that OPP solicitors and Crown prosecutors should consider when determining public interest. These considerations range from the seriousness of the offence and the defendant's degree of culpability, to the mitigating and aggravating factors (such as youth, age, intelligence and mental health), the attitude of the victim, and what outcome would best maintain public confidence in the courts. Judge09M reflected on these factors, claiming:

> The key consideration is the public interest. [A prosecutor should] want to make sure that whatever plea resolution is reached, it properly reflects the wrongdoing which is supported by the evidence. It realistically takes into account the risks that the prosecution may result in a full acquittal, and that the judge is ultimately given proper scope to sentence the person.

Prosecutor04M likewise stressed the importance of determining the public interest in accepting a negotiated guilty plea, while recognising the difficulties that arise for prosecutors in balancing these sometimes conflicting considerations:

> You've got this public interest to consider. … You have a balancing act, but you do have to, in my mind, have to strip it back and deal with the reasonable prospect [of conviction] and just divorce the emotional side of it. But certainly, there's a policy and expectations by the public about what we do.

The Client's Interests

Defence practitioner participants highlighted the importance of the individual client and their unique interests as a primary consideration in determining whether to engage in plea negotiations. They noted that this varies among cases, depending on the individual needs of the client, as well as their background (such as deportation as a result of a conviction), the repercussions of a guilty plea (such as loss of licence or being placed on the sex offenders' register, both of which might impact on employment), the costs of pursuing the case through a contest and the delays inherent to proceeding to trial. As Defence03F explained:

> The key consideration always has to be: what's in your client's best interest? That's always my primary consideration … what's in my client's best interest? … It's my job to protect them. And so, when you're looking at the negotiations you have to figure out what is the best outcome for them in terms of what does the evidence show? What are the circumstances? What can we best achieve? … It's really important that they always feel that it's their choice, because otherwise they won't be at peace with it, they can't be. If they feel that they've just done it because you say that they have to or that they've got no options, that's not a good outcome for me. So, what they can live with is always at the forefront and making sure that they feel empowered that it was them who made the choice and not me.

Defence11M provided a similar overview:

> The main thing you need to keep in mind is your client's personal position, not applying some general defence formula because everyone has different interests and different considerations to be taken into account. So having a detailed conversation and finding out what your client wants is really important before anything [else].

This approach was also evident in Defence09F's comments:

> Every client is different. Some clients don't care what the charge is, as long as the summary is read in a way that suits them. Others couldn't care less about the summary or the charges, just so long as they're not going to go back to jail. Others don't care about going back to jail so long as they're not going to be registered as sex offenders. … One of the most important things when you're getting your client's instructions is to say, what about this is it that really concerns you? Are you saying to me I didn't do this or I don't want to plead guilty, or are you saying I would be amenable to pleading? … You need to establish at the outset what their primary concern is in relation to the matter.

Personalities

A key consideration identified by participants as something that needs to be factored into any decision about whether or not to resolve the matter through a plea negotiation is the personality of the opposing counsel and the judicial officer. Defence12FR explained:

> You want to consider, if you've got a more lenient magistrate or judge on at that time, then that might be an advantage to the client if they accept an offer or negotiation on that day. If you've got, likewise, a reasonable prosecutor, you might be more likely to negotiate or accept something and that's just based on how people operate, the practical implications.

Defence23M similarly observed:

> There are hundreds of different prosecutors in Victoria, so the personalities of every prosecutor are different and some are eminently lovely to negotiate with and they come at things in the spirit of resolution, and others want to stick by their guns until the final moment and then withdraw on the steps of court. So it just depends on the personality of the defence counsel and the prosecutor and to some degree the magistrate [for sentencing considerations].

Prosecutor06M also noted the significance of personality, maintaining that "there's some practitioners that take a more reasonable approach; there's others that won't. And therefore, you obviously gauge your negotiations based on that". The majority of participants were of the view that the outcome of negotiations depends upon which prosecutor and defence practitioners are involved: "it really does come down to the personality" (Defence02FR). As Defence08MR maintained, "it's idiosyncratic. It depends on the prosecutor, it depends on the lawyer, it depends on a whole range of factors. … It depends so much on the personalities and also the skill sets of the lawyers". Many defence practitioner participants pointed to the different personalities of the prosecutors as having a significant impact on the types of discussions and outcomes they are privy to in resolutions:

> The personalities of every prosecutor are different and some are eminently lovely to negotiate with and discuss and they come at things in the spirit of resolution, and others want to stick by their guns until the final moment and then withdraw on the steps of court. (Defence23M)

Some participants, like Defence15M, went so far as to say that the prosecutor's personality affects whether they would even attempt to engage in negotiations. He explained, "you need to be aware of who you're dealing with. There's certain prosecutors that, if they were on duty on a given day, you might try and avoid, lest you lock them into a discussion" (Defence15M).

The differences in personalities and how this affects plea negotiations were also evident in participants' reflections on their personal approaches to and experiences with early resolutions. For example, in discussing his previous experiences with negotiating cases involving sexual offences against children by a parent or step-parent, Judge02MR noted, "I used to mark those as capable of resolution if it was biological, but not if it was non-biological [defendant not biologically related to the victim] … but that was just my instinct, it was just experience. Others did it differently". Similarly, in reflecting on his approach to negotiations, Prosecutor04M observed, "how I negotiate is different from other prosecutors. I'm a little bit more methodical about how I approach things". These comments support the findings of a US study in which 200 state prosecutors in eight different offices were interviewed (Wright and Levine 2014: 1076, 1073):

> We treat prosecutors like widgets, one the same as the next. In reality, prosecutors are individuals with their own priorities and commitments. … A prosecutor's individual character traits, family background, and religious faith may all play a part in her [sic] decision-making. But organisations also matter; for instance, some prosecutors' offices and court systems are arranged in ways that encourage prosecutors to think of themselves as team members, while other offices are organised to inspire the prosecutor to think of herself [sic] as an autonomous professional, not tightly linked to others in the office. Thus, the exercise of discretion may differ – systematically and predictably – as one travels from office to office, and from prosecutor to prosecutor.

In terms of the impact of personality differences on negotiations, participants pointed to the relationships one develops with opposing counsel as making all the difference in "how it turns out" (Defence16F). As Defence16F further explained, "you can't pick your prosecutor. … It really depends on your relationship with the prosecutor and it's about how you manage that". A similar view was expressed by Judge15M at the roundtable, who noted that "a lot of it [negotiations] depends upon the trust between the practitioners". This was particularly evident in our discussions with rural and regional participants, who suggested that their negotiations were often advantaged because there was a smaller pool of people in the legal community, which enabled opposing counsel to develop more established relationships, thereby making the negotiation process smoother and more likely to result in a "practical" and "reasonable" outcome (Defence25MR). As Defence14FR explained:

> It is a personal relationship that you build with the prosecutors. Certainly, we know the County Court prosecutor who services our region – because we're a circuit court – we know him well. He knows our office and therefore we can have some fairly frank discussions with him that are helpful and we know that he's not an unreasonable prosecutor. So if there's a middle ground to be found, the chances are we're going to find that. … With our local prosecutors in our Magistrates' Court, we know them all. They all know us. Half of us are Facebook friends, like we're all invested in each other's lives to some extent, and those relationships are really important to the outcomes that you will get. … We have an enormously friendly bench around here and we have really reasonable prosecutors. Therefore, you get some different outcomes here than you would anywhere else.

Prosecutor02FR also described working in a rural area as offering "unique" advantages:

> Being in a rural area everybody – all of our informants – are in the same building that we're in. … I actually encourage having conversations with informants and to be able to sit down and identify those issues and engage them in the process, because you tend to find that you get a lot more happy customers by being able to do that. … All our defence practitioners are within a stone's throw of the police building and most days of the week, every single defence practitioner that's in the town is actually in the building. So they may see you and approach you and say, hey, listen, I want to speak to you about that matter. It makes it a lot easier. … In Melbourne [capital city of Victoria], they don't have that luxury.

As flagged by Prosecutor02FR, several participants with experience working in both metropolitan and rural or regional areas pointed out the differences between the two environments in relation to plea negotiations, with all claiming that the rural and regional areas were more conducive to "frank and open" (Prosecutor02FR) and "reasonable" (Defence08MR) discussions. Defence08MR claimed:

> At [*names rural location*], it's a small prosecution team, limited number of lawyers, everybody knows each other. You can often reach a reasonably practical solution, probably more so than in Melbourne where there's a much bigger team of prosecutors and they're much more likely to say, well, we don't care, just take what we're offering, you know, or book it off.

Prosecutor02FR likewise commented on the differences between rural and metropolitan negotiations resulting from the relationships developed between lawyers and police:

> Some of the more metro[politan] prosecution offices, because they don't have that ability to be able to build the relationships with all of their customers, being the other police units, then I think that's where people might get themselves, you know what I mean, a bit emotional about when things are withdrawn.

Drawing on his experiences, Defence25MR identified the size of Melbourne as making it very difficult to "build relationships with prosecutors" because "there's of course a much bigger team [of prosecutors]". He maintained that:

> Out here in [*names regional town*], I've known them for a year and I think they know that I'll make it pretty obvious if I think my client is wasting their time effectively in the negotiation setting or if I think they should actually take something and they'll consider it properly. So you build a relationship and you feed off that. ... You have to be much more careful because you're going to be seeing them the next day and the day after that as well. So you have to make sure that your arguments don't get blown out of proportion and you don't talk shit [*laughs*].

The benefits of the relationships developed in country environments were also identified by stakeholders at the roundtable:

Prosecutor13F:	I think that's also why plea negotiations work so well in the country because people know they've got a designated prosecutor at the early stages, people have got to know each other and trust each other and I think that –
Judge15M:	You can shake your head at the defence barrister as you walk down the street – you can do all sorts of unrecorded things.
Prosecutor13F:	That wasn't quite where I was going [*laughter*].
Judge16F:	That point is important, though, because she's [Prosecutor13F] saying it's about people having the time and the opportunity to negotiate too. One of the problems again in the city is ... the number of prosecutors.

The apparent differences between rural or regional and metropolitan locations in relation to how plea negotiations are carried out, as well as the ways in which personalities can shape the negotiation process, including the likelihood of discussions occurring and the outcome, raise some interesting questions around consistency. As Prosecutor04M observed:

> You may find if you chuck ten lawyers in a room and gave them the same circumstances, not everyone is always going to come to the same conclusion. You are going to have the factors of different prosecutors, different levels of skill, different barristers. … So you are going to have different outcomes.

Similar questions have been raised by Flynn (2016: 570), who describes this as the "human nature effect". A key finding in her study of prosecutorial discretion and plea negotiations in Victoria was that there are inconsistencies in the ways in which prosecutors approach and view plea negotiations, despite the existence of internal policies guiding behaviour. She maintains that the "striking contradictions between what is instructed in internal policies and the contrasting conduct and perspectives of prosecutors … permit inconsistent conduct and outcomes" (Flynn 2016: 570).

Participants provided several examples of the different personalities of practitioners resulting in differing views being taken in negotiations, even within the same case. Defence04M, for example, reflected on a recent murder trial in which he was involved:

> I had one particular prosecutor who said he was prepared to resolve the matter on a manslaughter [plea]. The client wasn't prepared to accept it [at that stage], but the next prosecutor that came along, because the first got reallocated, he wasn't interested in dealing with it on a manslaughter. So the outcome really can depend on who the prosecutor is.

Prosecutor06M likewise offered examples of occasions when he had "stepped in" to assist defence practitioners in reaching an early resolution when they had come up against "more difficult solicitors":

> I've had cases where a defence practitioner has rung me up and said, look, I've got this matter with so-and-so solicitor in the office, I don't seem to be getting anywhere with it, or, what do you think? Do you think we can resolve this sort of thing? So I've stepped in occasionally and then I've spoken to the solicitor and said, look, I've had a call from the defence. I hope you don't mind, but this is what they say and maybe we should look at this and see whether it can be resolved.

In this regard, it is noteworthy that such intervention occurred despite its prohibition in the *Director's Policy: Resolution*, which states:

> A Crown prosecutor must not discuss resolution with an accused's legal representative unless the Crown prosecutor is briefed to appear in the prosecution.

> An Office of Public Prosecutions ('OPP') solicitor must not discuss resolution with an accused's legal representative unless the OPP solicitor has conduct of the prosecution.

A key aim of the criminal justice system is to achieve equality and consistency. The above comments from participants suggest that, when plea negotiations occur, the outcome is at least somewhat dependent on the people involved. Reflecting on his time as a prosecutor, Judge02MR maintained that negotiations involve "a lot of intuition. There's no formula, it's your gut. You go with your gut all of the time". While such an approach raises a number of concerns, similar arguments could apply in the context of a trial where the outcome depends somewhat on the individual personalities of 12 members of a jury. Likewise, sentencing has been criticised for being dependent on the individual judge—indeed, several participants described judges as either "sympathetic" to the defence (Defence03F) or "hard" on the defence (Defence09F). In this regard, it could be argued that plea negotiations are reflective of the "human nature effect" (Flynn 2016: 570) inherent to the broader criminal justice system, seen, for example, in the prosecutor's decision to prosecute, the jury's verdict and the judicial officer's sentencing judgments (Hogarth 1971). Perhaps the key difference in relation to plea negotiations is that both the trial and sentencing hearing are highly visible and open to external scrutiny and appeal, therefore inconsistencies in approaches to plea negotiations may create a greater sense of unease and potential for injustice.

Factors Shaping the Negotiation Process

Overcharging: The "Hamburger with the Lot"?

Overcharging has been a common criticism of plea negotiations globally. Citing Freedman (1975: 88), Flynn and Fitz-Gibbon (2011: 916) define overcharging as "the situation in which a prosecuting agency charges an accused with a more serious offence or an accumulation of offences, which creates a strong incentive for the accused to enter into plea bargaining". As Ashworth (2010: 261) observes, "to some extent it remains in the prosecution's interest to bring a number of charges against a defendant, since they may then agree not to proceed with some of the charges in exchange for the defendant's agreement to plead guilty to the others".

The main concern of overcharging raised by critics relates to the police charging defendants with every possible offence and alternative offences linked to the offending conduct, "in order to strongly encourage [the defendant] to plead guilty to a bargained version of these charges" (Flynn and Fitz-Gibbon 2011: 916). Internationally, this process is referred to as "coercive plea bargaining" (Caldwell 2011), in which "bluff and tactics – rather than truth, justice, guilt or innocence" (McConville et al. 1991: 165)—guide the plea negotiation process. Coercive plea bargaining is based on the assumption that any prosecutorial offers made to the defendant are only a negotiation on the multiple charges that would be unlikely to stand up to the rules of evidence applied at trial. Graham (2014: 704) presents an overview of two key forms of overcharging, both of which he argues can be used "to facilitate a plea bargain": horizontal, which refers to the practice of "multiplying unreasonably the number of accusations against a single defendant", and vertical, which involves charging "a single offence at a higher level than the circumstances of the case [support]".

In the Australian context, less than half (46 per cent) of the participants (comprising representatives of the prosecution, defence and judiciary) in Flynn and Fitz-Gibbon's (2011: 916) study acknowledged that overcharging occurs, with only eight participants identifying it as a concern. The remainder of the participants who did acknowledge that overcharging occurs attributed it "not to the deviousness of the prosecution, but rather to the inexperience or the overzealousness of the police" (Flynn and Fitz-Gibbon 2011: 916). Most commonly, criticisms of overcharging in Australia have emerged in relation to murder charges laid against battered women who have killed their partners/ex-partners in response to prolonged periods of abuse, where there is a clear basis for the alternative charge of manslaughter (NSW Legislative Council 2013). As Sheehy et al. (2014: 668) observe, across Australia "the overwhelming majority of cases involving battered women accused are still prosecuted as murder, even though murder convictions are rare and the majority of these cases are resolved by the acceptance of guilty pleas to manslaughter". This concern is also raised by Kirkwood et al. (2013) in their analysis of Victorian homicide cases involving a woman killing an abusive male partner, in which they argue that women are often subjected to overcharging. Kirkwood et al. (2013: 43) found that in all the homicide cases they reviewed, the initial charge was murder despite the evidence being incapable of sustaining this charge—an outcome supported by the fact that in the majority of the cases, "the Crown was willing to accept a plea of guilty to a lesser offence".

In this study's case file dataset, the mean number of charges a defendant ultimately pleaded guilty to, in relation to the number with which they were first charged, reduced by 50 per cent (mean of 6.42 charges reduced to a mean of 3.24 charges). Consequently, the question was raised as to whether overcharging—intentional or otherwise—was a problem in Victoria.

Overwhelmingly, participants acknowledged that Victoria Police tends to charge every possible offence that fits the offending conduct. As Defence03F noted, "all the time. … It's like police, they get their little thing and go, oh yeah I think I can charge all these things. It's like a hamburger with the lot and they just throw it all in there". Defence19M claimed that within "Victoria Police, overcharging is endemic". Defence24M similarly observed, "every day – [in] 95 per cent of cases they [Victoria Police] do it". Defence04M also maintained that this practice is "very [common]. … In the first instance, you will have the police charging everything under the sun, that's very common and so you get indictments that are overloaded". Judge03M likewise explained that:

> Police lay every charge in the book. In a typical injury case they charge everything from assault to common law assault to recklessly causing injury, intentionally causing injury, recklessly causing serious injury, intentionally causing serious injury, and doing the latter things in circumstances of gross violence.

Some participants questioned whether overcharging is a mechanism used by the police to "beef up statistics" (Defence09F):

> If you are laying a certain number of charges it beefs up your stats, whether or not you return a conviction or you obtain a plea of guilty in relation to any of those charges. I certainly have experience and views about certain members and certain units who are much more problematic in that regard and sometimes charges just don't even make sense. … These days it's the minority I would say of cases where you actually just get the charges that should be there in the first place. (Defence09F)

Other participants noted inadequate training and understanding of the law among police as one of the reasons for the prevalence of overcharging:

> I guess you've got a police officer who's probably never been in a courtroom or only just to give evidence on a bail app[lication] or at a trial. They don't really understand what they need to prove that charge half the time I don't think, so there's probably some issues around knowledge. (Defence03F)

Defence24M similarly claimed:

> They're not lawyers, so that means that often they don't understand the legal elements of a charge, so you use the machine gun approach or a hamburger with the lot … in the hope of getting something.

Most of the prosecutorial participants felt that overcharging was not as common now as it used to be. Prosecutor09F claimed, "that's changed. I think there's a little bit more support or training around charging what's on the brief and not doing that sort of hamburger with the lot where there's just a mountain of charges". Likewise, Prosecutor10FR observed that "years ago there was the practice of just throwing as many charges as they could, but I think that's really tamed back in the last, I don't know how long. But yeah, there's not often things that aren't supported somewhere within the brief". In contrast, however, defence practitioners and some judicial participants argued that overcharging was as common as ever and that, problematically, it is used as a negotiation tool by the prosecution. Judge01M explained:

> There's a real concern about overloaded indictments and overcharging in order to put yourself in a better bargaining position, and I fear that some indictments that I've seen smack of the prosecutor throwing the book at the accused with a view to ultimately negotiating it down.

In this vein, Defence24M argued:

> There's a culture of doing it. It's been going on for as long as I've been a practitioner, which is over 30 years. I think that there's probably a whole lot of reasons for it … but I think that there are specific cases and occasions where people are deliberately overcharged in the hope that that would get them to plead [guilty].

Defence04M similarly noted that overcharging occurs "as a sort of way of potentially trying to see if they [the prosecution] can resolve the matter", while Defence23M observed that police "throw [in] everything they can, in the hope that a plea will get entered to something".

The majority view, however, was that overcharging is not a deliberate or malicious approach; rather, it is "a product of the adversarial system" (Judge09M) and "the way Victoria Police have done things for a long, long time" (Prosecutor02FR):

> Police of course, it's their role to charge … that's not with a view to securing a plea, that's just being defensive and wanting to ensure that a conviction is secured. … I know of no practice where people have deliberately overcharged with a view to securing a [guilty] plea to a lesser offence. (Judge09M)

The view that charging a defendant with multiple and alternative offences is a "defensive" approach aimed at ensuring that a conviction is secured was common among participants. As Defence04M observed:

> I've often thought that the overcharging, the old 'hamburger with the lot', is done really as a defensive mechanism to ensure that if they are not committed [to trial] or they are acquitted on certain charges, we've got some lesser alternatives. One can readily understand that.

In addition, participants considered this type of charging to be a "process", and something Prosecutor01F identified the police were "doing a pretty good job at". She explained:

> You've got to remember, it's a process. When they get it, they may arrest somebody and they're investigating. I mean they're damned if they do and they're damned if they don't. … They lay the charges and they don't want to be accused of not laying the appropriate charges. … By and large, they're getting pretty good at that. … They're better trained I think. They're much better educated. … And if they're unsure, they do have a mechanism where they can ring us up and ask us for advice as well.

The idea of overcharging as a "process" was also recognised by Judge02MR, who described the charging practices of the police as a means to ensure "flexibility":

> Because of the way the police initially charge, they'll go from the most serious to the least serious and in between there might be a negotiation point. Because if you have an assault with injury, you're likely to get intentionally and recklessly cause injury, assault with a weapon, assault by kicking, aggravated assault of a female, unlawful assault. So just with that one scenario, you may have up to six to eight charges arising, and then you might have a threat thrown in as well. So the accused might ultimately plead guilty to recklessly cause injury, the threat goes in as part of the context, but the charge is withdrawn. It's done so there's that flexibility.

There are also some practical reasons underpinning the charging process, including that most summary offences cannot be amended after 12 months, which may result in multiple charges being laid to ensure the charge is there, should it be needed. It may also be entirely appropriate to charge a defendant with both intentionally and recklessly causing injury offences, but it may be difficult to prove intent, thereby resulting in the reckless charges ultimately proceeding. Additionally, if there is a tendency for Victoria Police to charge with all relevant offences, this may be perhaps more reflective of the many alternative offences that exist in Victoria, as opposed to any sinister or malicious motive designed to force a defendant to plead guilty to a reduced number of charges. As Judge02MR pointed out above, there are many charges laid in relation to the one act. For example, an assault has numerous alternative offences available, including common assault[8]; aggravated assault, assault in company, assault by kicking, assault with a weapon[9]; assaulting or threatening to assault a person with the intent to commit an indictable offence[10]; resisting, obstructing, assaulting or threatening to assault an emergency worker on duty or a person lawfully assisting an emergency worker on duty[11]; assaulting or threatening to assault a person with intent to resist or prevent arrest[12]; common law assault[13]; causing serious injury intentionally in circumstances of gross violence[14]; causing serious injury recklessly in circumstances of gross violence[15]; causing serious injury intentionally[16]; causing serious injury recklessly[17]; and causing injury intentionally or recklessly.[18] If the police do not charge the various alternative offences to reflect all the possible outcomes, the prosecution may ultimately fall through or fail. As Prosecutor06M suggested:

> Police are fairly accurate in charging. They will always and should always have alternatives, of course. … There's a lot of overlapping offences and sometimes there's nuances that you really need [and] it needs legal expertise to look at.

While most of participants recognised this charging practice as "standard" (Defence25M) and "acceptable" (Prosecutor06M), there is the potential for it to place undue pressure on the defendant to plead guilty in exchange for a reduction in the number and extent of charges on the indictment. It can also result in distress for victims when the charges are withdrawn or reduced, and they perceive that their victim status and experience are being "downgraded" (Flynn 2012: 86). As a prosecutor in Flynn's (2012: 86) study of plea negotiations stated, "the victim might prefer it were recorded that they were a victim of a rape rather than an indecent [sexual] assault, or if they are a secondary victim, that their family member was the victim of a murder, not a manslaughter. That is more … [about] recognition of what occurred". Flynn (2012: 86) maintains that this practice can result:

> Not only in the 'downgrading' of the offences, but also the downgrading of the victim's status. Accordingly, this can impact on a victim's right to be recognised as a legitimate victim of the full extent and number of crimes that were committed against them.

Overcharging can also create false hope for victims who may struggle to understand how and why the charges are altered. In this vein, the NSW Legislative Council (2013: 164) observed that "overcharging and subsequent acceptance of pleas to reduced charges can be frustrating and disappointing for families [of victims]". In light of these concerns, and the data, which suggest that there is some overlap in offences, there may be a basis for revisiting the number of offences used to cover the various types of offending conduct in Victoria. Alternatively, there may be room to consider following the statutory charging process adopted in England and Wales, where the Crown Prosecution Service (CPS) (the equivalent of the OPP) in conjunction with the Association of Chief Police Offices advises police prior to charges being laid as to appropriate offences based on the law, and also reviews the brief submitted by police to determine what charges the defendant should face in serious and complex cases (College of Policing 2015).

Statutory Charging Process

In England and Wales, under the *Code for Crown Prosecutors*, the police are responsible for charging "all summary offences irrespective of plea and any either way offences [indictable offences tried summarily] anticipated as a guilty plea and suitable for sentence in a Magistrates' Court". The *Director's Guidance on Charging* (2013) provides information on the offences and categories that the police are able to charge without seeking advice from the CPS. For all other matters, the police are required to contact the CPS for guidance on charging decisions. For serious and complex cases, police officers will meet with a CPS lawyer in person (College of Policing 2015). For advice in relation to less serious cases, the police officer may contact the CPS lawyer by phone or via a secure digital service following the arrest of the suspect to discuss whether there is sufficient evidence to charge the defendant and what the charge(s) should be (College of Policing 2015). As part of this process, the CPS may require the police to collect further evidence before a charging decision can be made. All advice is recorded for internal transparency purposes (College of Policing 2015) but is not disclosable as it is subject to public interest immunity between the police and the CPS (College of Policing 2015).

Research into the statutory charging process in England and Wales has been mixed. Some has reported that the process has negatively impacted timeliness and efficiency by creating delays for police in being able to access a CPS lawyer, thereby adding "a significant delay in the time from arrest to the disposal of the case" (House of Commons Justice Committee 2009: 12). In conducting a review of the statutory charging process, the House of Commons Justice Committee (2009: 16–17) noted the concerns raised by some police that "the CPS is over-cautious, or target-driven, and as a result prefer less risk, i.e. lower charges that are more likely to lead to a guilty plea or conviction". Citing a submission from the Police Federation, the report states:

> There is a perception amongst many officers that, to use a current buzz phrase, many CPS [prosecutors] are 'risk averse' when it comes to charging decisions and the CPS will only pursue the 'most certain of cases', perhaps because of how their performance targets worked. … Cases that could realistically be charged as serious offences are either not charged at all, or downgraded to something that is easier to prove. (House of Commons Justice Committee 2009: 17)

McConville and Marsh (2014: 154) have also criticised the legitimacy of a process that essentially gives the CPS "free reign over both charging decisions and plea negotiation". They contend that "handing over the process of State-induced guilty pleas to the CPS was unreflective and damaging to the interests of justice" (McConville and Marsh 2014: 154). In spite of these potential limitations, the "significant benefits" of statutory charging in England have included a reduction in discontinuance rates, an increase in guilty plea rates and an increase in conviction rates (Police Association of NSW 2013). Accordingly, there may be some basis for considering a similar scheme for serious cases in Victoria to address some of the limitations pertaining to police charging practices identified by our participants, albeit this should be considered with caution, taking into account the justice concerns identified by McConville and Marsh (2014).

Summary Versus Indictable Offences

As discussed in Chap. 2, the OPP is responsible for prosecuting matters in the indictable stream, and police prosecutors are tasked with prosecuting matters in the summary stream (including indictable offences tried summarily). As part of this study, it was useful to consider what factors affect the way in which plea negotiations are engaged in at the different court levels and what the major differences in the approaches and outcomes of negotiations between the summary and indictable jurisdictions are.

Most commonly, participants suggested that negotiations in the Magistrates' Court were less formal and often happened on the day on which the matter was listed for a pre-trial hearing. As Defence07M observed, "in the Magistrates' Court, I'd usually do it on the day. County Court usually well before. … If it's a summary matter, the most effective way to do it without wasting anyone's time is to do it at court". Defence11M similarly claimed:

> With the OPP, which obviously is the County Court and Supreme [Court], you're better off dealing with it in writing. It's a more academic approach that's given to the matter and assessment of the merits, and in the Magistrates' Court with summary matters, it's more face to face with police prosecutors.

Defence02F likewise explained that:

> My experience with police prosecutors is their preference is to negotiate on the day, so they don't want to have any emails hanging around before the date. … They just want to have it dealt with on the day, whereas, obviously it's very different in the committal stream where you're negotiating two weeks, three weeks in advance and you try to establish where the case is going quite early.

Interestingly, in pointing to the more serious matters heard in the higher courts, participants implied that it was necessary to "pay more attention to negotiations" (Defence25MR) and "negotiate much more thoroughly and much more based on the evidence" (Defence18M) in the higher courts. As Defence19M suggested, "if you're gambling with a decade of jail, you're not mucking around. … It's a different process". When asked to expand on this comment, Defence19M said:

> In the Magistrates' Court, you need to be able to jump in, negotiate on the day, why am I going to be here? What's the lay of the land? And back out, that's a rubbish negotiating forum, I'll go somewhere else. Whereas with the Crown, you can't be doing that sort of thing. It's got to be a much more evidence-based and considered decision about, well, what is our position? What is our bottom line? What are we going to say to the Crown? It's a much more formal process and so it should be, because the matters are so much more serious.

Participants also pointed to the speed at which matters need to be dealt with in the Magistrates' Court, given the number of cases it hears each year, as affecting how negotiations are carried out. As Defence02F maintained:

> The pressures of the Magistrates' Court system to try to resolve matters before it goes to contest, the policy of trying to or not having any delays in the courts puts a lot of pressures on the magistrates to try to not resist adjournment applications and to try and resolve it, finalise things as much as possible.

Defence14FR similarly observed:

> In the Magistrates' Court, there's a bit of an impetus on everybody to keep these matters moving, resolve these matters. They're either going to contest or they're resolving. Let's just keep them going and sort this out, whereas the timelines are so drawn out in the County Court, especially in circuit towns, there is more time to think and there are more requirements that things are done in writing.

In this fast-paced environment, Defence25MR reflected on plea negotiations in the summary jurisdiction as being "less about the evidence and the law". He explained:

> In the Magistrates' Court, it's much faster, it's more immediate, there's no law quoted really, not very much at least, it's just a matter of trying to reason with each other and reach a reasonable position. If a client says no he says no and then you move on. In the higher courts, there's a lot of law quoted, it's about what charge is appropriate in the circumstances as much as anything else.

Participants also argued that the seriousness of indictable matters often means that the investigation is longer and there are more people involved in handling the matter, which requires more time to negotiate, whereas the summary matters often lack that level of involvement or detail—hence matters resolve on the day. This may be due in part to the heavy workload of police prosecutors, many of whom are unfamiliar with the details of each individual case until they have the file in front of them on the day. Defence14FR observed:

> The nature of County Court matters in my experience is that they've been investigated usually in far more detail. So your negotiations I think tread a far more fine line than in the Magistrates' Court, where sometimes you're getting in there, they have not taken any statements from anybody, nobody's been to see a doctor and you're trying to prove serious injury. That's just not going to happen. So there's sort of more of that, well that's just patently ridiculous. So let's just remove that one and let's talk about these two. In the County Court, it goes through more sets of hands, then a longer timeframe on it and therefore, yeah, I think a lot of that negotiation to some extent is done by the OPP with the informant before it even gets to us when they say, look that's just absurd. We're not going to get up on that, so we're not even going to put it to them [the defence].

In addition to noting the impact of differences in the type of case on negotiations, a key theme emerging from the defence practitioner participants was that they had to adopt different negotiation styles with police prosecutors, compared with OPP prosecutors. Some participants saw this as a benefit, in that discussions with police prosecutors were often more informal:

> It's much more informal and that doesn't happen so much in the higher court. … I think that it's the pomp and ceremony of the whole process, like you need to have the correct terminology for the thing that you're talking about. Whereas when you're discussing a case with the [police] prosecutor, you'll use more everyday language. (Defence17F)

Others, however, suggested that this lack of formality made the process more difficult. References to police prosecutors as "difficult" (Defence09F) and "not having legal degrees" (Defence03F), and comparisons of them to the "professional people" (Judge08M) working in the higher courts, revealed a common perception of police prosecutors as "outsiders" to the rest of the legal community. The data suggest that this view ultimately affected the way in which defence practitioners approached and engaged in negotiations with police prosecutors. As Defence06MR explained:

> I would have to use a lot more energy and effort, looking up cases and law and all of that for the people downstairs, for the police prosecutors, because they just don't get it. Whereas if I'm speaking to the OPP, on the whole, they get it, they know, we're all on the same page, we're talking about the same things, we all have the same sort of reference. Whereas downstairs, you really have to, you know, put a lot of effort in, and that wastes time.

Defence08MR similarly noted that:

> The OPP are probably more attuned to some of the legal arguments. Obviously, you know, police prosecutors aren't lawyers, so they sort of haven't, you know, gone and sat through hours and hours of lectures on intention or recklessness.

Defence09F identified several factors that influence the nature of negotiations in the summary stream:

> In the Magistrates' Court where you've got police prosecutors who might not necessarily firstly know the law terribly well – they're not lawyers – and they don't necessarily always have a good appreciation of – these are the elements you need to be able to satisfy beyond reasonable doubt in order to proceed with this charge. You have some very gung-ho police prosecutors who say, basically I'll run it anyway. There's no accountability there; police prosecutors will run anything. I just think there's less accountability, there's less supervision, there's less review and so things that shouldn't get run in the Magistrates' Court just get run anyway. There's also a presumption amongst a lot of police prosecutors that, well, your client's just going to plead anyway because they'll get a favourable [sentence] indication and I don't have to worry about it, I don't have to do anything. That doesn't happen in the County Court and the Supreme Court, as I said, there's much more review, the charges are necessarily more serious so people aren't just going to stick their hand up to it, and you're dealing with lawyers who understand the law.

Defence09F went on to note that OPP prosecutors are more willing to engage in negotiations and discuss resolution possibilities, whereas police prosecutors rarely approach the defence to resolve a case, and take the view that if the defendant does not plead, they will "simply run the matter anyway". She maintained:

> It's not the same way as it operates in the higher courts, where the OPP or the CDPP are always the ones coming to you saying, can we resolve this? What can we do about this? It's very much more one-sided and the police's position tends to be, well, if you don't like it, then we'll run it. Plead [guilty] or we'll run it. It's a lot more one-sided, whereas it's a more collaborative, we all want the best outcome here, for the most part anyway, in the higher courts. I would say there's definitely a different perspective between Magistrates' and County/Supreme Courts, but again I think that's a difference between having police officers as prosecutors who might not necessarily grasp all the complexities associated with the law. I mean they know charges and they lay charges and that's fine, but they're not lawyers and it can be quite difficult trying to negotiate with someone in that kind of environment.

The reluctance of police prosecutors to negotiate was also highlighted by Defence10FR, who claimed that "the biggest hurdles to negotiating would be, you know, having a police prosecutor that is not interested or not responsive or not receptive". Defence03F similarly maintained that "police prosecutors are completely unreasonable most of the time with resolutions". Defence25MR also pointed to the difficulties of negotiating with police prosecutors:

> The police prosecutors are much more difficult to reach a negotiated agreement with. I think part of that really might be I suppose the court culture and the fact that most people who run cases out here are found guilty ultimately and so they can be pretty comfortable that they can run this and win, and so it gives them less incentive to try and resolve it.

Defence06MR likewise argued that:

> There are so many times that I've got the response of, look, I know this informant, he's a good informant, he wouldn't be saying it if it wasn't true. … So that just shows you how frustrating, when you've got a real issue to be determined, [it] can be very difficult between police prosecutors. … In the OPP, I know that there are a couple of people that, you know, weren't much chop as lawyers, but, on the whole, I think if you've got – if you're up against another lawyer, I think they can see a resolution far more regularly than police officers can.

These comments suggest that there are significant differences in the negotiation approaches and styles utilised in the different courts which all shape the nature, detail and type of discussion involved, primarily as a result of the speed and nature of matters heard in the Magistrates' Court and the involvement of police prosecutors, who do not necessarily have a law degree.

Contest Mentions and Summary Case Conferences[19]

Two main factors that were identified by participants as shaping the negotiation process in the summary jurisdiction were the contest mention and summary case conference pre-trial processes (see Figs. 2.11, 2.12 and 2.13 in Chap. 2). Wood (2013: 33–4) argues that the summary case conference has encouraged "an early identification of guilty pleas; listing certainty for matters set for trials; more efficient resource allocation; [and] a reduced [court] backlog". As discussed in Chap. 2, the purpose of the summary case conference is for the prosecution and the defendant (or their representative) to manage the progression of the case (e.g. to avoid unnecessary adjournments or resolve matters at an early stage).[20] While not directly acknowledged in the legislation, it is anecdotally argued that the summary case conference is a key point for early plea negotiations to commence between the parties, and the legislation stipulates that "anything said or done in the course of a summary case conference; or any document prepared solely for the purposes of a summary case conference is not admissible in any proceeding before any court … unless all parties [agree otherwise]".[21] Also discussed in Chap. 2, the contest mention is a relatively informal court hearing with the magistrate, defence practitioner, defendant and police prosecutor, which aims to define the case issues, including the possibility of an early resolution.[22]

Primarily, participants saw these two pre-trial processes as positive initiatives that encourage resolutions and early guilty pleas because "it brings it [the case] to a head – the prosecution have to make a decision [and] the defence have to make a decision" (Judge02MR). In discussing the contest mention, Judge06M maintained that:

> It works very well. It's responsible for resolving large numbers of matters that would otherwise have gone to contest if the system wasn't there. It focuses the mind of both sides: the lawyer has to be prepared and understand what the case is about, has to be in possession of all the materials; the prosecutor's got to be across the case as well so that everybody understands what the evidence is, who the witnesses are and what they're all going to say. And then a proper conversation can be had and sometimes a prosecutor will, once it's seriously looked at, appreciate that there's real evidentiary weaknesses in parts of the case or all of the case and sometimes, you know, it takes the defence until that point in time to have all the evidence for the defendant to realise there's no defence there.

Defence02F likewise described the contest mention as "working really, really well". She explained that:

> It's legally aid–able [funded] those appearances, so it puts it outside of the pressures of the duty lawyer system. And it means that police prosecutors are forced to turn their minds to it before the date of the hearing and that way they are able to negotiate on things instead of just taking our views and then saying that they've got to get back to us.

Defence25MR similarly identified the contest mention as a key point at which to hold "proper negotiations". He maintained that:

> It's really the first stage at which you can have proper negotiations. It's the first stage at which the prosecutor will actually have read the brief, listened to the [police] interview and know what the case is. Before that, they're just picking it up for the first time when you sit down with them.

Furthermore, the contest mention was said to be a much more successful initiative than the summary case conference for a number of reasons, the two most common being that: (1) VLA lawyers are not specifically funded for the summary case conference, so many defendants are unrepresented at this stage, usually relying on assistance from a duty lawyer, and it can be difficult to engage them in discussions given their limited understanding of the law and the criminal justice process, and (2) at that early stage in the criminal justice process, police prosecutors are often not privy to all the evidence and not abreast of all the relevant case materials to make a decision or have a meaningful discussion. Defence09F expanded on these limitations in comparison to the contest mention process:

> Contest mentions I think are valuable because a lot of the time when you're trying to summary case conference a matter you have very little evidence available to you, the prosecution hasn't gone and got statements, they haven't gone and actually investigated things and they'll say, well, only if you book it off, will we go and do this. It's reactive, it's not, here's all the evidence and you can decide what to do with it. With these prelim[inary] briefs that we're getting now there's nothing on it, so there's a preliminary summary of facts, you might get a statement from the informant if you're really lucky and that's it. You don't know what you're dealing with and you won't get anything further until you go to contest mention.

Comparing the summary case conference with the contest mention system, Defence15M also pointed to the prosecutors being more abreast of the material as a beneficial aspect of the latter:

> Often they will have read the briefs, so at the very least you've got a prosecutor and they will be a more senior prosecutor who's actually looked at the material before they've come to court, and that does let you have a more sensible discussion.

The summary case conference is not a hearing per se. Rather, it is an out-of-court discussion between the prosecutor and the defence about the case. Defence10FR explained that, "generally speaking", all their summary case conferences are completed "by email, so there's a record of the discussion in the file". She further explained:

> Within a Legal Aid office, because we often don't have grants of aid for our clients, the duty lawyer needs to pick up the file on the day and run with it. So if there's a written discussion it's much easier for someone else to pick up and follow than a discussion that I might have with a prosecutor that's then not recorded or – I mean I always record but, you know, it's just easier if there's an email that people can look at. And that's largely because it keeps the communication clear and because of the way this office operates.

The link between summary case conferences and plea negotiations was identified by Prosecutor02FR, who claimed that "the summary case conference process was introduced for early resolution and negotiations to occur. The whole point is to engage with defence as early as possible to identify what the issues are and hopefully resolve those".

Resources and Funding

While the summary case conference is designed to avoid wasting court time by requiring that discussions occur out of court, participants identified several limitations of this arrangement, specifically relating to funding and the heavy workloads of police prosecutors, which hinders their capacity to respond to resolution offers out of court. Defence23M explained:

> There's not enough [police] prosecutors there. They're all in court so no one is doing the case conferencing out of office, no one is seeing it. You turn up to court and they'll say, I've never seen that email. And so the whole purpose of a case conferencing system was to have an out-of-court discussion so you're not all turning up to court trying to resolve things on the day. Whereas in reality, it means we're just doing it with a different prosecutor at court. It comes down to not enough resourcing.

This view was supported by Prosecutor04M, who maintained that the high workload restricts prosecutors involved in summary case conferences from being able to fully engage with the process: "when you have 200 plus cases in court at summary case conference and you're chasing your tail, you don't have a chance to look at it in depth". The view that prosecutors' high workloads mean that the process does not work as effectively as intended was similarly identified by numerous participants at the roundtable. In highlighting this concern, Defence30M provided a hypothetical comparison to the indictable stream. He claimed:

> Imagine for a moment, though, that you walk into the committal mention list at the Magistrates' Court and there's two OPP prosecutors and a line of 100 defence practitioners lining up to speak to the OPP prosecutors who don't read the hand up brief until the moment that you get to the front of the line and they'll request to have a discussion. … That's how it operates in the summary stream and that does affect the quality of the negotiations. It's not a criticism of the [police] prosecutors, it's just that the prosecutors do not have the manpower [sic] or the resources to actually have touched upon the material that they're dealing with until the lawyer that they're dealing with gets to the front of the line.

In the interviews, Defence16F similarly observed that "the police prosecutors aren't properly resourced to prepare for them [summary case conferences]. I feel sorry for those prosecutors, because their loads are so high". Judge04FR likewise expressed concern that the current system has "prosecutors run off their feet". She maintained that "they [prosecutors] can't be answering any phone calls or negotiating things out of court, so you've just got a whole lot of wasted adjournments which is just unnecessary churn through the court system, which is the most expensive bit". In this vein, Defence30M observed that:

> It works in theory, and I like the idea when it works properly. From our experience, it works really well in Melbourne but some of the other suburbs it doesn't because the emails don't get responded to in an efficient way. It's no criticism of course, it's simply a resourcing issue.

In addition to the limitations on police resourcing, the absence of VLA funding for summary case conference work was identified by Prosecutor09F as resulting in wasted court time:

> The issue is you have people [unrepresented defendants] with no court experience, or not a lot of court experience, and so they come for a summary case conference, you know, you can't talk to them about legal issues, they don't

> understand the processes of the court, they don't understand the system of adjournments and they want to plead not guilty on the day and have a contested hearing on the day that they first arrive. So it blows out the summary case conference in time because within our role you can't give legal advice, so you can't tell them what to do or what may happen or anything like that. You have to be really careful in regards to the discussions that you have with them. And then the magistrate, it takes a longer time for them because they have to ensure that the accused at all times understands all of their options.

The absence of specific funding for VLA representatives in the summary case conference was also identified as hindering achievement of the aim of the conferences by reducing the ability of practitioners to engage in plea negotiations. Defence05M explained that "the practitioner is not being paid apart from a low preparation rate, so that means it's left to the practitioner to try and negotiate by email or by telephone and it's not as easy to negotiate in that way. It's a bit more stark by email and telephone than face to face". In a similar vein, Defence06MR argued that "opportunities for negotiation, genuine negotiation, are lost as part of the regrettable way that Legal Aid's [funding is] structured". This is reflective of the findings of Flynn's (2010b: 53) study on Legal Aid funding and the pre-trial process, in which she observed that:

> Victoria's Legal Aid funding structure requires that all counsel are reimbursed for their work based on an approved fee that is scaled to the perceived level and complexity of the tasks performed. Thus, a substantially lower payment is made for pre-trial attendance and preparation than for the trial preparation.

At the time her study was published, the payment rates for VLA solicitors for preparation and attendance at a committal mention was $286, compared with (for County Court matters) an average of $444 for other pre-trial preparation and attendance (except for a committal hearing, which was $665), and $1311 for trial preparation (Flynn 2010b: 53). Flynn argued that, as a result, the funding structure "hinders the capacity of Legal Aid counsel from preparing and engaging in pre-trial hearings or plea bargaining discussions because the funding is prioritised to support contested trials … and pre-trial hearings play a secondary role" (Flynn 2010b: 68). Tague (2008: 257) has also raised concerns about the fact that the lower payments available to a defence practitioner during pre-trial proceedings may result in fewer early guilty pleas (see also Flynn et al. 2016). At the roundtable, this issue was similarly explored by Defence28M, who maintained that "early intervention with proper funding at the front end makes for a more efficient system. We have a system that's skewed [in terms of funding] towards the back end running trials. I just think we need to have a paradigm shift in the way we fund VLA".

Defence03F commented on the absence of funded preparation time for summary case conferences, and claimed that this means "you can end up sending things to contest mention maybe prematurely, because you're funded then to turn up for that one appearance". Judge14M similarly raised this concern at the roundtable, arguing that "Legal Aid funding impacts on contest mentions. We want cases to be summary case conferenced before they go to contest mention. The difficulty is with Legal Aid, they're not funded to do a summary case conference". This lack of funding, as Defence09F maintained, means that "everything goes to contest mention, because until you get to contest mention you don't actually know what you're dealing with".

Magistrates

While primarily identifying the positive aspects of the contest mention, participants pointed to the success of the process being reliant upon the personality of the magistrate involved—as Judge02MR noted, "the problem with contest mentions is it's very dependent on the magistrate". Defence05M likewise commented, "it comes down to practicality and different magistrates" (Defence05M). In particular, the effectiveness of a contest mention is based on whether or not the magistrate actively encourages an early resolution. As Defence13FR explained, "it depends upon the magistrate who you've got and how open they are to resolution". This view was also taken by Defence24M, who observed that "there'll be a range of competence, a range of experience, a range of issues there, but that's part of the process and I think it's a flaw in the contest mention process". Defence03F similarly maintained that contest mentions are:

> Running pretty well, but only when they've got a decent magistrate. If they put someone in there, that has no interest in resolving matters, they do not care and so everyone ends up going off to contest, because there's no incentive and for that process to work, there really has to be incentive.

There was some evidence in the data to suggest that magistrates with a strong predilection for settling cases were being appointed to the contest mention list in Melbourne in order to clear the court of cases by encouraging more defendants to plead guilty at an early stage, usually in response to a favourable sentence indication. As Defence20M observed, "if you want a matter to go to contest[ed hearing] it seems to require quite a lot of effort on the client, and a sort of determination to see it go through to [a] contest". Prosecutor02FR also identified this focus, claiming that "it's just that our main business at the moment now is not running contested hearings, it's all about the contest mention". Defence18M even referred to the Magistrates' Court as "peddling what we call fast-food justice". Numerous participants also commented on the "busy mention lists" (Judge02FR). As Defence15M claimed, "the mention list is extremely busy. … It takes about three months to get a contest mention date at Melbourne at the moment". Clearly, this is a limitation, as justice delayed is justice denied. On the whole, however, participants recognised these processes as providing a forum for plea negotiations while also identifying the need for some changes in relation to funding and resourcing for both VLA and Victoria Police to ensure that these processes remain effective.

Early Resolution Culture at the OPP

In the indictable stream, the key factor participants identified as influencing both the frequency and nature of plea negotiations was the early resolution culture embedded within the OPP. This culture is evident in the OPP's policies guiding prosecutorial conduct that include discussions on early resolutions and their importance.[23] In the mid-2000s, the OPP introduced an Early Resolution Unit (ERU), which was tasked with proactively identifying and finalising matters that could resolve prior to trial. The ERU was disbanded in early 2016, although this was not a well-known fact among participants, including those from the OPP, during the interviews. Initially, the ERU had a primary focus on offences involving theft, armed robbery, aggravated burglary, assault and attempted murder (Victorian OPP Annual Report 2007: 38). These offences align with those commonly subject to negotiation as identified in this study's case file dataset, which may explain why the ERU focused on these areas.

Within the ERU, a number of Early Resolution Advocates (ERAs) were responsible for managing most negotiations with defence practitioners in the first instance. Judge02MR outlined how this unit operated:

> The OPP triage every file that comes in and then rank it one to four; four is the highest level of risk to the organisation, one is the lowest. The ones and twos are generally where not many counts have been charged and the accused has made admissions or there's an overwhelming case. … A three might be a sex matter where there's multiple victims, a four might be the same but might have, for example, [a] QC briefed on behalf of the accused so it puts the OPP at greater risk of failing prosecution. It might be that it's got high public media interest.

All homicides, for example, where there's culpable driving, or murders, or manslaughters, will go into four. … The OPP then allocate those files, the ones and twos, to the Early Resolution Advocates. … They were very experienced [solicitors].

Prosecutor06M similarly described the role of the ERAs as follows:

It's just a more formalised role in that what we [ERAs] do is something that everyone should be doing and a lot of people are doing it who aren't in our section. The section was set up because it was a group of fairly long-term, very experienced people that probably knew the roles as far as resolution is concerned, more so than the more junior members. Basically at the filing hearing, … matters are shortly thereafter allocated and … there's a form that the filing hearing people use, advocates use, that has a box for potential early resolution. … They tick a box. After talking to defence and … hearing something very little because the briefs haven't been served but reading the summary, hearing from the defence, speaking to the informant at the filing hearing, they try and make an assessment as to whether it's capable, and defence might say, we want to resolve this. So the box is ticked. Generally, those sort of cases come to us [the ERU], as well as others. … The Allocation Manager decides. At the early stage, it's more likely than not that you don't get that indication [of a potential negotiation] because the defence aren't prepared and understandably aren't prepared to play their cards until they've seen the brief. … We get the filing hearing sheet and attached to that generally is … the police summary and there may have been a bail application, so we might get even additional material but, at the very least, we've got a police summary. As an Early Resolution Advocate, you read through the summary and sometimes there's issues that arise, and perhaps pieces of evidence that you might want to confirm that the police are going to obtain. There might be a few blanks, generally some requisitions and enquiries in relation to the matter at that stage. You send that off or you say to the police, look, I've read the summary, these are my questions at this stage. Once that's done, basically nothing happens until the brief is served. … What I do is I generally go down to the Crown prosecutor with brief in hand and say, after reading it and making up my mind as to what charges I think are appropriate at that stage, I often go down and get a bottom line as to what we may be prepared to accept in resolution and then hopefully the defence get in touch with us and we start discussing as to where we are. … There are situations where you may be a bit more proactive and you put a bottom line to the defence.

In describing the work of the ERU, all participants reflected on the quality of the ERAs, defining them as "proactive" (Judge10F), "pragmatic" (Defence11M) and "sensible" (Defence22M), and significantly helping facilitate plea negotiations. As Defence11M maintained, "the people were pragmatic and sensible and easy to deal with. ... If you can't strike a deal with them, you're not going to strike a deal, as simple as that". Judge03M likewise claimed:

> They selected people who were realistic, who'd express an independent view in an early stage, because very often police have an inflated view about the outcome and perhaps the evidence that supports that outcome. Highly realistic and competent solicitors settle a larger number of cases. I don't think they did so in a way that undermined the interest of justice or led to people pleading guilty to insignificant offences where they should have pleaded guilty to more serious offences. It simply brought forward in time when the matter ultimately resolved. If it hadn't settled on that basis at that stage, it would have settled on a similar basis two years later.

Throughout the interviews, it became clear that the ERU had been disbanded, with several defence practitioners identifying this as a shame, due to the quality of lawyers who worked within the unit and the level of consistency their work brought to the resolution process. As Defence05M claimed, "there will still be negotiations and there'll still be good outcomes, but I wouldn't be surprised if the plea negotiation rate fell, not to a great extent, but fell. And that's because of [a] lack of consistency and knowledge of who you're dealing with". Defence03F similarly maintained:

> Dealing with them was great. We would resolve matters on really good terms and early in the process. It was a good unit. ... They would sensibly get instructions from a Crownie [Crown prosecutor] that they knew would be sensible about the resolution and so it just meant that it worked. ... Now it takes far longer for something to get allocated and so instead of having your initial remand summary and looking at it and going, we can figure this out and just ending up with a plea brief rather than a full hand-up brief, none of that happens now, because the files don't get allocated early. So, it's definitely caused delays and I think there's probably more adjournments of things because of it. And I think probably more things proceed to contest stages when they don't need to.

Defence18M also commented on the disbandment of the ERU as creating more delays:

> I had a substantial amount of involvement with that unit. ... I thought it worked really well. I was really surprised that they abandoned it. We haven't really got an explanation as to why. ... They had good people in there, who were

> experienced and you could talk to, it worked really well I thought. ... Now it just makes things a bit harder to get to the person that you want to have a conversation with. Often it takes a while for the files at the OPP to be allocated, you often don't know who it is that you're supposed to be speaking with, and then they don't really have the clout. Whereas you had those experienced people in the Early Resolution team, they were able to go to a Crownie [Crown prosecutor] and say, this is what we think should happen. Also they were proactive. If they saw a pathway to resolution, they didn't wait for the defence and that's stopped now. We're back to how we used to be.

At the roundtable, Judge16F also noted some of the problems associated with the late allocation of files within the OPP as hindering negotiations:

> One of the problems is that because of the volume of cases and the number of prosecutors and the time at which a case will be allocated to prosecuting counsel is late, often just before trial. If it hasn't been negotiated and resolved through the list with the assistance of the solicitor who it's been assigned to for the prosecution, then it may take quite some time after that and maybe only days before trial, or the day of trial, where the barristers who have both actually been briefed and [are] on top of the materials will sit down and bang heads.

While there is evidently a strong shift towards an early resolution culture at the OPP, identified by the then DPP (Champion 2012: 1) himself—"it goes without saying that the resolution of cases by negotiated settlement is an extremely important area of the work we do"— one way of increasing the effectiveness of this culture may be to ensure that cases are assigned as early as possible, to provide a consistent point of contact for the defence from an early stage.

In discussing the rationale behind the disbandment of the ERU, Prosecutor06M explained that "the office [OPP] seem to have taken the view that it's [as early resolution culture] sufficiently permeating through the office to actually, in effect, do away with the early resolution section". Prosecutor03F provided a similar explanation: "my understanding is that everybody's supposed to – the onus is on everybody to try and negotiate. All solicitors try and negotiate, not just specialist solicitors. ... So now everybody's [considered] an Early Resolution Advocate, rather than having specialists who do it". While some concerns were expressed as to the removal of specific ERAs (particularly in relation to the delays in files being allocated within the OPP), most participants recognised that a new culture of resolution has developed at the OPP and that each division does now focus on resolution. As Judge03M noted:

> My sense is that the culture of the OPP across the board now is more realistic than it may have been in earlier points. You don't need one or two individuals, or half a dozen individuals, to be promoting early resolution, if the whole office understands the significance of having matters determined speedily, and justice not being delayed.

Judge07M likewise said, "the work of all the OPP is focused on identifying issues and identifying resolution. … They are oriented towards settlements, and that's good". In a similar vein, Prosecutor06M noted that, in his experience, "the new crops of solicitors are fairly keen on entering into the negotiation process. I think it [a resolution culture] is filtering through and I think people are trying to negotiate things generally".

During the final phase of the research process, a new OPP structure was implemented (in March 2016) together with a key focus on early resolutions. The new structure includes the ERAs, who previously worked within the dedicated ERU, now being dispersed into the different divisions within the OPP. As explained to us during one of our consultations with members of the OPP:

> A need for the expertise of these experience advocates was identified under the new structure to review, prepare and resolve cases where a resolution required the most experienced solicitors in the office. Accordingly, ERAs (rebadged as Principal Resolution Advocates (PRAs)) were embedded in each new trial division and were allocated the most complex (CAR 3 and 4) matters for preparation and resolution where possible. The less complex matters are now allocated to junior staff and the PRAs provide support, training and guidance in the skills of negotiating and resolving these matters.

Under this new structure, all cases are reviewed and allocated to a solicitor within ten days of the OPP receiving the case, which may address some of the concerns raised by participants regarding an early contact point to discuss cases and may in turn have a positive impact on early resolutions.

Notes

1. The *Sentencing Act 1991* (Vic) s 5(2)(e) states that in sentencing a defendant, a court must take into account whether the defendant pleaded guilty and, if so, the stage in the proceedings at which the defendant did so, or intended to do so.
2. See, for example, *Director's Policy: Resolution; Director's Policy: The Crown's Role on Plea and Sentence Hearings.*

3. A pre-trial hearing in the Magistrates' Court (either an oral hearing or it proceeds on paper) for indictable offences to test whether the Crown's evidence is strong enough to support a conviction.
4. A pre-trial hearing in the Magistrates' Court for indictable offences that provides a forum for parties to identify the key issues for resolution, as well as those matters not in dispute.
5. As will be discussed in Chap. 6, the main cases that were identified as difficult to negotiate related to cases involving homicides, where it is often too complicated to resolve on other terms, and sexual offences, due to the lack of alternative charges and obstacles like the sex offenders' registry and high acquittal rates.
6. Because the study did not include access to OPP files, this section cannot report on the involvement of the victim in plea negotiations.
7. See Appendix 1, clause 11.
8. *Summary Offences Act 1966* (Vic) s 23.
9. Ibid. s 24.
10. *Crimes Act 1958* (Vic) s 31(1)(a).
11. Ibid. s 31(1)(b)(ba).
12. Ibid. s 31(1)(c).
13. Ibid. s 320.
14. Ibid. s 15A.
15. Ibid. s 15B.
16. Ibid. s 16.
17. Ibid. s 17.
18. Ibid. s 17.
19. The contest mention involves a magistrate, defence practitioner and police prosecutor meeting in a relatively informal manner in court to identify any matters or issues that could resolve without having to proceed to a contested hearing. The key aims of the contest mention are to refine the case issues and, where relevant, to estimate the likely length of a contested hearing. The magistrate can also provide a sentence indication at this hearing if requested by the defence. The summary case conference is a required out-of-court communication that occurs before a contested hearing in the Magistrates' Court between the prosecution and the defence, with the aim of managing the progression of the case smoothly, including resolving matters at an early stage.
20. The summary case conference is regulated by s 54 of the *Criminal Procedure Act 2009* (Vic).
21. *Criminal Procedure Act 2009* (Vic) s 55.
22. Ibid.
23. See, for example, *Director's Policy: Resolution, Director's Policy Discretion, Director's Policy: The Crown's Role on Plea and Sentence Hearings.*

6

Negotiation Outcomes

This chapter discusses patterns in the outcomes of negotiations, including identifying offences most commonly negotiated and those offences where negotiations are less likely to occur. In doing so, this chapter builds on the forms of negotiations presented in Chap. 4 to provide a unique insight into which types of crimes most commonly feature in negotiations. This is important as it highlights potential trends in negotiation outcomes.

Across the 50 de-identified case files, 325 charges were laid. Guilty pleas were entered to 162 charges. This is a reduction of almost 50 per cent. Forty-seven de-identified case files contained information on the charges pre and post the guilty plea. Of these 47 cases, 89 per cent ($n = 42$) had charges withdrawn. The mean number of charges per case prior to a resolution was 6.42. The mean number of charges to which a defendant pleaded guilty post a resolution was 3.18. As a result, the mean number of charges withdrawn was 3.24. The highest number of charges withdrawn in an individual case was 11 (the defendant was originally charged with 29 offences).

Most commonly, the final set of offences to which the defendant pleaded guilty contained fewer charges than the police had originally laid. While the majority of the cases involved the most serious charge being withdrawn in exchange for less serious alternatives, this was not always the case. Instead, in some cases, the defendant would plead guilty to the most serious offence in exchange for all other charges being withdrawn, as in case 024-HN:

A. Flynn, A. Freiberg, *Plea Negotiations*, Palgrave Socio-Legal Studies,
https://doi.org/10.1007/978-3-319-92630-8_6

The defence offered to plead guilty to recklessly causing serious injury if the remainder of the charges were withdrawn. This offer was made on the basis that intoxication impaired the defendant's intent, that the incident occurred very quickly, and the event was spontaneous and not premeditated. The OPP rejected the offer on the basis that they could prove intentionally causing serious injury. The matter was booked in for a committal hearing, but resolved at court on the day of the hearing. The defendant pleaded guilty to intentionally causing serious injury (the most serious charge) in exchange for all others being withdrawn.

Other examples included case 032-LC and case 031-MT, where the defendants pleaded guilty to armed robbery and lesser alternatives were withdrawn, and case 037-MH, where the defendant pleaded guilty to intentionally causing serious injury and lesser alternatives were withdrawn.

Most Common Offences Negotiated

Within this study's case file dataset, the most common offence types that were negotiated to lesser offences or withdrawn included:

- Theft/attempted theft—8.4 per cent (n = 15).
- Intentionally causing serious injury—8 per cent (n = 14).
- Intentionally causing injury or recklessly causing injury—6.7 per cent (n = 12).
- Drug use/possession—6.1 per cent (n = 11).
- Recklessly causing serious injury—5.6 per cent (n = 10).

While it is important to note that the de-identified case files were randomly selected, therefore affecting the broader applicability of these findings, similar offences were present in the interview data, thereby suggesting that the case file findings are reflective of more general practice in relation to the types of offences prone to negotiation.

In the interviews, participants identified intentionally causing serious injury as a commonly negotiated offence because, in such cases, there are so many other alternative charges. As Judge03M observed, "the offence which appears to be frequently negotiated is intentionally causing serious injury to recklessly causing serious injury". This view was supported by Defence09F, who commented that "I don't think I've ever had a case where a client's pleaded [guilty] to an intentionally cause serious injury. It always resolves to a recklessly cause serious injury or under". The main reason for these offences commonly being negotiated is because the more serious charge is associated with intent, whereby the focus is on the mental state of the defendant, rather than the act itself. In such cases, the question must be asked: Can the prosecution prove that the defendant intended to cause the serious injury, or was the defendant reckless to the injury they could cause from the act? In this regard, Defence05M explains, "there's lots of variables in terms of serious injury as opposed to injury, in terms of reckless as opposed to intentional, so there's a few different alternatives".

A similar argument was made in relation to aggravated burglary, as another common offence that is negotiated. As Defence01M observed:

> Aggravated burglary, the offender will say I was there but I was invited in. … Or I was there but I wasn't reckless as to the possibility that someone was present. I rang the doorbell, I knocked on the door, there were no lights on, so that recklessness element goes and then you've just got a burglary.

Aggravated burglary was likewise identified at the stakeholder roundtable as one of the most common offences to negotiate. As Prosecutor13F maintained, "most of my negotiations involve aggravated burglaries". This view was supported by Defence29F, who claimed, "the sheer number of aggravated burglaries that we see linked I suppose to the ice epidemic; it's commonplace from my experience. I couldn't say numbers, but coming across my desk would be quite a few". In the interviews, armed robbery was also said to be a common subject of negotiation because of the alternative offences available and also due to the emergence of technologies like CCTV—"it's everywhere" (Defence02F)—which capture more evidence:

> Armed robbery resolves all the time. Your client says, yeah, okay, I did that but I didn't have a weapon, so it'll resolve to a robbery because there's insufficient evidence to prove the existence of a weapon. (Defence01M)

Drug crimes were also mentioned by judicial participants in the interviews and participants in the stakeholder roundtable as commonly negotiated. As Defence30M maintained, "the drug trafficking stuff is, for us anyway, a very common charge to negotiate". In this regard, Judge15M suggested that the prevalence of this offence was perhaps not reflected in the case file statistics because "all the entrepreneurial drug traffickers are privately funded and not legally aided, so that'll skew the statistics". Defence30M supported this view, but also flagged that VLA "deal with quite a large number of unlawful non-citizens who are charged with cultivating commercial quantity which is what it ultimately resolves to, but there's also a trafficking tacked on as the head charge". This view was evidenced by the dataset, in which three of the five drug trafficking cases involved foreign nationals.

Two of the main reasons identified for drug offences being commonly negotiated were because the trials, and associated forensic testing requirements, are generally lengthy and expensive:

> Drugs are always negotiated. It is very hard to get a big drug trial to actually run. They negotiate on the drip-feed and they resolve on the drip-feed. As in, one [person] rolls and then others remember that they participated too. ... We're not really listing those big drug trials on a basis that they'll run. (Judge10F)

Judge13F similarly maintained that "[a] drug trial, if it runs, can often be very lengthy and expensive and so often there's an incentive by both the Crown and the defence to settle it and perhaps let some of the offending conduct go". Both these statements are quite significant in that they reveal an acknowledgement by the court that there is an expectation of settlement by negotiated resolution in drug trials, which, as Judge13F observes, will result in some offending conduct being let go. This demonstrates the tension between court efficiency and expectations of justice, where there may be some apprehension that "policy efficiency arguments" may "prevail over common law principles" such as the right to trial or "the presumption of innocence" (Johnson and Edwards 2013: 6). Wren and Bartels (2014: 66) have noted similar concerns among critics of plea negotiations: "the principle of efficiency [can be seen to] suppress other central values, such as the presumption of innocence, public trial and fair labelling".

Difficult Offences

One of the main offence types that participants identified as being more difficult to negotiate included the more high-profile and serious offences, such as murder, or those that have received a high level of media attention or public interest. As Prosecutor05M explained, "murder cases ... they do end up sometimes as lesser charges. But often, unless they're willing to plead to murder, then there's a trial". This view was similarly expressed by Defence11M, who claimed that "murder charges are the ones that run [as a trial] more often than not and where you're less inclined to be able to resolve it on any terms". This finding is also reflected in the SAC's analysis (2015: 19) of guilty plea outcomes between 2004 and 2014, where it found that murder had the lowest guilty plea rate of all proven offences (48 per cent).

On the whole, however, the data obtained in this study suggest that sex offences—which primarily involve male defendants and female victims—are the most difficult to resolve, with 66 per cent of participants identifying these as the most challenging in this regard. This is perhaps unsurprising, given the number of sex offence matters that proceed to trial in the County Court and the low conviction rate. In the 2014–15 financial year, 40 per cent of County Court trials involved sexual offences, despite only 23 per cent of criminal initiations in the court involving sexual offence matters (County Court 2015: 21). In the same reporting period, only 56 per cent of sexual offence trials resulted in a guilty verdict, compared with 65 per cent of matters that proceeded to verdict in the general crimes list (County Court 2015: 21), thus representing some benefit to "risking" a trial. This benefit in "risking" a trial was articulated by Judge15M during the roundtable, who stated that "you're 50 per cent going to get off if there's corroboration. If not, you're 80 per cent going to get off. If there's no corroboration, they'll get acquitted basically". Such outcomes are not limited to the case study jurisdiction. In England and Wales, for example, of the 4231 sexual violence trials proceeding in 2011, only 38.7 per cent resulted in a conviction (Ministry of Justice 2013).

In addition to the low conviction rates, interview participants highlighted the lack of corroborating evidence (because the offence usually occurs in a one-on-one context), and delays in reporting the offence to police, which can reduce the quality of the evidence, as obstacles to plea negotiation in sex offence cases. As Defence02F maintained:

> Sex offences [are the most difficult] because obviously it usually happens when it's one-on-one, rarely are there any CCTV footage and sometimes the complainant makes the statement, it's not believed and then 15 years later there's another piece of evidence [that] produces itself. … Sex offences are usually the ones that don't resolve.

Another key obstacle to negotiations in these cases is the absence of alternative offences to rape—thus, there is no "middle ground" (Defence09F) or "wriggle room" (Defence25M). As Judge08M explained:

> Rape sex offences are very hard to negotiate because they're so black and white. I mean with a murder, you've always got manslaughter, but sex offences are hard to negotiate, with very little room to move. You can negotiate on the number of charges, but there's no room to move on the type. Sometimes you can occasionally move a rape down to an indecent [sexual] assault if the circumstances support that, but it's hard to do.

As noted by these participants, there is no alternative offence to rape in Victoria other than sexual assault, which involves touching of a sexual nature but does not include penetration.[1] This was articulated by Defence04M, who claimed that there is not "something a bit less" than rape. He went on:

> A rape case would be difficult to settle on something other than rape. In fact, I don't think I've ever settled a rape case. ... The difficulty with rape is, depending a little bit on the factual situation, but generally speaking, it's hard to think of a lesser count. I mean, unless there's, for example, there hasn't been penetration. If there hasn't been penetration, then you can say, well, it's only – maybe it's only some sort of sexual assault, but generally speaking it's hard to see. Whereas with murder, you've got manslaughter with intentionally cause serious injury, you've got recklessly cause serious injury, you've got lesser offences, but with rape, it's sort of a bit difficult to sort of say there's something a bit less. (Defence04M)

Defence11M expanded on this view:

> Sex offences are difficult because the alternatives are not as apparent ... it either occurred or it did not occur. Mens rea – state of mind – won't often come into it and therefore there isn't that easy way in which to present a plea negotiation to the OPP. It's very hard to find a middle ground.

Defence practitioners also pointed to the difficulties in getting clients to admit guilt by entering a guilty plea, particularly in child sexual offence or incest cases. As Defence03F observed:

> Incest is one of the really common ones that people will not plead [to] and it's because it's something about sex offenders and particularly incest that actually owning up to that is really difficult. Whereas, if they're convicted by a jury they can always maintain their innocence to themselves and to those around them and say the jury got it wrong.

The data are supported by the guilty plea rates seen in the County Court between 2008 and 2015 (see Fig. 6.1), where there is a noticeable difference between the number of guilty pleas entered to general offences, which averages to 72 per cent over the seven years, compared to the number of guilty pleas entered to sex offences, which averages around 45 per cent.

This difference is also reflected in national statistics, with the most recent ABS yearbook (2004–05) to contain such information showing that adjudicated defendants with a principal offence of sexual assault and related offences were second only to homicide cases in being least likely to resolve by guilty

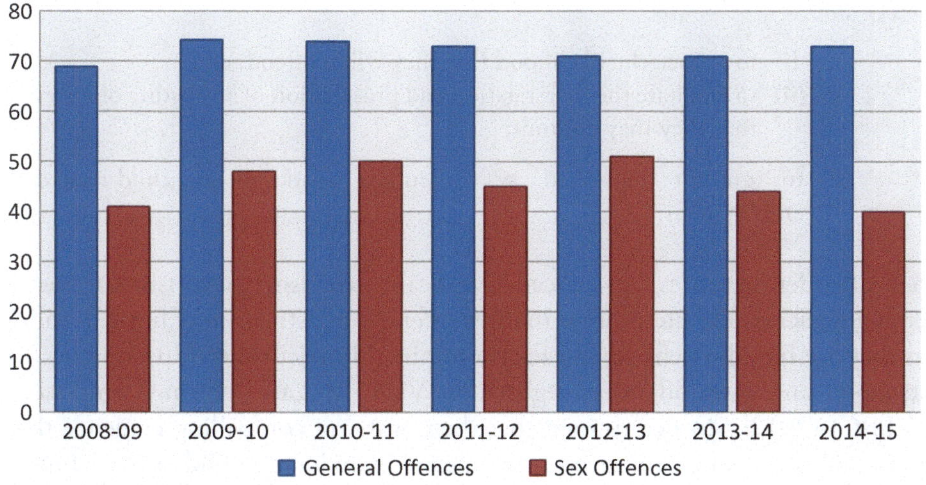

Fig. 6.1 Victorian County Court guilty pleas 2008–15

plea nationwide (50 per cent homicide and 58 per cent sexual offences).[2] Similar statistics are also evident elsewhere. In England and Wales, for example, approximately 70 per cent of defendants plead guilty, but this figure drops to approximately 38 per cent for defendants charged with sexual offences (Ministry of Justice 2013).

The SAC (2015: 27) also suggest that the comparatively low guilty plea rate for sexual offences is reflective of the "dynamics of prosecuting such cases", listing the following examples:

> The complexity, the likelihood of delay before the offence is reported, the difficulty of proving guilt where a case comes down to one person's word against another (partially in relation to those offences that occurred many years prior to proceedings commencing), a reluctance on the part of sexual offenders to acknowledge or admit what they have done, and the serious consequences of being found guilty (such as facing a sentence of immediate imprisonment and the possibility of being placed on the Sex Offenders' Register).

The *Sex Offenders Registration Act 2004* (Vic) came into operation on 1 October 2004. The Act requires defendants who commit a Class 1[3] or Class 2[4] sexual offence to "keep police informed of their whereabouts and other personal details"[5] for 15 years (if the defendant committed one Class 1 or two Class 2 offences); eight years (if the defendant committed one Class 2 offence); or indefinitely (if the defendant committed two or more Class 1 offences, one Class 1 and one or more Class 2 offences, or three Class 2 offences). The purpose of the Act is:

(1) (a)

(i) to reduce the likelihood that they will reoffend; and
(ii) to facilitate the investigation and prosecution of any future offences that they may commit;

(b) to prevent registered sex offenders working in child-related employment.[6]

Sex offender registries have faced significant criticism. A consistent theme emerging across the literature is that sex offender registries are of limited utility as they are broadly defined and have a minimal impact on recidivism rates. In its report on the sex offenders' register, the Victorian Law Reform Commission (VLRC) (2012: 56) determined that there was "no compelling evidence that registration schemes are an effective means of reducing child sexual abuse". Other research suggest that the schemes are flawed because they are framed around stranger perpetrators and amalgamate defendants with a low and high risk of reoffending together, thereby diverting police resources (Law Institute of Victoria [LIV] 2011a; Ombudsman Victoria 2011; Powell et al. 2014; Vess et al. 2011; VLRC 2012: 55; Freiberg et al. 2015: 212). As Vess et al. (2011: 418) argue, "one of the primary criticisms that has been directed against sex offender registries is that they are too broad, and cover a heterogeneous range of offenders, many of whom present a relatively low risk of sexual reoffending". The Law Institute of Victoria (LIV) (2011a) also argues that "the mandatory nature of the registration scheme fails to take account of one important fact: not all sexual offenders are the same", which may have the unintended consequence that serious and dangerous defendants go undetected "in the vast sea of registrants" (LIV 2011a). For these reasons, it has been argued that judicial discretion should factor into the decision as to whether or not a defendant should be placed on a sex register, as opposed to an automated decision that captures every sex offender. The research in favour of judicial discretion usually points to examples of children sending consensual naked images of themselves to others being captured by child pornography offences, and the child becoming subject to registration as a sex offender. Ultimately, much research considers the schemes to be at odds with empirical research, and simply a tool used by politicians wishing to be seen to be responding to sexual violence in the community:

> In the face of limited evidence on the effectiveness of registers it could be that they are expensive policies built on no evidence base, and the result of public concerns and political expediency to be seen to be doing something. Politicians may speak of their usefulness … but such statements stand alone from research results. (VLRC 2012: 56)

What has yet to be explored in the literature is how the sex offenders' register affects plea negotiations and what role it may play in relation to the low guilty plea rate for these crimes.

This study's interview data suggest that the register is one of the main reasons for the lack of guilty pleas in sex offence cases. As Defence20M maintained, "people don't want to be on the register and they're not going to plead [guilty] if they're going to be on the register". In fact, the sex offenders' register was commonly identified as "an obstacle" (Prosecutor03F), "a barrier" (Defence16F), "one of the biggest hurdles to successful negotiations" (Defence21M) and "a significant impediment to any kind of resolution" (Defence20M) due to the significant implications it has for those who plead guilty. As Defence05M explained:

> The *Sex Offenders Registration Act* is an impediment to the ease of negotiations in sex cases. There's plenty of impediments in sex cases but that's another one and it's into the mix, and people, notwithstanding that they might have to go to jail for offences, do not want to go on the register, so that is an impediment.

Defence24M argued that the register is an "insuperable obstacle to negotiation". He claimed:

> Because there is no discretion, and clients rightly say, what's the point of me doing that? And you say, well there's a penalty and they go, right, well, that's all very well but I'm going to be on the sex register for 15 years. I don't want that for any time, I'll take my chances. So that is a very good example of legislation which directly inhibits any sort of negotiation for charges that will get onto that [register].

Similar observations were made at the roundtable, with several stakeholders recognising the sex offenders' register as a significant hurdle to guilty plea resolutions. As Defence28M observed, "if you go onto the sex offenders' register for life, why not just have a go? It can't get any worse, you're only going to have one life and you've got a 50 per cent chance at least of getting off". Judge15M similarly maintained:

> I think in the County Court it will stop people pleading in the first place. I had one the other day, for example, of a family, 20-year-old offending, grandparents [were] ... living with the kids, grandad gets done for one of these, won't plead to it, gets convicted, and is on the sex offenders' register. He can't live with the kids; him and his wife are in a caravan for the rest of their lives probably. I was told afterwards that was why he couldn't risk pleading guilty.

The link between a register and a potential decrease in guilty pleas was discussed by the president of the NSW Council for Civil Liberties, Stephen Blanks, in the context of a proposed register for domestic violence offenders in NSW. Arguing that "a proposed registry for domestic violence offenders could encourage more perpetrators to plead not guilty" (Olding and Saulwick 2015), Blanks maintained that "it will be a huge incentive on everyone charged with domestic violence offences to plead not guilty, which is quite counter-productive" (cited in Olding and Saulwick 2015).

There are some limitations to the mandatory sex offenders' register in relation to resolving cases by guilty plea—the benefits of which can be quite demonstrable for victims of sexual offences who are spared from going through a trial, and the secondary victimisation commonly experienced during that process (Daly 2011; Flynn 2015). And in light of the general concerns expressed in the research about the sex offenders' register, particularly that it fails to affect recidivism rates, these findings raise some questions about this process and may highlight a possible explanation for the low rate of guilty pleas in sex offence cases.

Family Violence

Interestingly, and perhaps reflecting an unexpected consequence of the recent focus on family violence in Victoria (and Australia more generally)—see, for example, the Royal Commission into Family Violence (RCFV) (2016)—participants maintained that there is minimal room to negotiate on family violence issues, because there is a perceived "public interest" in the matters being seen to be treated with the utmost seriousness. As a result, there has been a change in police charging practices and approaches to prosecuting family violence matters:

> Family violence, that's an area where there should be little or no negotiation. (Judge12M)

> There's a spotlight on family violence. Now that means, in a practical sense, it is harder to achieve negotiated outcomes. (Defence24M)

> Family violence, while it used to be more appropriate to have a negotiation, is tending to now be not appropriate. (Prosecutor04M)

> Family violence is extremely difficult to negotiate. (Defence19M)

The shift in police charging and prosecution policies in relation to family violence was attributed not only to the public interest, but also to a fear among police of the consequences of the family violence escalating. As Defence24M explained:

> When you have inquests like the Batty inquest, where successive police officers are taken to court and asked to explain why they did or didn't do X and Y, one of the consequences that has is that people become very over-protective and defensive and will not negotiate in situations where they ought to, because of the fear that they'll find themselves on page one of the *Herald Sun*,[7] or before a Coroner, or some similar forum where they're going to be put under the spotlight, so it's much easier to not make a decision than to do it.

The Batty inquest refers to the Coronial Inquest held into the murder of 11-year-old Luke Batty, who was tragically killed by his father after a cricket training session in Tyabb, south-east of Melbourne in February 2014. As part of the findings, "the Coroner made 29 recommendations into the systemic problems that contributed to Luke's death, including a call for better coordination between police, courts and the Department of Human Services when they deal with family violence cases" (ABC 2015). This case became a basis for numerous changes in policies relating to family violence, and Luke's mother, Rosie Batty, became a high-profile advocate for these changes and was the Australian of the Year in 2015. Defence14FR similarly noted the influence of Luke Batty's death on plea negotiations in this area:

> The police's policy in relation to family violence means that negotiations in those matters are far less likely to get you anywhere. The police have really taken a very hard and fast approach to that and so there's not a lot of room to move in those matters. Really, you're either pleading or you're not … and our prosecutors are saying things to us about – they made sort of a passing comment to me one day about [how] they don't want to be the prosecutors who let somebody off on this, who then turns into the next Rosie Batty. They are really conscious of the public's expectation that the police will protect victims of domestic violence and so family violence matters. It is difficult to get offences withdrawn. It's not impossible, but it's certainly the one where you've got your biggest push up hill.

This view was supported by roundtable participants, who reflected on the difficulties that exist in negotiating family violence matters. As Prosecutor11F maintained, "in family violence there does tend to be that extra layer of difficulty added because people want to make sure they've made the right decision, because it's family violence". Prosecutor13F claimed that "the reason for the prosecution moving on with cases [taking them to trial] that once would've just been flicked off as just being domestic violence is for the very good reasons that victims ended up in body bags. So we're just much more careful".

The concern raised by participants that family violence matters can escalate to further violence and even homicide is supported by the report of the RCFV (2016: 41), which stated that "there is a demonstrable link between family violence [and] homicide". The report continues:

> As might be expected, the coronial investigations of family violence homicide have revealed that many parties involved in fatal family violence incidents had previous contact with the justice system. Many had contact with the police, courts and/or community corrections within six months of the fatal event. (RCFV 2016: 41)

In Victoria, specifically, the RCFV (2016: 55) report noted that, of the 250 murder cases prosecuted by the OPP in the previous three reporting years, approximately ten per cent (n = 23) "were related to family violence".

However, in discussing the shift in police prosecutor attitudes and Victoria Police policy involving the prosecution of family violence matters, some participants pointed out that the decision to primarily pursue all cases to contested hearing and avoid engaging in negotiations was often at odds with the victim's preferences. As Defence15M noted:

> In family violence matters, the approach now is very much that even if complainants change their mind and don't want those matters to proceed, they often will proceed all the way up to contested hearings. … The approach of the police is that they'll be prosecuted more forcefully.

Defence19M likewise claimed:

> The prosecution have a blanket policy, essentially, we don't care if we don't have statements, we don't care if we don't have evidence, we don't care if we don't have anything; we're proceeding. We don't care what the victim's attitude is. We're batting on; which is kind of ironic, given that the process is supposed to be there for the victim.

Some participants recognised the rationale for overlooking the interests of the victims in these types of cases:

> Even where the complainant is actively saying to the police, I am not coming to the court, I do not want to give evidence, I do not want him charged, we're back

together now, they'll proceed. And there's … good policy reason for that, so I'm not being critical. Because often people involved in family violence take that approach because they're petrified or because they're … living under the control of the perpetrator. So I presume that's the reasoning behind that approach. (Judge11F)

But others highlighted how this has resulted in family violence offences being treated "differently to other crimes". As Defence19M argued:

Family violence had been treated in the past, in the distant past, very badly. But in the more recent past, it had been treated as a crime quite similar to other crimes. So, if a victim doesn't want the matter to proceed, and the prosecution is satisfied this isn't by coercion, but they just genuinely do not want the prosecution to continue, and it will do more damage to them than good, then the prosecution would often be discontinued or resolved on a more sort of lenient basis, whereas now, they just bat on. They just put the victim in the witness box and [essentially] just [say] come on, get amongst it, which is quite interesting because the process is designed to protect the complainant, to stop the violence, but a lot of the time, it actually has an inverse effect.

Defence14FR also explained that, even in cases that have remarkably similar offences, if there is family violence involved, the "negotiation will be significantly different":

It's a much harder battle than it is – if two blokes had a fight versus a bloke's allegedly beaten up his missus, they'd have the same sets of charges and the negotiation will be significantly different.

Defence24M commented on how public interest concerns can change the way negotiations play out, but that this shifts as public interest waivers: "these things go through trends, if you like, or go through phases is perhaps a better way of expressing it". This differential treatment of family violence was also noted in the roundtable discussions, with Judge16F claiming, "what it [not negotiating] is in fact doing is recognising risk and valuing violent family dynamics".

The findings reported in this chapter raise some interesting questions about negotiations and the public interest. If negotiations are considered a legitimate way for a case to resolve, then why is the practice at odds with the public interest in family violence matters? If the fear of getting it wrong and the matter escalating exists in relation to these offences, surely similar arguments can be applied to all offences. And if some people perceive that resolving matters by plea negotiation is a lesser form of justice in family violence matters, then why is this view not held about all plea negotiations? This is not to suggest that there is something unjust about plea negotiations, but the current approach to family violence implies that perhaps there are circumstances where plea negotiations are considered a less appropriate criminal justice process or, at the very least, are not reflective of public interests, which may be better met by a contested hearing or trial. These issues are discussed in more detail in Chap. 9.

Notes

1. Under s 40(1) of the *Crimes Act 1958* (Vic), sexual assault is defined as:

   (1) A person (A) commits an offence if –

   (a) A initially touches another person (B); and
   (b) the touching is sexual; and
   (c) B does not consent to the touching; and
   (d) A does not reasonably believe that B consents to the touching.

2. The Royal Commission into Institutional Responses to Child Sexual Abuse also found that in NSW, the conviction rate for sexual assault other than child sexual assault was 50 per cent and the conviction rate for child sexual assault was 60 per cent, compared to an overall rate for all offences of 89 per cent (Royal Commission 2017a: 10).
3. Class 1 offences include rape, incest, sexual penetration of a child under 16, sexual penetration of a 16- or 17-year-old, sexual penetration of a person with a cognitive impairment by providers of medical or therapeutic services, sexual penetration of a person with a cognitive impairment by providers of special programs, compelling sexual penetration if the person who the offence is committed against is a child, persistent sexual abuse of a child under the age of 16, facilitating sexual offences against a child, aggravated sexual servitude, sexual intercourse or other sexual activities with a child outside Australia, persistent sexual abuse of a child outside Australia and sexual intercourse or other sexual activities with a young person outside Australia where the defendant is in a position of trust or authority.
4. Class 2 offences include sexual assault of a child, sexual assault by compelling sexual touching against a child, assault with intent to commit a sexual offence against a child, threat to commit a sexual offence against a child, indecent act with child under 16, indecent act with 16- or 17-year-old child, grooming for sexual conduct with a child under the age of 16, abduction or detention of a child, production of child pornography, procurement of a minor for child pornography, possession of child pornography and causing or inducing a child to take part in sex work.

5. *Sex Offenders Registration Act 2004* (Vic) s 1(a). Personal details include name; date of birth; address; telephone number; email addresses; any internet usernames, instant messaging usernames or chat room usernames; personal details of any children who the defendant has contact with; job (including details of the job, name of employer, address of workplace); and car details.
6. *Sex Offenders Registration Act 2004* (Vic) s 1(a)(i), s 1(a)(ii), s 1(b).
7. A popular tabloid newspaper in Victoria.

7

Plea Negotiations and Sentencing

Plea negotiations and sentencing are inextricably linked. While it has been argued that sentencing is not a part of plea negotiations in Australian jurisdictions, the data collected in this study, also discussed in Chap. 3, contradicts this view and demonstrates that discussions on sentencing are, in fact, a component of negotiations. This chapter examines connections between various sentencing regimes, policies and plea negotiations. In particular, it examines the effect of mandatory and presumptive sentencing on plea negotiations, the existence of judicial indications of sentences to defendants prior to the entering of a guilty plea as an extension of the plea negotiation process; the role that sentencing outcomes play in discussions, including the effect of the High Court's decision in *Barbaro*[1]; and the requirement that courts must state the sentence they would have imposed but for a guilty plea, as part of a transparent sentence discount process.[2]

Mandatory and Presumptive Sentencing

Mandatory and presumptive sentencing regimes are subject to extensive academic critique.[3] Freiberg and Murray (2012: 20–1) claim that "mandatory and presumptive sentences have been impugned on numerous constitutional grounds including that they may usurp an essential judicial function of sentencing and may impair public confidence in the courts' integrity". Criticism is also levelled at the way in which mandatory and presumptive sentencing regimes can "disproportionately impact on the disadvantaged" (VLA 2016c: 6; see also Solonec 2015). Commonly, critiques of mandatory sentencing

A. Flynn, A. Freiberg, *Plea Negotiations*, Palgrave Socio-Legal Studies,
https://doi.org/10.1007/978-3-319-92630-8_7

regimes focus on how the policies shift power from the court to prosecutors, whereby the "pre-trial decisions, where the charges are negotiated [become] more significant" (Aas 2005: 19). As Flynn (2016: 574) explains, "the inflexibility of mandatory penalties means the charging decision has a greater impact on the accused's likely sentence". Indeed, research examining the effect of mandatory minimum penalties on prosecutorial discretion and plea negotiations suggests that these policies have two main outcomes: an increase in the number of trials (Harris and Jesilow 2006) and a shift in discretionary powers (McCoy 1990).

During the data collection period for this study, there were two main presumptive sentencing policies in effect in Victoria. The first was baseline sentences, which set a median sentence for seven nominated offences (see details below), and the second was a mandatory non-parole period for gross violence offences (unless there are exceptional circumstances).

The *Sentencing Amendment (Baseline Sentences) Act 2014* (Vic) took effect for seven nominated offences committed on or after 2 November 2014. Under the legislation, a baseline prison sentence (a median sentence) was specified for murder (25 years); incest with a child, step-child or lineal descendant aged under 18 years (10 years); incest with a child, step-child or lineal descendant aged under 18 years of a de facto spouse (10 years); sexual penetration of a child aged under 12 years (10 years); persistent sexual abuse of a child aged under 16 years (10 years); culpable driving causing death (9 years); and trafficking in a large commercial quantity of a drug of dependence (14 years). The Act also prescribed minimum non-parole periods for the baseline sentences of 30 years (if the total effective sentence (TES) is a term of life imprisonment), 70 per cent of the TES if it is 20 years or more and 60 per cent of the TES if it is less than 20 years. Under the legislation, a court could impose a sentence that was above or below the median sentence, provided that it stated its reasons for such departure.[4] In the case of *DPP v Walters* (a pseudonym),[5] the Court of Appeal ruled that the legislation was "inoperable" for reasons relating to the means of determining a "median sentence"; and in 2016, the SAC recommended the repeal of the baseline sentencing provisions in their entirety.[6]

In January 2014, the *Crimes Amendment (Gross Violence Offences) Act 2013* (Vic) introduced two new offences into s 15A and s 15B of the *Crimes Act 1958* (Vic)—intentionally causing serious injury when committed with gross violence and recklessly causing serious injury when committed with gross violence. The legislation also amended s 10 of the *Sentencing Act 1991* (Vic) to require that a statutory minimum non-parole period of four years' imprisonment be applied to adult defendants and a two-year minimum detention sentence be applied to juvenile defendants (aged 16 or 17 years) found guilty (by plea or trial) of either of these offences.[7]

Consistent with criticisms voiced by some commentators (Flynn 2016; Freiberg and Murray 2012; Harris and Jesilow 2006; SAC 2008; Solonec 2015), participants identified a number of problematic outcomes of these provisions, including an increase in the number of trials and a reduction in the number of guilty pleas:

> More people will plead not guilty. (Judge02MR)

> Why would you plead? There's just no point to it. I would expect many more trials to run. (Judge08M)

> More trials, less people pleading guilty. (Judge13F)

Additionally, several judicial participants said, in the context of baseline sentencing, that they would openly query any guilty pleas offered by the defendant and direct them to instead consider running a trial. As Judge05M maintained:

> I think it is garbage … [and will] make plea negotiations impossible. … You can't plead [guilty] to culpable [driving]. You'd be an idiot. If someone came and tried to plead [guilty] to culpable driving in front of me, with baseline sentencing, I'd say, are you mad? I'd almost refuse to accept the plea. Why are you going to walk in there with nine years when most people get four or five for it? Preposterous!

Defence22M similarly commented on the lack of intervention by judicial officers to encourage guilty pleas following the introduction of these sentencing regimes. Citing an example of a drug trafficking matter that was subject to the baseline sentence of 14 years' imprisonment, he explained:

> We've got a commercial drug trafficking [case]. We've gone to initial directions hearing immediately post-committal and the judge is advising us to consider a plea of guilty based on him having [had] a quick look at the summary. We then say, it's baseline your honour, and the judge says, I'll fix a [trial] date. There's no intervention, … whereas if there was no baseline, the judge will say, well, why don't you engage in some discussions? These things [mandatory sentencing regimes] stifle pleas and negotiation discussions.

Judge07M likewise maintained that mandatory sentencing regimes "impede the negotiation process" and that "any mandatory aspect does [impede the negotiation process]. … The defence thinks, let's just run the trial, we may as well have a dash". A similar view was put forward by Defence07M, who claimed that "people may as well run trials. They've got nothing to lose". Indeed, this theme of having "nothing to lose" (Defence02F, Defence09F, Defence08MR, Defence12FR, Defence18M) when mandatory penalties are in place was commonly expressed by the defence practitioner participants.

Jonathan Simon (2007: 36) argues that "various forms of mandatory sentencing schemes have made the prosecutor's determinations of criminal charges the dominant influence on the ultimate prison sentence". In the US context, Rakoff (2014) has equated this situation with providing "prosecutors with weapons to bludgeon defendants into effectively coerced plea-bargains". Similar concerns have been voiced in relation to the mandatory sentencing regimes introduced across Australia, and Victoria specifically. For example, in a submission to the SAC, the LIV (2011b: 13) stated that these mandatory sentencing regimes mean that "prosecutors hold the discretion, as to which charges should proceed, and pre-trial decisions and plea-bargaining become increasingly important". They continued:

> Offenders, who believe they may have a complete defence, may be discouraged from contesting the matter if they are advised that the charge carrying the mandatory minimum sentence would be withdrawn in the event they plead guilty to a lesser alternative charge. … Prosecutors are therefore given more power in the plea-bargaining process. … By agreeing to withdraw a charge that attracts a mandatory sentence, prosecutors could secure a plea to a lesser charge, despite any gaps in evidence or the possibility of a [strong] defence. (LIV 2011b: 13)

VLA (2016c: 6–7) also raised concerns about discretionary powers shifting "to prosecutors and law enforcement agencies where there is reduced transparency and accountability, and where inconsistencies in approach are hidden (for example through the plea bargaining process)". Participants in this study shared this view, noting the powerful position in which prosecutors are placed within negotiations, and the pressures presumptive sentencing regimes can place on defendants to plead guilty to any alternative charge available to them. In the context of baseline sentences, Judge10F claimed:

> I'm very concerned that people will plead guilty to dangerous driving causing death in circumstances where they should be pleading not guilty, because they

can't risk the baseline. That can't be right. There's already that pressure in relation to gross violence offending and others, and sometimes I worry that the charge is sort of flown like a balloon to try and get a negotiated situation. … It's a very big call if you're charged with culpable [driving] and the prosecution will take a dangerous drive causing death [guilty plea], to instead run a culpable [driving trial] in a baseline state.

Judge11F expanded on this point, maintaining that:

It means there's a much greater bargaining tool in plea negotiations to take a plea to a lesser charge so as to avoid baseline. It may skew the process in the sense that, pre baseline, people may have been prepared to plead to the more serious charge as the appropriate one because it was the right one. It puts a different and I think quite unfair factor into the negotiation process between the Crown and defence – [with] either the Crown wrongly accepting a plea to a lesser charge to avoid baseline, or the risk of the Crown unfairly holding out for a plea to the higher charge because it wants the baseline.

Defence13FR also identified this as a concern, and provided an example where her client ended up pleading guilty to intentionally causing serious injury in order to avoid the mandatory non-parole period linked to the gross violence offence, despite the Crown not having what she considered to be a particularly strong case. She explained:

The gross violence non-parole period is helpful in the negotiation process from a prosecution perspective, but not in a positive way. My client was willing to accept a less serious charge, even though I didn't think it was a particularly strong Crown case and I thought we could've easily run it to trial and probably come out … with a not guilty verdict. But he, in the end, took a plea to something less, because he didn't want to run the risk of being found guilty of the gross violence charge and then go into custody for a lengthy period of time. … He ended up getting a Community Correction Order for the lesser offence, and just a bit of a talking-to from the judge. But ultimately, that was a bit disappointing, because that was one that I think, but for the gross violence charge, we probably would've gone to trial, and we would've succeeded.

This example highlights a significant issue in that defendants may be unfairly induced to plead guilty to escape the potential mandatory penalty, clearly raising doubt over the appropriateness of retaining these types of sentencing policies.[8]

The data suggest that mandatory sentencing regimes also affect the way in which both prosecutors and defence practitioners approach the negotiation process. For defence practitioners, it means that they will only encourage their clients to plead guilty if the prosecutor will accept a guilty plea to an alternative offence that does not carry a mandatory penalty; otherwise they will suggest running a trial. As Defence09F maintained:

> My advice to clients would be, don't plead, you may as well run it. … You're going to get such a heavy whack anyway that you may as well take your chances and run a trial. It has a drastic impact. More people are going to dig in their heels about pleading because what's the benefit? You're not going to get a discount,[9] you're going to get a mandatory sentence. I think we will see a lot fewer matters resolving, a lot more matters running just for the sake of putting the prosecution to their proof because what do people have to lose?

Defence18M expressed a similar view, noting that "no one will plead [guilty]; no one that's represented by me anyway". Defence12FR likewise maintained, "it's pretty straightforward –it makes me less likely to negotiate". Defence08MR also discussed his approach to negotiations in these situations, claiming:

> There's no incentive to plead to those gross violence offences, so you're always going to be pushing to negotiate either to get the gross violence element removed or you'll contest it, because you've really got nothing to lose because you're unlikely to get much more than that. … Anything that interferes with the discretion of the court to sentence I think starts to move into problematic territory.

In this vein, Defence02F observed that mandatory sentencing regimes make it difficult to explain any benefit to the client of their pleading guilty, even when the prosecution case is strong. She observed, "it's almost like, well, if I'm facing ten years what do I have to lose? It makes it a lot harder for us to explain to the clients the merits of the case, the strength of the evidence and also to try and kind of reason with them if the evidence is strong". Defence05M claimed that the consequences of this situation are, "without a shadow of doubt, that a tremendous amount of trials will be listed".

For prosecutors, the greater reluctance of defendants to plead to the higher charge means that they either need to run more trials or accept guilty pleas to lesser alternative offences. Mallet (2015: 547) argues that:

> Prosecutors are often reluctant to prosecute some offences due to the penalty being disproportionate to the gravity of the offending. Due to the inflexibility

of mandatory sentences, they will instead file charges for different, but roughly comparable, offences that are not subject to the mandatory sentencing regime. As a result, inconsistency will shift from the quantum of the sentence to what charge is laid in the first place.

Prosecutor06M expressed similar concerns:

In circumstances of gross violence, the defence are loathed to plead for obvious reasons – because of the statutory non-parole period. I've had a number of cases where police have charged the circumstances of gross violence and they're often resolved for intentionally cause serious injury, if anything, and not for the gross violence because of that reluctance [on the part of the defendant to plead].

The Law Council of Australia (2014: 35) has argued that, because "mandatory sentencing offences may result in more contested cases, prosecutors and police may feel additional pressure to negotiate with the offender and/or the defence and agree to pursue lesser charges to prevent court delay and a backlog of cases". There may be some validity to this claim, as many defence practitioners in this study identified this as a common negotiation point. Defence11M commented, "we're talking about intentionally causing serious injury in circumstances of gross violence. I've already done it twice. Just negotiate the prosecution to drop that charge and present on intentionally causing serious injury". Defence19M maintained that, "in my experience, the Crown are very willing to negotiate that gross violence offending, otherwise they'll face running many more trials". He continued, "I've got a client who's whacked someone … it's a horrific offence. But what incentive do we have to just plead guilty to the head charge? We will receive four years on the bottom before we plead, so we've negotiated it down" (Defence19M). Defence19M also described the Crown as "good" by agreeing to withdraw the gross violence offences and accept a guilty plea to intentionally causing serious injury in many cases because of the non-parole period attached to the higher offence, and the fact that the court retains the "ability to impose, say, a youth justice centre order, or a significant two-year term of imprisonment, plus a Community Correction Order or some other sentencing option that's more suited than a mandatory penalty". The absence of guilty pleas to gross violence offences was also noted by Judge15M at the roundtable, who commented:

I've always had the concern, it would lead to situations like [in] America, you know, we'll charge you with murder one and we'll take murder three, and this sort of stuff. I was always concerned that the gross violence would be thrown in

> as a tool to try and force people to plead guilty to lesser offences. I don't know whether that's what's happening or not, but certainly very, very few [gross violence offences] are being heard as [guilty] pleas in the court.[10]

These responses raise serious questions about the effects of mandatory sentencing regimes, and how they may affect the quality of justice provided—in terms of both pressuring defendants to plead guilty to lesser charges and influencing prosecutors to accept guilty pleas to lesser charges to reduce court backlogs. As Defence23M acutely observed:

> Gross violence charges that have been laid have, in my understanding and experience, uniformly resulted in matters either not resolving or resolving to a guilty plea on lesser charges. … It's an irony that you've got this tough-on-crime policy that's having a negative effect on victims by making us take everything to trial or leading to a plea to a lesser charge.

The data thus suggest that there is a need to revisit the mandatory and presumptive sentencing regimes and consider whether they are achieving their purposes or creating more problems in the justice process.[11]

Sentence Indications

The Higher Courts

Following the recommendations of the SAC (2007), sentence indications were officially introduced in Victoria's County and Supreme Courts in July 2008 as a means of encouraging early guilty pleas.[12] Under s 207 of the *Criminal Procedure Act 2009* (Vic):

> At any time after the indictment is filed, the court may indicate that, if the accused pleads guilty to the charge on the indictment at that time, or another charge, the court would or would not (as the case may be) be likely to impose on the accused a sentence of imprisonment that commences immediately.

This means that under this provision, a court can advise a defendant of whether s/he would be likely to receive a custodial or non-custodial sentence if s/he were to enter a guilty plea, but the court is not able to specify the length of sentence or what a non-custodial sentence would entail. The indication can only be requested once by the defendant (unless the prosecutor consents otherwise) and the application itself is subject to the approval of the prosecution.[13] To facilitate plea negotiations, the defendant can request an indication for a charge that is not listed on the indictment.[14] The court can refuse to grant an indication if the judge deems there to be "insufficient information of the impact of the offence on any victim of the offence".[15]

In discussing the possibility of introducing a sentence indication scheme in Victoria in its ten-year reform agenda, the then Labor government stated that "a sentence indication procedure will assist the defendant to weigh up his or her options that should lead to earlier resolution of matters" (Victorian Department of Justice 2004: 29). In this regard, sentence indications operate as a systems-oriented reform, in that they focus on "strengthening and increasing the efficiency of existing criminal justice processes" (Harris 2003: 31).

There has been considerable support expressed for sentence indications nationally and internationally (ALRC 2006; Freiberg and Willis 2003; Mack and Roach Anleu 1995; New Zealand Law Reform Commission 2005; Spears et al. 1994; UK Office of the Attorney-General 2007). As Flynn (2010a: 47) observes:

> This support is based primarily upon their potential to attract early guilty pleas by better informing an accused person's pleading decision; the benefits of which can extend to reducing the often drawn-out criminal process for victims and accused persons, and also offer a mechanism to respond to court delays and the increased workloads of legal practitioners.

As a result of these potential benefits, sentence indication schemes operate in both summary (see, e.g. Tasmania, the ACT and New Zealand) and indictable (see, e.g. New Zealand, and by case law authority in England and Wales) jurisdictions (ALRC 2006: 412; New Zealand Law Reform Commission 2005).[16] NSW also employed an indication scheme for three years in the mid-1990s,[17] although this was "ultimately abandoned in 1996 on the basis that inappropriate sentences were being indicated, and it failed to achieve its anticipated efficiency gains, particularly once the Director of Public Prosecutions began appealing many of the sentences imposed" (Flynn 2010a: 50).

The main justification for introducing sentence indications into the criminal justice process is to increase the early guilty plea rate. This is achieved by providing the defendant with more information to make an informed pleading decision at an early stage, which subsequently reduces court backlogs and workloads (Flynn 2009). While this potential does exist, questions have been raised as to the capacity of sentence indications to work effectively outside the summary jurisdiction. Jamieson (2009: 170), for example, questions whether "the processes of sentence indication adopted in summary environments can be adequately adapted to the more formal and complex arrangements that apply in indictable proceedings". Likewise, in the context of the Victorian scheme, Flynn (2009: 263–4) has argued that, "in theory, sentence indications for indictable offences may appear a powerful mechanism to assist in minimising delays. However, there is a significant contrast evident between the possible benefits and the many disadvantages inherent in [such schemes]".

Since its introduction, there has only been one formal review of the sentence indication process in Victoria. This was conducted by the SAC (2010), and was based on the scheme's operation from 1 July 2008 until 30 June 2009. The review was informed by interviews with legal stakeholders and statistical data obtained from the OPP. During the 12-month review period, the SAC (2010: 15) determined that 27 indications were given (18 non-custodial and 9 custodial), over 92 per cent of which (n = 25) were given in the County Court. Eighty-five per cent of defendants pleaded guilty after receiving their indication, with all 18 non-custodial indications resulting in a guilty plea and five of the custodial indications leading to a guilty plea (SAC 2010: 26). Of the four cases where the defendant initially pleaded not guilty, two later pleaded guilty before another judge, while two matters proceeded to trial and resulted in guilty verdicts (SAC 2010: 27). The most common offences for which an indication was sought were intentionally causing injury, and intentionally causing serious injury, followed by drug trafficking and robbery offences (SAC 2010: 18).

Overall, the number of cases resolved by sentence indications in the 12-month SAC review period made up less than 1 per cent of the 2231 criminal cases resolved during this time. However, once the guilty pleas and cases resolved prior to the sentence indication stage of proceedings were removed, the SAC (2010: 23) estimated that the indication process in the County Court had affected 4.2 per cent of cases. The report acknowledged that, "while there has been some impact in terms of increased resolution of cases, the contribution that this would have made on case flow has been limited … [and] the impact of the scheme on the case load of practitioners involved in sentence indications has been minimal" (SAC 2010: 23–4). The SAC (2010: 82) further stated that "those involved in the scheme, whom the Council was able to speak with, reported minimal impact on case load and workload across the system as a whole". Despite this, the SAC recommended that sentence indications be retained on the basis that they have the "potential to facilitate the resolution of an increased number of cases" and the "capacity to increase the proportion of guilty pleas in matters that have not resolved after the first hearing in the higher courts" (SAC 2010: 23).

It appears that little has changed since the SAC report. Of the 50 de-identified case files, none involved a sentence indication being given or requested. The interview data similarly revealed that very few participants had been involved in a matter where a sentence indication was requested or given in the higher courts. As Judge08M observed, “I’ve never given one and it’s not being utilised in the County and Supreme Courts”. Defence18M similarly maintained that “it’s unquestionably under-utilised”. Participants pointed to two main limitations of the current system as explanations for the under-utilisation of sentence indications: (1) the overly broad nature of the indications and (2) that an indication requires the consent of the prosecution.

Almost all participants reflected negatively on the limited amount of information judges are able to provide in the indications. As Prosecutor05M maintained, “I think they’re a bit narrow. The only indication that can be given is immediate custodial or not immediate custodial … [so] you can only use it in a very limited set of circumstances where people are on the cusp”. Defence18M likewise claimed:

> The set-up for sentence indications in the high courts is poor, it’s too restrictive, it doesn’t work because all they can say is jail, or not. I’ve had a couple where judges have got to the end of the whole thing and said, look, I can’t decide. I just can’t say what I would do. That’s then unsatisfactory, because the accused is left in a quandary, they don’t know whether they’re going to get jail, or not, and the purpose of the legislation was to give people certainty.

This limitation of sentence indications was also identified by Flynn (2009: 254) who argues that:

> The broad nature of the indications limits their usefulness in providing significant information and clarity to defendants to inform pleading decisions. … Defendants who receive custodial indications will be in no better position to assess the length of time they will spend in custody before or after receiving an indication, especially if prison is already a likely outcome of the crime.

This view was echoed by Defence22M, who argued that “because you’re in that jurisdiction, imprisonment is often the primary sentencing consideration. And it’s just imprisonment or non-imprisonment, so there’s not enough flexibility”. A similar comment was made by Defence30M at the roundtable: “I don’t know many people that use sentence indications at all. You know what’s going to go to jail and what’s not going to go to jail generally in the higher courts”. The usefulness of having just a custodial or non-custodial indication was also discussed in the SAC (2010: 22) in its review, in which it was noted that:

> The pool of potential sentence indication cases is reduced even further by the nature of the offences within a case as well as the likelihood of an immediate custodial sentence being perceived by the defendant. If the likelihood of an immediate custodial sentence is perceived to be extremely high (such as in a murder case) or extremely low (such as in a relatively minor theft case), it is unlikely that the defendant would request a sentence indication. Sentence indication is most useful for borderline cases in which it is uncertain whether an immediate custodial sentence will be imposed.

Defence01M expanded on this point, citing drug offences as an example:

> Not having a range certainly undermines the utility, and the best example of that would be large drug trials, where, for example, in Commonwealth matters, the maximum period of imprisonment is life, meaning that the legislation gives the imprimatur to a judge to impose a huge sentence. And a sentencing indication that it might not be anywhere near that which perhaps the accused and even his legal advisors think, would be a very good idea. Very conducive, I would have thought, to [encouraging] a [guilty] plea.

The second main limitation identified by participants was that the process requires prosecutorial approval, which defence practitioner participants said can be very difficult to obtain, although less so in cases prosecuted by the CDPP. As Defence24M observed:

> It's restricted because the OPP, or the Director, are the gatekeeper of the whole process and that means that you can only get a sentence indication if they agree to it. If they say, no we don't agree to it, it doesn't happen under the legislation … so it's a rare beast.

During the 12-month review period, the SAC (2010: 15) found that 12 per cent of the 31 applications for an indication were not consented to by the Crown, resulting in no indication being given.

In addition to prosecutors not approving indications, participants also pointed to judges being unsupportive of the scheme. Prosecutor07M maintained, "the Act is structured on the basis that the Crown has to agree to the sentence indication … but I think the problem is probably the judges. My sense of it is that the judges haven't embraced it". Defence03F likewise argued that "County Court judges aren't a huge fan of the sentence indication". This view was also represented in the comments of judicial participants, who highlighted the limitations of the system as the reason for it not being actively utilised in the higher courts. Judge10F explained, "the utility of them at the County Court is seriously compromised by what I'm allowed to say … I'd like to be able to say more, but I'm very conscious that I can't, so I don't". Judge08M went further, labelling the process "a complete waste of time", due to the constraints on what can be said.

In terms of improving the scheme, participants suggested that amendments making it more reflective of the process operating in the Magistrates' Court (discussed below) would be of benefit. This could include removing the requirement on the prosecutor to consent to the indication being given and permitting the judge to provide a more detailed indication. Judge01M maintained:

> If you're going to have sentence indication the judge should be able to say, I haven't come to a final view about the matter, that will depend upon a full plea and this is a kind of summary. But I can tell you now that, as things look to me at this stage, without binding myself about it, I'm looking at [sentencing you to] between three and four years.

Defence05M likewise argued that "there needs to be a broadening of the scope in which a sentence indication can be given, as in not just prison or no prison … whether a CCO is within the range and what matter, and length of jail". Prosecutor05M was also of the view that "if there was the ability to give a broader indication, it probably would be used a bit more, and I do think it could be used more".

The Magistrates' Court

Sentence indications for summary offences have informally been given in Victoria's Magistrates' Court since the introduction of the contest mention system in 1993 (Flynn 2010b). However, they were officially introduced in legislation alongside the indictable sentence indication scheme in July 2008. Under s 60 of the *Criminal Procedure Act 2009* (Vic):

> At any time during a proceeding for a summary offence or an indictable offence that may be heard and determined summarily, the Magistrates' Court may indicate that, if the accused pleads guilty to the charge for the offence at that time, the court would be likely to impose on the accused:

(a) a sentence of imprisonment that commences immediately; or
(b) a sentence of a specified type.

Similar to the indictable process, the court must have regard to the impact of the offence on any victim of the offence and may "decide not to give a sentence indication … if the Magistrates' Court considers there is insufficient information before it of the impact of the offence on any victim of the offence".[18]

Almost all participants identified the summary sentence indication process as primarily beneficial and something they regularly engage in. As Judge02MR explained, "I would do it 20 to 40 times a week". This view was supported by stakeholders at the roundtable, including Defence30M, who observed, "we resolve everything in the Magistrate's Court because we have this [sentence indication] discussion". On the whole, participants pointed to three main benefits of the scheme for (1) defendants, (2) defence practitioners and (3) the courts.

Beneficial for Defendants

Participants identified a range of benefits arising from the granting of sentence indications in the summary jurisdiction for defendants, including that it helps inform their decision, and, as Defence02F argued, it allows "the accused to take ownership over their decision to plead guilty". She explained, "when the Court says, if you plead guilty this is what you're going to get, it helps them cope with the decision to plead guilty or it assists them with making the decision to take it to a contested hearing, but they feel more in control of their choice". Defence14FR also saw the process as encouraging defendants to "feel safer pleading guilty", because "they know what's happening to them before they make that decision [to plead]". She went on:

> The client needs to know what's happening because their fear of jail motivates a lot of not guilty pleas. If the client knows that the courts are not talking about jail, they're far more likely in that sort of category of, it's a bit grey, or it's pretty black but the client's just seeing white, a sentence indication will resolve those matters almost every time. I can't remember the last time a client refused a sentence indication.

Further to assisting represented defendants, the sentence indication process was considered by many participants to be beneficial in providing unrepresented defendants with a greater understanding of their case and the likely outcome. As Prosecutor04M claimed, "it helps a lot with self-represented people". Prosecutor09F expanded on this view, drawing on some of the key problems that arise for unrepresented defendants in the court system (discussed in more detail in Chap. 8). In particular, she highlighted how an indication can offer a mechanism for defendants to better comprehend the implications of their guilty plea, without the prosecutor or magistrate having to (inappropriately) take on a defence representative role:

> Sentence indications work for [an] unrepresented accused because they're always concerned they're going to go to jail because a lot of offences have jail attached as a sentence, but they don't realise that they can also get a fine. And being a prosecutor you can't give legal advice to people, so you can't say, when you go into court if you plead guilty to this, it's likely you're going to get a fine. You can't say that. ... I often – in [summary] case conferencing, we'll say to someone, you know that there's three roads today. There's pleading guilty where you just go in and we'll read the summary and the magistrate will give you X. There's pleading not guilty where you'll come back on another day and it'll go before a magistrate and you tell your story. Or there's the middle road which is a sentencing indication. The magistrate will tell you if you plead [guilty] what your sentence is likely to be and you can choose then and there whether you take this road or this road. (Prosecutor09F)

Beneficial for Defence Practitioners

Defence participants also commonly identified sentence indications in summary matters as a way to assist them in explaining the outcome of a guilty plea to their clients, in effect, a "client management tool" (Defence19M). As Defence19M further claimed, it can help in situations where you have "a client whose instructions are ridiculous, and you think, look, what we'll do is we'll just go into court, I'll ask for a sentencing indication, then you can make a decision once you have this certainty about what's going to happen". Prosecutor02FR similarly noted that:

> The other bonus to it from a defence perspective, it's not them saying it to their client, their client's actually hearing the thought processes of the magistrate and that this is what the magistrate is thinking. ... In that respect, it makes people realise where that magistrate is setting the bar and what his [sic] expectations are.

Prosecutor09F identified this client management tool as helping "keep things resolving and moving matters through [the court]". She explained:

> It works for defence when they've got a belligerent sort of accused who won't listen and then they can say, well, you know, let's have a sentencing indication and then that makes it clearer to the accused that it's not going to be the biggest deal in the whole world if you plead guilty. I think they're a great thing for early resolutions.

Defence05M also identified indications as a way to encourage early guilty pleas and plea negotiations, because it can "allow you really to put your toe in the water and see how hot it is at any time". He considered this a particularly beneficial aspect of the summary scheme compared to the indictable offence process, where you are "ramshackled [sic] by the prosecution saying yes or no to it" (Defence05M).

Beneficial for the Courts

The final common theme to emerge from the data was that when indications encourage early guilty pleas, immense efficiency benefits are provided for the court process overall. Judge12M maintained:

> In those courts, there's thousands of cases that go through those lists every year, so its legitimacy lies in the fact that it really is bringing about earlier what will ultimately certainly happen. It's bringing [it] forward and that's delay reduction and that's a benefit to all, including victims. It's bringing forward the inevitable, that's the way I'd best put it.

Defence23M similarly claimed, "it resolves matters. That's the reality of it. It speeds things up. It means matters don't unnecessarily go to contest, or just get delayed for disclosure. It does resolve a lot of matters earlier that should resolve".

Limitations

The main limitation of the summary sentence indication scheme identified by participants was that its effectiveness—as is the case with contest mentions (discussed in Chap. 5)—is dependent upon the magistrate. Prosecutor02FR claimed, "it is very magistrate dependent. There's some magistrates that won't do it, and will just basically say, look I'll force you to test the case and see how you go. You'll have others that will make strong sentencing indications even without being asked". In this regard, some participants expressed concern about the fact that magistrates sometimes give an indication even when the defence does not request one, which they feel places undue pressure on defendants to plead guilty, even when they may have a strong case. Defence03F maintained:

> You say, I don't want it Your Honour, this has to go to contest. And the magistrate will say, well, you know my practice, and you just get the indication anyway. … I mean sometimes you've got clients who, they've got a good case, but they hear, oh you'll get a bond or whatever, and they think, oh well, that sounds pretty good, and that's the whole point of it, to get the guilty plea.

The concern that sentence indications may place pressure upon a defendant to plead guilty was also flagged in Parliamentary Debates before the indictable or summary schemes were introduced. At the time, then leader of the National Party, Peter Ryan, claimed:

> What this legislation will do is introduce a system where people who are disadvantaged and not able to make the judgments which are so fundamental to their future will be under enormous pressures to plead guilty, simply because they think that course of action is better than going to trial. … The indication that has been given to them convinces them to think, although I didn't commit this crime, I'm better to take this option of pleading guilty to the charge because it will spare me the effects of a trial in all its forms, personal, financial and otherwise. (Parliamentary Debates, Legislative Assembly, 6 December 2007, 4348)

In the context of the indictable sentence indication scheme, the SAC (2010: 53) review did not find any evidence of improper pressures being placed on defendants to plead guilty after receiving an indication. Likewise, in this study, many participants did not consider that sentence indications in either court would unduly pressure a defendant to plead guilty. However, as evidenced in Defence03F's comments above, there were some examples and perspectives offered which suggested there is in fact some pressure placed on a defendant in this context, but the outcome is usually a positive one—reflecting the view that a degree of pressure is acceptable, if it results in a positive sentencing outcome for the defendant.[19]

In describing the differences in magistrates' approaches, participants claimed that some magistrates will give rough indications, while others will provide a "very, very thorough and very particular indication" (Defence23M). Defence23M explained:

> Some magistrates will say to the degree, if your client was to plead guilty, I will convict and fine him $1000. … It's down to that level of detail. Or it is, I was thinking of a corrections order with treatment only. That will probably be more common, or they might even go so far as to say how long the loss of licence would be if that's the sticking point. Some magistrates will say, I'm thinking of a custodial order, that's it, like you get in the higher courts.

Drawing on some recent examples of indications, Judge02MR likewise maintained that magistrates differ in their approaches:

> A lot of magistrates will not give figures. They'll say what the range of penalty is [or] they'll say, it's an immediate term combined with a Community Correction Order. I tend to give figures, particularly if it's looking at an immediate [custodial sentence]. … One that I had, the accused had assaulted his partner. I said, you're looking at eight months [in prison] and 12 months CCO. And another one recently, I said, look, you're looking at 18 months' [imprisonment] with a non-parole period of X if you were to plead [guilty], that's the best I can do. … At the end of the day we've got four options – we're not exactly putting a square peg in a round hole – it's either a bond, a fine, a CCO and/or imprisonment.

Similarly citing his own experiences in providing sentence indications, Judge06M explained that he will often look for the "sticking point" or "tension" that is preventing the defendant from pleading guilty. In describing his approach, Judge06M referred to it as "a personal preference. It's my style, it's how I exercise my authority under the *Criminal Procedure Act* [2009 (Vic)] that allows for sentence indications". He explained:

> I want a barrister to tell me in one or two minutes what the key issues are. I don't want the whole thing rehearsed. Then I'll give them an indication. Sometimes the indication that they want is, is it jail or is it not jail? Sometimes, is it a licence disqualification or not? There's always a point of tension, you can see generally why they're asking for a sentencing indication and it's usually in circumstances where there's some weakness in the prosecution case. The defendant who's as guilty as sin is entitled to stand mute and have the prosecution prove its case and if there's a flaw in the evidence then a defendant might say, well, if I don't go to jail, I'll plead. I've done it, I'll plead, but if I'm going to go to jail, damn it, let's make the cops prove their case because there's a chance they won't. In those situations, that's when I'll often be asked for a sentencing indication and I'll give that indication. And I will always build in a discount of some

> kind if the sentence indication is acceptable, to recognise the utility that the community enjoys by that decision [to plead guilty].

Some participants raised concerns about the ineffective reporting systems surrounding indications, which can allow defendants to end up receiving multiple indications from different magistrates. This issue was linked to a concern over what was referred to as "magistrate shopping", which was a major limitation of the indictable scheme that operated in NSW in the 1990s (Flynn 2010b: 56; Weatherburn and Lind 1995), whereby indications were sought and rejected until a preferable indication from another judge was given. As Judge06M explained:

> There are some flaws. I don't think we reliably … prevent magistrate shopping. I think it's possible to get a sentencing indication from me, for instance, and not accept it and then the punter might say, no, I don't accept that, so it goes off to a contest stream. I suspect there are times when another magistrate will be asked to also give a sentencing indication on the same case. I think that happens because of bad file management. My practice is to write on the front of the file when I've been asked for a sentencing indication. Another magistrate should never know if they're hearing a contest that a sentencing indication was previously sought, but they should certainly know that a sentencing indication was previously sought if the punter tries to ask for another one. And the court doesn't have a good system, a good electronic system. … I think people can probably do a bit of shopping if they're clever about it.

Defence08MR similarly claimed:

> Some magistrates very much take the view, what, you're going to try me and then you're going to get someone in a couple of weeks? You're going to try someone else until you get the answer you want? So they're not going to do it.

Despite these concerns, most participants felt that the summary sentence indication scheme was an effective and relatively fair mechanism to encourage early guilty pleas, and were supportive of it being retained in its current form.

Prosecution Submissions on Sentencing

For many years in Victoria it was the practice that prosecutors did not make any submissions on sentence (Freiberg and Fox 1987). However, in 2008, in *MacNeil-Brown*,[20] the Court of Appeal of the Supreme Court of Victoria in a 3:2

majority (Buchanan and Kellam JJA dissenting) held that, if requested by the court, or if the prosecution reasonably believed the court would otherwise fall into error, prosecutors were required to submit what they considered to be the available range of sentences to impose on a defendant. In 2014, however, the decision of the court in *MacNeil-Brown* was overturned by the High Court in *Barbaro*,[21] in which the court stated that "the practice to which *MacNeil-Brown* has given rise should cease. The practice is wrong in principle".[22] The court further stated that, "contrary to the view of the majority in *MacNeil-Brown*, the prosecution's conclusion about the bounds of the available range of sentences is an irrelevant statement of opinion, not a submission of law".[23]

In *Barbaro*, the two defendants, Barbaro and Zirilli, had pleaded guilty to various offences related to large-scale ecstasy importation and trafficking, following plea negotiations with the prosecution. As part of their negotiations, the prosecution had indicated that the sentencing range they would submit for Barbaro was between 32 and 37 years (with a non-parole period of 24–28 years), and between 21 and 25 years (with a non-parole period of 16–19 years) for Zirilli. However, in hearing the pleas, the presiding judge, King J, refused to hear the prosecution's submission on range, stating instead, "can I make it clear that I do not seek and will not seek any indication of sentencing range from anyone. … I don't consider it appropriate".[24] King J then imposed a sentence of life with a minimum non-parole period of 30 years for Barbaro and a head sentence of 26 years with a non-parole period of 18 years for Zirilli. Both defendants appealed to the High Court, asking it to consider whether King J's refusal to hear the prosecutor's submission on sentence range was a breach of procedural fairness and a failure to take into account a relevant sentencing consideration.

The appellants' first line of argument was that plea agreements had been made and the cases resolved to guilty pleas because they expected that the prosecution would advise the court on an appropriate sentencing range and they were disadvantaged by not being able to rely on the submission. In responding to this argument, the High Court stated that:

> The applicants' allegations of unfairness depended upon giving the plea agreements and the prosecution's expression of opinion about sentencing range relevance and importance that is not consistent with these principles. The prosecution decided what charges would be preferred against the applicants. The applicants decided whether to plead guilty to those charges. They did so in light of whatever advice they had from their own advisers and whatever weight they chose to give to the prosecution's opinions. But they necessarily did so knowing that it was for the judge, alone, to decide what sentence would be passed upon them.[25]

Further clarification on the *Barbaro* decision was provided by the Court of Appeal of the Supreme Court of Victoria in *Matthews v The Queen; Vu v The Queen; Hashmi v The Queen.*[26] In this case, the appellants were concerned with whether the sentencing discretion of the judge is vitiated when the prosecution provides the sentencing judge with the available range of sentences. In each appeal (heard together), it was argued that the judge took into account an irrelevant sentencing consideration. The Court of Appeal held that a quantified range of submission would not vitiate sentencing discretion unless it could be demonstrated that the sentencing judge was swayed by the prosecution's submission in arriving at the sentence. The court also clarified that the limitation on the prosecution only applies in relation to submissions regarding the available range of sentences, not the appropriate type of disposition, and that the prohibition against sentencing ranges does not apply to defence submissions on sentences. Further clarification was also provided in *Director, Fair Work Building Industry Inspectorate v Construction, Forestry, Mining and Energy Union,*[27] in which a unanimous decision of the High Court held that *Barbaro* does not apply to civil penalty cases, recognising the fact that negotiation and compromising proceedings following negotiations between regulators and defendants are not unusual in civil penalty proceedings, as well as the importance of promoting predictability of outcomes in such proceedings.

As flagged in Chap. 3, this study sought to understand the effect that the *Barbaro* decision had on plea negotiations, particularly in light of concerns raised in the wake of the High Court's decision that it would restrict or constrain such negotiations. As Ananian-Walsh and Gover (2015: 418) argue:

> In *Barbaro*, the High Court sent shockwaves through criminal law practice by radically restricting the circumstances in which a sentencing judge may consider, or even hear, counsel's submissions on sentencing range. The practical impact of this decision was that an accused could no longer rely on pre-trial discussions or agreements on sentencing range in considering whether to enter a plea of guilty.

In contrast, it appears that the effect of the *Barbaro* ruling on the plea negotiation process in Victoria has been largely negligible, other than removing discussions on range. Plea discussions continue to occur as regularly as they did pre *Barbaro* and guilty pleas appear to be entered as regularly as they were pre *Barbaro.* The data also revealed that discussions over sentencing submissions as to the type of disposition to impose (such as a CCO or time served) continue to form a key part of negotiations post *Barbaro.*

In addition to considering how the decision has affected plea negotiations, legal practitioner perspectives on *Barbaro* were sought in the light of the negative commentary that emerged in the wake of the 2014 High Court decision. In his analysis of the High Court's decision, Bagaric (2014: 133) argues that it "undermine[s] the fairness and effectiveness of the sentencing process". He claims that describing "the sentencing range as a statement of opinion", and not a submission of law, is "flawed to the point of being unintelligible". He claimed that if this is the court's view, then the same could apply "in relation to most submissions made by lawyers in Australian courts in the adversarial process" (Bagaric 2014: 133). Judge01M, in this study, expressed a similar view, claiming that "just to characterise it [the submission] as an opinion is nonsense. It's not an opinion, it's a submission and it should be a submission based on proper legal principles in the same way that other submissions are based on proper legal principles". Bagaric (2014: 135) was particularly critical of the court's decision, arguing that:

> The reasoning in *Barbaro* is misconceived. The outcome of the decision will introduce even higher levels of obscurity into the sentencing realm. The decision is likely to discourage guilty pleas and therefore increase court backlogs. All Australian jurisdictions should introduce legislation to overcome the impact of the decision.

In April 2016, the Queensland State Government did just this, passing legislation overturning the High Court's decision. Under the *Criminal Law (Domestic Violence) Amendment Act 2016* (Qld), the *Penalties and Sentences Act 1992* (Qld) was amended to reinstate the ability of the court to receive a submission from both the prosecution and defence on the bounds of the range of appropriate sentences that should be imposed. In introducing the legislation, the Attorney-General and Minister for Justice, Yvette D'Ath, maintained that:

> [We] have listened to the concerns of the legal profession and the judiciary and have secured vital legislative reform that will return sentencing procedures to those in place in Queensland prior to the 2014 High Court decision. … This will allow for better and more fulsome [sic] submissions to be made on sentencing. It reflects the significant contribution which should rightfully be made to the sentencing process by lawyers on both sides of the bar table. … It will improve consistency in sentencing. (Queensland Government 2016)

In this study, the data revealed that the Victorian legal community holds quite diverse views on the *Barbaro* decision. For example, Judge03M stated, "I wholeheartedly support the outcome of *Barbaro* and the approach of the High Court", while Judge07M declared, "I favoured and was comfortable with *MacNeil-Brown*". This difference of opinion was aptly summarised by Judge07M:

> The reaction to *Barbaro* in the legal community has been mixed. People who are against are saying, this is silly and we should be able to get what information we need. It's hard enough [sentencing]. We should get as much information as we can. Then some are saying, it's never been done this way, it wasn't done this way in the past when I put on my barrister's robes in the 1950s, so we shouldn't change it. And then there was the ridiculous proposition, no one's going to tell me how to sentence. But the thing is, people have been telling you, or making submissions to you, as to how to sentence for years and the Court of Appeal has been telling you how to sentence for years.

Many of the concerns underpinning the *MacNeil-Brown* ruling focused on the inconsistencies in the quality of the ranges provided by the Crown. Judge01M maintained:

> We were getting an untutored, unstructured, unexplained range of 11 to 12 years, that's not a range. A range is eight to 12. And so we got 'ranges' of 11 to 12 years and judges were giving ten and a half [years]. What do you do with that? And then sometimes we'd get the Crown coming along and complaining, you've given ten and a half and we submitted 11 to 12.

At the roundtable, Judge15M similarly criticised the prosecution providing a firm sentence rather than ranges: "one of the main problems that arose was that we weren't getting ranges, we were getting proposed sentences", which fell outside the *Mac-Neil Brown* requirements. Further to these issues, Judge03M argued that he "never supported the provision of sentencing ranges from the prosecution" because he believed them to be "haphazard". He explained:

> I thought they were an inappropriate function for prosecutors to engage in. Prosecutor A might say four years and prosecutor B might say two years. Those decisions were made after five or seven minutes of discussion between an instructing solicitor and a Crown prosecutor.

Judge11F also commented on the "disparate and inconsistent practices from the Crown on submissions on sentencing range", arguing that "sometimes they were good, [but] more often than not they were not thought through and a bit of examination showed that". This view was also expressed by Judge16F at the roundtable, who stated:

> Had there been more consistency and good types of sentencing ranges that were being put up and a proper analysis of where they fitted, I'd certainly have more enthusiasm for it coming back. But it was so inconsistent that it was just unreliable. And there was never a sense of accountability that it had been properly considered and thought through. You didn't know whether it was a fly-out-the-door, off-the-cuff opinion from a senior prosecutor. You didn't know whether they had all the defence material that was available that was being put or an understanding of the way the plea was going to be put, and you had no confidence that it was actually gained by looking at the sentencing stats with comparable factual cases.

One of the reasons for such inconsistency may be the additional work the practice added to the prosecutor's already heavy load. As Prosecutor01F maintained, "as Crown prosecutors, as a prosecuting agency, we found it very time consuming to give a *MacNeil-Brown* range". Prosecutor13F highlighted a similar concern at the roundtable, noting that "it was almost impossible to be able to go to the amount of time and effort that the court was saying was required". This opinion was supported by Prosecutor14M at the roundtable, who described the process as "an enormous resource burden on the Crown".

Further to inconsistencies, many participants were firmly of the view that the role of the prosecutor should not extend to the sentencing arena:

> The job, or the task, of identifying the range was shifted from the judge, who hears the plea, who goes away and reflects upon the material, who has read all the material, who's had the opportunity to question counsel about the matters, that job was transferred across to somebody who had nothing to do with the matter except for one day and he [sic] wasn't involved in the actual hearing of the matter. I just think that was never right.

Defence09F similarly maintained that:

> There was certainly a view, at least amongst defence practitioners, that it was never the Crown's role to determine what the sentence should be. They decide which charges are proceeded on, yes, they get it to that point, but the function

> of the court and of the judge is to impose sentence and to do so with judicial discretion and having regard to all the circumstances of the case. And it's not for the Crown to decide how that discretion is employed.

This view was shared by Defence01M, who firmly believed that "the prosecution ought not to have the right to set a figure". These comments pertaining to the prosecutor "determining" and "setting" a sentence were made despite the prosecutor's role under *MacNeil-Brown* being to provide a submission on the sentence range possibilities, not to determine a sentence.

One of the most interesting reflections on the practice was given by Judge05M, who discussed the psychological effect this shift in the prosecutor's role had on judges, such that "a lot of the judges always came in at the bottom of the Crown range, and some of us would never follow the Crown range". He explained:

> I spent most of my time trying to work out how not to fit within the Crown range. ... Apparently it was rather unnerving as to what, as to what psychologically judges were doing. And that's my understanding of it. Now there's probably proper stats on all that, I don't know, but that was anecdotally what we were being told. That was our [the judge's] reaction [to not fit the prosecutor's range].

Participants also pointed to concerns that the ranges were often too high, which placed the court in an awkward position in sentencing "because the sentencing judge knows if they go below that range, that the Crown's likely to appeal and they know if they go within that, that there's not necessarily much we can do because that's the Crown's sentencing range" (Defence09F). Defence01M similarly maintained that "I always thought that the range put by the Crown was absurd. ... I think the whole concept of putting ranges is not very helpful to anyone". Judge13F expanded on this view, claiming that:

> The problem was that it became a sort of a – it seemed like a bit of a dark option that the Crown would always state a range that was higher than what was really reasonable. The defence would then be forced to come in to a figure just below that just because it would seem ridiculous to come in very far below it and we'd have to sentence somewhere in the middle.

Most participants who were in favour of the *MacNeil-Brown* decision spoke of the usefulness of the ranges in assisting judges to make informed decisions. Judge01M argued, "*MacNeil-Brown* was a very good judgment in principle. ... I know that judges wanted ranges, because they felt comforted by ranges – not because they assisted them, but because they felt comforted". Judge02MR similarly maintained:

> I've found it difficult following *Barbaro* when I'm not aware as to what a tariff is, where I'm not as familiar as I am with the state, criminal offences, like with the Commonwealth offences, … because if you're not familiar, how do you get any guidance?

Judge07M also viewed *MacNeil-Brown* as providing a useful tool in preparing sentencing judgments. He explained that "having someone telling me that this is the seriousness of this offence which would bring about a sentence of about this length, so that's where we pitch it. So, you synthesise everything and go from there. How can that be anything other than rational"? Judge10F likewise claimed that, "as a sentencing judge, I quite liked getting range, but I never felt constrained by it". At the roundtable, Judge16F similarly reflected on the usefulness of ranges when the prosecutor presents an overview of the sentencing statistics. She explained:

> Sensible prosecutors will put up the sentencing stance and that gives you the statistical range and sentencing snapshots. It means if you're thinking 15 years for a culpable driving and you see, well, no-one's ever given 15 years for a culpable, you're out of range. You don't have to be a rocket scientist to work that out. But if you're looking at whether it's custodial or non-custodial and you see from the stats that 35 per cent of offenders for this type of offence get a non-custodial, then you know that, on the face of it, you're not falling outside what is within range. (Judge16F)

Judge15M supported this view at the roundtable, saying that the presentation of useful statistics by the prosecution "stops outrageous [sentencing] decisions".

The interview participants also pointed to the usefulness of a range in high-volume courts:

> When done responsibly and properly, it is a legitimate and extremely helpful practice. … In high-volume courts where a particular judicial officer is sitting in a court –because he [sic] hears a lot of cases, doing a lot of sentencing on a given day, for example, prosecution submissions can – particularly prosecutors that you know and you trust and who are responsible about it and of course most of them are – are just helpful and practical, and you can cut to the chase more quickly. You can spend less time considering matters that they might be able to tell you shouldn't be a concern, so it is very helpful, particularly in a busy court. (Judge12M)

While not supportive of the decision in *MacNeil-Brown*, Judge05M did acknowledge that it was useful, but only in matters where the sentence range he had in mind was above the prosecutor's submission: "the only time that assisted me was if I was about to give someone 15 years for incest, and they'd say look eight would be enough".

In addition to submissions on sentence range assisting the court, Defence02F identified some other benefits of having the Crown provide a range from the point of view of the defence:

> In my experience and opinion, it makes our job harder when we are doing the plea, when we're doing plea submissions. [Before *Barbaro*], you had someone else on the other side either saying yes or no or suggesting another number, you have a second opinion about whether or not you're going down the right track with what you're proposing to the court.

Defence09F likewise observed that the range could be very useful when it was a "reasonable" prosecutor presenting before "an unreasonable" judge. She claimed:

> Pre *Barbaro*, sometimes you'd think, great, they've [the prosecution] given me a great range and this is wonderful because now this particular judge who I don't think is a very good draw is going to give me a result consistent with that because they don't want to be appealed by us, they don't want to be appealed by the Crown, so they'll fall into line, they'll go within range.

While identifying some of the benefits of the *MacNeil-Brown* ruling, many participants maintained that the *Barbaro* decision had not changed the process in a negative way, because, as Judge01M claimed, prosecutors can still assist judges to avoid error by "drawing the attention of the court to any comparable, truly comparable, cases and drawing the attention of the court to useful statistics coming out of bodies like the Sentencing Advisory Council". He continued:

> They can talk about the type of penalty, they can say this is a case that warrants immediate custodial disposition, they can say this is a mid-range murder or a low-range murder or a high-range murder. … These are the aggravating factors, these are the mitigating factors, here are comparable cases which will assist you, here are what the Sentencing Advisory Council says. … It hasn't changed much at all. It's just knocked out the bit where the judge is told the range is X to X.

Judge07M likewise explained that "the prosecution do [still] say, this has got to be jail and in many of our pleas they're saying to you, this is not a combination sentence or it's a custody plus parole. So we still get a feel of it". These comments support this study's broader findings about *Barbaro* in relation to the effect on guilty pleas and the plea negotiation process, which reveal that the *Barbaro* decision has not had a significant effect on the frequency of discussions or reduced discussions pertaining to sentencing submissions. Rather, it has simply changed the nature of the discussion away from ranges to instead encapsulate broader indications such as time served and CCOs.

Section 6AAA

Section 6AAA of the *Sentencing Act 1991* (Vic) was introduced in 2008 and requires the court, when sentencing a defendant to a "less severe sentence than it would otherwise have imposed because the offender pleaded guilty",[28] to "state the sentence and the non-parole period, if any, that it would have imposed but for the plea of guilty".[29] This reform was introduced with the aim of demonstrating the value of a guilty plea by requiring judges and magistrates to indicate what the sentence would have been, but for the guilty plea being entered. As the SAC (2015: 77) explains, "by making discounts for guilty pleas more transparent, section 6AAA was expected to encourage people who intended pleading guilty to do so as early as possible, without encouraging inappropriate guilty pleas".

In 2015, the SAC conducted a review of the s 6AAA practice. The review was informed by an analysis of 9618 cases sentenced in the higher courts between 30 June 2009 and 1 July 2014. The SAC (2015: 15) found that, over the reference period, the rate of guilty pleas did not increase; however, there was a shift in the timing of when guilty pleas were first entered, with a significant increase in earlier guilty pleas. In its analysis, the SAC (2015: 22) noted that the "biggest jump" in early guilty plea rates occurred between the first and second year of s 6AAA's operation. While recognising that a number of reforms had been introduced over the previous ten years to encourage early guilty pleas and that it "is not possible to identify which of the reforms, if any, have contributed to the significant shift in plea timing" (SAC 2015: 22), the SAC (2015: 22) contends that this increase in early guilty plea rates was "consistent with the intended outcome of the section 6AAA".

In terms of s 6AAA's impact on sentencing, the SAC (2015: 77) review found that in one-third of the cases with a s 6AAA statement, the guilty plea changed the sentence type the defendant received (e.g. from imprisonment to a youth justice centre order). In the remaining two-thirds, of which almost all were imprisonment cases, the SAC (2015: 77) found that:

> The sentence type did not change but the offender would have received a longer sentence had he or she not pleaded guilty. The most common discount for sentences of imprisonment was between 20 per cent and 30 per cent (in 44.9 per cent of cases), and between 30 per cent and 40 per cent in a further 26.8 per cent of cases.

Overwhelmingly, the s 6AAA statement was described by the participants in this study as "artificial" (Judge13F), "speculation" (Judge08M) and "superficial" (Defence09F). Judge13F maintained:

> I don't think it's particularly useful because it's better if the judge just states, you know, I have given significant weight to your plea of guilty blah, blah, blah. I don't really think that [s] 6AAA is particularly useful because I think it leads to an artificial kind of judge having to artificially try and dream up a figure that they might have otherwise imposed.

Judge12M likewise claimed, "you might say, apart from the plea of guilty I would have imposed a sentence of 18 months. Whether you would have is the question that one can't answer really. … So, it is artificial". These comments support a range of judicial commentary in sentencing post the introduction of s 6AAA, whereby numerous judges have referred to the "artificiality", and "theoretical" and "hypothetical" nature of the s 6AAA statement. For example, in *R v Nguyen*,[30] Coghlan J stated:

> Pursuant to s 6AAA of the *Sentencing Act 1991* [(Vic)], I state that, had it not been for your pleas of guilty, I would have imposed a sentence of eight and a half years with a non-parole period of six years. In this case, that indication is somewhat artificial because there are so many other features relevant to this sentence, as I have outlined above.

Priest JA likewise described the statement as a "somewhat artificial (although legislatively mandated) exercise" in *The Queen v Prately*.[31] Kaye J referred to the exercise as "somewhat artificial, because of the necessary interrelationship of your plea and other mitigating factors" in *DPP v Carleton*.[32] Croucher J noted that "there is a degree of imprecision and artificiality in that [s 6AAA] exercise" in *The Queen v Deing*.[33] And Lasry J declared the statement to be "a thoroughly artificial exercise" in *The Queen v Bacak*.[34]

Throughout the interviews, a number of participants raised concerns that judges simply "pluck a figure out of the air" (Defence02F), challenging the accuracy of the s 6AAA statement. Defence16F claimed, "I think sometimes, though, the judge is just making it up as they're talking. … I mean, sometimes it's obvious that they've forgotten about it and they're thinking, quick, quick, got to add X years". Defence11M also stated, "I don't believe in s 6AAA because there is zero consideration given to it". He continued:

> A judge or a magistrate will simply just see what they've given and add on 20 to 30 per cent without giving any regard whatsoever to it. Therefore, the figures are artificial. Any empirical studies that come back that say, oh well we're seeing tangible benefits of 30 per cent based on this is absolute rubbish. They're [judges and magistrates] doing it to cover their arses to what they're required to do under [s] 6AAA.

This view was (perhaps surprisingly) supported by some of the judicial participants, who drew on their own experiences with giving the statement to criticise its existence. Judge01M maintained:

> It's totally artificial. Nobody puts any thought into it. We do it, but it's a nuisance more than anything else, and what we do, I don't know if I'm letting the cat out of the bag, is we take a figure that we've come to and then we announce it [s] 6AAA and we sort of add a couple of years and say had it not been for. … But let me tell you, that is the least part of the exercise. Nobody ever puts any real thought into what the [s] 6AAA figure would be.

Judge05M likewise described the statement as "rubbish", claiming that:

> Sometimes I'll deliberately give a much bigger figure than I probably would have, just to encourage people [to plead]. First sentence on a circuit that's not a bad idea sometimes. … I do that a bit … Realistically, I've always thought it [s 6AAA] was just nonsense.

Concerns regarding judges initially escalating the sentence were also raised by defence practitioners, including Defence21M, who claimed:

> There's a temptation for judges to inflate what they would have given somebody. So sometimes I find the [s] 6AAA statements remarkable where they're like, I've imposed a sentence of five with three, but I would have given you nine with seven, or eight with six, or something. And sometimes I think to myself, really? So sometimes it seems to me that for some judges there's an imperative

to overstate what the sentence might have been to make it look like it was the right decision to plead guilty.

The practice of "building in some nonsense discount afterwards" (Judge06M) was similarly noted by Judge06M, who described the s 6AAA statement as "a complete fiction, utter fiction. It's a joke. … I don't believe anybody, anybody would dispute that. It just doesn't work".

Participants also pointed to the difficulties of making the s 6AAA assessment, on the basis that a judge cannot possibly predict what sentence they would have imposed following a guilty verdict at trial. As Defence25MR maintained, "I don't know how the s 6AAA could be realistic really". He continued:

> How can you consider the effect of the complainant [victim] on giving evidence without actually seeing the claim and giving evidence, for example? They seem pretty arbitrary, they seem pretty artificial. I don't put much stock in them. It seems to me that the judge or magistrate is just adding a few numbers and saying, this is what I would've given you. I don't really see how they can work effectively.

In a similar vein, Judge07M maintained that, after a trial:

> You know much more about the person and you think, well, the complainant or the victim is here. … You can, sort of, understand the whole dynamic and so the sentence that you might have given if you'd heard the cold, unemotional facts are maybe more severe than if you hear the trial. … Some of us have thought that. Now, you've got to really work on that intellectually. You've got to make sure that this is the sentence I would have given had it been a trial. I don't think we get much support on that decision.

Defence15M also described the statement as "arbitrary" on the basis that, in the Magistrates' Court context:

> You don't know what would've come out in a contested hearing. It might've been a contested hearing that raised purely a point of law that was relevant and needed the magistrate to decide that point, and there would be no criticism of the client for running the hearing in that context.

Defence22M similarly identified the statement as "arbitrary" and a "crystal ball exercise", arguing that the judge "can't know if we'd gone all the way to trial what they would have given you".

The difficulty of making this assessment has also been acknowledged in a range of judicial comments in sentencing, particularly when other relevant mitigating factors are taken into account, such as remorse and providing assistance to the police/prosecutor. For example, in *R v Trezise*,[35] Coghlan J stated:

> I indicate that had you not pleaded guilty to this offence, I would have imposed a sentence of ten years with a non-parole period of six years. That calculation is extremely difficult because there are so many other factors that come into the process of sentencing you for this offending.

In *R v Davis*,[36] Coghlan J likewise maintained:

> I am obliged to state what sentence I would have imposed had you not pleaded guilty. Your case, and those of its kind, prove extremely difficult ones in which to make that assessment because at the conclusion of a trial, many of the features which influence this plea would be absent.

The difficulty factor was similarly noted by King J, who described the task as "almost impossible" in *R v Spark*,[37] while Kaye J acknowledged in both *R v Watson*[38] and *DPP v Meulenbrock*[39] that providing the s 6AAA was "a difficult task"[40] and "particularly difficult to comply with"[41] because the guilty pleas in both cases were "inextricably connected"[42] to other mitigating factors. Accordingly, one suggestion in this study from Judge07M was that the statement would be more effective "the other way around". He explained:

> We should be able to say, you've pleaded not guilty, this is what you're getting. But if you'd pleaded guilty, this is what I would have given you. I would have given you a significant benefit. You've got to wear it now. That would have a much stronger impact and be more reflective of what the sentence would have been.

As the following excerpt from the roundtable transcript demonstrates, many stakeholder participants were opposed to the s 6AAA statement:

Defence30M:	Well I think you should eliminate 6AAA.
Defence28M:	So do I.
Defence30M:	It's meaningless really.
Defence27M:	It's worse than meaningless.
Q:	*Why is it worse than meaningless?*
Defence28M:	Because no one believes it.

Judge15M: Yeah, everyone knows it's nonsense. You haven't got a clue what you would've done if they'd pleaded not guilty.

Defence28M: It's true.

Despite the majority of the interview and roundtable participants considering the s 6AAA statement to be ineffective, some participants did point to the benefit it provides in making judges reflect on the sentences they are imposing. As Judge03M maintained:

> It probably has a benefit for judges in thinking about the penalty that would have been imposed if there'd been a trial. I think it's a protective device for judges, because you have to think then about, if this person had not pleaded guilty what they would have received. I think it probably has a sort of an aspect of mental discipline, forcing judges to reduce a sentence in acknowledgment of the guilty plea.

Judge02MR similarly noted that, on occasion, "I've put the sentence on, I've then gone to do [s] 6AAA and I've thought, well, no actually, I wouldn't have given him this, so I've readjusted everything. It's normally down, because you can't inflate a [s] 6AAA". In this regard, the statement can be seen as a positive initiative in ensuring that the sentence does include a discount in recognition of the efficiency gained through a guilty plea. Judge16F also reflected on this benefit at the roundtable, claiming:

> For me it is actually an exercise in intellectual honesty because when I do my [s] 6AAA thinking, and if I look at it and think I wouldn't have given that much if the person had pleaded not guilty and been found guilty, then I have to, and I do, reduce the sentence that I'm giving for the guilty plea. … I've been surprised at the number of times that doing that analysis has made me reduce the sentence that I'm going to give on plea.

This comment however was responded to by Defence28M as follows: "well, judge, I think you are a rare person to do that because the others tend not to, well at least I don't think they do".

While the artificiality of the s 6AAA statement was highlighted by most participants, the value of having the discount articulated by the sentencing judge or magistrate was acknowledged by a number of participants as a way to provide transparency and "peace of mind [to defendants] … so they realise what would have happened had they not pleaded guilty" (Defence07M). This view was also expressed by Judge16F at the roundtable, who maintained that "[s] 6AAA has made an enormous difference in achieving an effect of transparency". Defence14FR claimed that the statement "makes the client feel better. I think it's really helpful when the court says that sort of thing, particularly ones where the client has made a difficult decision. … I think that that's helpful to the client". Participants noted that the benefits of articulating the discount are particularly evident and "really effective" (Defence18M) in cases involving a co-defendant, where one of the defendants has pleaded guilty. As Defence18M maintained:

> When you have co-accused, some that are trying to go to trial and others that are not, you might have a judge say, I'm giving you five, but I would have given you eight. The co-accused's then thinking, oh shit, I'd better jump on board now.

Defence02F similarly claimed:

> If the court has already sentenced a co-accused and has then announced the [s] 6AAA in relation to the co-accused and says, oh, if you hadn't pleaded guilty this is what you'd be getting and then your client is then charged with the same offence a year on and you're telling the client, look, this is what the co-accused got, the judge gave him this, it can be helpful to get the risk of the trial across.

In addition to the statement being "helpful" for defendants, Defence14FR pointed to it providing the defendant with "some control and some power" over the decision to plead guilty, so they can "walk away feeling like they've made some decisions versus having those things imposed upon them". She argued that this can result in "better outcomes in terms of compliance with CCOs and things like that" (Defence14FR). Defence16F also identified the statement as giving the defendant a distinct recognition of their decision to plead guilty, which she considered to be "very beneficial to the accused". She explained:

> I think it's very helpful, particularly if the judge or judicial officer then says to the client, it's really good that you pleaded guilty, for these reasons, and blah, blah, blah. And if you hadn't, this is what you would've got. I think for those clients, they then come out feeling like their decision has been vindicated, even if I know realistically it was a no-brainer, for them to feel, yes, I made the decision, is important … for them to feel, mmm wow, that was a good decision.

This identification of benefits by the defence practitioner participants raises an interesting question as to whether it might be of value to retain the statement, despite the legal community feeling that it is "artificial", in order to provide greater transparency and peace of mind to the defendant. In considering this benefit, Defence06MR said, "oh, it allows all of us to point to the client and go, you're so lucky, you know, you're so lucky, you would have gotten, you know, two years more than that if you had of [sic] had a contest and lost". However, he went on to argue that "the reality is that's not true, they wouldn't have got that at all … it's rubbish, it's an inflated figure". A similar discussion emerged at the roundtable:

Prosecutor13F:	I think it's useful in the sense that it does reinforce to the accused that they did do the right thing by pleading guilty –
Judge15M:	I've got no trouble with that, it's the use of it. Now if I've got an accused who I know has been giving the barrister or the defence a really hard time in terms of pleading and eventually pleads, I'll say, I've given you a six with a four, cross my fingers and say, but under [s] 6AAA I would've given you 12 and eight if you hadn't pleaded. They'd go home as happy as Larry.
Defence30M:	It [that statement] is false though?
Judge15M:	That's right.

The SAC (2015: 77) review of s 6AAA found that, overall, there was strong compliance by the courts in making the statement following a guilty plea, that it worked positively in tandem with other reforms to increase the proportion of guilty pleas entered at an early stage in proceedings, and that "there is no indication that defendants are under increasing pressure to plead guilty" because of the statement. The data in this study likewise suggest that the process has some benefits for defendants and defence practitioners in providing better recognition of the sentence discount provided for the defendant giving up their right to a contested trial/hearing, and it can also encourage the judge to reflect on the sentence they would have imposed. However, these benefits may be outweighed by the lack of confidence most participants had in the accuracy of the s 6AAA statements, and both the concerning number of judicial participants in this study and comments made by the judiciary in sentencing judgments, that attest to the artificial nature of the statement.

Notes

1. [2014] HCA 2.
2. *Sentencing Act 1991* (Vic) s 6AAA.
3. A mandatory sentence is one that must be imposed under any circumstances. A presumptive sentence is one that the court should impose unless there are exceptional circumstances that warrant a departure from the presumptive sentence.
4. *Sentencing Act 1991* (Vic) s 5A(4).
5. [2015] VSCA 303.

6. These provisions were entirely abolished by the *Sentencing Amendment (Sentencing Standards) Act 2017* (Vic). However, this Act introduced a number of presumptive sentences for a similar range of offences as the baseline provisions. In sentencing for a standard sentencing offence, a court is required to take the standard sentence into account as one of the factors in sentencing and must refer to the standard sentence in sentencing a defendant. It must also fix a set non-parole unless it is in the interests of justice not to do so. This sentencing regime is more flexible than the one it replaced but is still likely to be regarded by defence counsel and the courts as unnecessary restrictions on the sentencing discretion.
7. A court is not required to impose the mandatory sentence if "special reasons" exist, namely, that the defendant has assisted or has given an undertaking to assist law enforcement authorities, the defendant is between the ages of 18 and 21 at the time of the commission of the offence and proves that he or she has a particular psychosocial immaturity or impaired mental functioning, the court proposes to make a secure treatment order or residential treatment order in respect of the defendant or that there are substantial and compelling circumstances that justify doing so, *Sentencing Act 1991* (Vic) s 10A; see, generally, SAC (2012) (baseline sentencing report) and SAC (2011) (Statutory Minimum sentences for Gross Violence Offences). Since the introduction of these pieces of legislation, the Victorian Parliament has added a number of other offences and circumstances in which presumptive sentences will apply, including certain offences against emergency workers and custodial officers on duty—*Sentencing Act 1991* (Vic) s 10AA; offences of breaching supervision orders under the *Serious Sex Offenders (Detention and Supervision) Act 2009* (Vic), *Sentencing Act 1991* (Vic) s 10AB; the offence of aggravated home invasion, *Sentencing Act 1991* (Vic) s 10AC; and the offence of aggravated carjacking, *Sentencing Act 1991* (Vic) s 10AD.
8. The *Crimes Act 1958* (Vic) s 422(1) provides that an alternative verdict of intentionally causing serious injury in the absence of circumstances of gross violence is available to juries under *Crimes Act 1958* (Vic) s 16. In addition, a person may be persuaded to plead guilty to an offence of causing injury (not serious injury) as an alternative—a charge that does not carry a presumptive sentence.
9. The *Sentencing Act 1991* (Vic) s 5(2)(e) provides that in sentencing a judge must take into account whether the defendant pleaded guilty to the offence and, if so, the stage in the proceedings at which the defendant did so or indicated an intention to do so. Section 6AAA requires a court, if it has imposed a less severe sentence than it would otherwise have imposed because the defendant pleaded guilty, to state the sentence that it would have imposed but for the plea of guilty.
10. It may be reflective of Judge 15M's observation that in the five-year period to June 2016, there were fewer than ten sentences imposed for these offences.

11. The increasing use of such measures would indicate that, in the face of populist pressures, such a suggestion is unlikely to be heeded.
12. *Criminal Procedure Act 2009* (Vic) ss 207–209.
13. Ibid. s 208(2).
14. Ibid. s 208(3).
15. Ibid. s 208(5).
16. See also *R v Goodyear* [2005] EWCA 888.
17. *Criminal Procedure (Sentence Indication) Amendment Act 1992* (NSW).
18. *Criminal Procedure Act 2009* (Vic) s 60 (2).
19. The nature of such pressure in the context of plea negotiations specifically is discussed in more detail in Chap. 8. See also McConville and Marsh (2014).
20. [2008] VSCA 190.
21. [2014] HCA 2.
22. Ibid.
23. Ibid. [at 42].
24. *Barbaro v The Queen; Zirilli v The Queen* [2013] HCA Trans 296.
25. *Barbaro* [at 47].
26. [2014] VSCA 291.
27. [2015] 229 FCR 331.
28. *Sentencing Act 1991* (Vic) s 6AAA (1)(a).
29. Ibid. s 6AAA (1)(b).
30. [2011] VSC 73 [at 30].
31. [2013] VSC 298 [at 38].
32. [2014] VSC 19 [at 38].
33. [2014] VSC 270 [at 47].
34. [2015] VSC 474 [at 39].
35. [2009] VSC 520 [at 49].
36. [2010] VSC 274 [at 38].
37. [2009] VSC 374 [at 24].
38. [2009] VSC 403.
39. [2010] VSC 113.
40. [2009] VSC 403 [at 38].
41. *R v Meulenbrock* [2010] VSC 113 [at 22].
42. Ibid.

8

Pragmatic Justice: At Any Cost?

Plea negotiation has a long history (Baldwin and McConville 1977; Buckle and Buckle 1977; Maynard 1984; McConville et al. 1994; McConville and Mirsky 2005; McCoy 1990; Vogel 2007). However, modern plea negotiations take place in an ideologically different context than in earlier times. What has changed over recent years is the increasing emphasis on economy and efficiency which can be understood as a manifestation of the effect of the new public management on the criminal justice system. Embedded in this pragmatic, managerialist approach are the ideals of efficiency, effectiveness, economy and professionalism (Hodgson 2010; McEwan 2011). More than a set of organisational practices, managerialism is an ideologically driven process that employs management theories to introduce change to the delivery of public services (Freiberg 2005: 15). Indeed "the public interest now demands that the considerations of public time and cost be taken into account in judicial administration" (Freiberg 2005: 26). The *Legal Aid Act 1978* (Vic), s 4(a) states that one of the objectives of VLA is "to provide legal aid in the most effective, economic and efficient manner" and similarly, the *Public Prosecutions Act 1994* (Vic), s 24(b) provides that in the performance of his or her functions, the DPP must, as well as having regard to considerations of justice and fairness, have regard to "the need to conduct prosecutions in an effective, economic and efficient manner". Incentives and procedures such as sentence discounts, sentence indications, pre-trial hearings, sanctions for non-cooperation, pre-trial disclosures and legal aid funding structures have recently been created to encourage an early guilty plea in order to free up court time and resources.

A. Flynn, A. Freiberg, *Plea Negotiations*, Palgrave Socio-Legal Studies,
https://doi.org/10.1007/978-3-319-92630-8_8

Such incentives have been subject to criticism. For example, McConville and Marsh (2014: 251, emphasis in original) argue that the "co-operation of defendants and their lawyers was [once] sought through an indeterminate hidden threat that otherwise something worse *might* happen"; in the wake of incentives like sentence discounts, such cooperation is "secured by an open threat that something worse *would likely* happen" (McConville and Marsh 2014: 251, emphasis in original). More broadly, McConville and Marsh (2014) argue that this pragmatic, managerial approach contrasts squarely with the traditional aims of the adversarial system, thereby bringing the legitimacy of the court system into question. They explain that "the starting point of any intelligent engagement with criminal justice should not be its end-point [i.e. increased efficiency] but its foundational principle, namely: because the State is claiming a right to punish one of its citizens we require it to *justify that claim*" (McConville and Marsh 2014: 229, emphasis in original).

Restrictions to government-funded legal services are occurring in many jurisdictions with significant implications for procedural and substantive justice. One of the most common criticisms of plea negotiations is their potential to place undue pressure on defendants to plead guilty, particularly the most vulnerable defendants coming before the court (Baldwin and McConville 1979; Flynn 2011, 2016; Mack and Roach Anleu 2000; McConville 2002; McConville and Marsh 2014). Such pressures are exacerbated by continuing constraints on Legal Aid services, which limit access to lawyers at all stages of the legal process, and leave defendants to navigate complex legal processes without support (Flynn and Hodgson 2017a, b; Flynn et al. 2016; Newman 2013; Smith and Cape 2017). A report commissioned by VLA completed by the NSW Law and Justice Foundation sets out some of these problems in relation to the Victorian Magistrates' Court:

> In June, we released an independent review of our adult criminal law services in the Magistrates' Court. The review, by the Law and Justice Foundation of New South Wales, painted a stark picture of this important public service. Put simply, there are unsustainably high levels of demand in the courts due to the cumulative impact of additional police, changes to sentencing and bail laws, increased drug use and increased family violence reporting. As a result, the Magistrates' Court jurisdiction is on the brink of crisis and, in some courts, the crisis is already occurring. The system is struggling with the current demand let alone the additional future pressure thousands of extra police will bring. (VLA 2017: 10)

Over recent years there has been a dramatic increase in unrepresented defendants attempting to engage in plea negotiations, particularly in the lower courts, raising a number of concerns around power and justice. This outcome also creates additional resourcing pressures within the system. As Flynn and Hodgson (2017a: 11) observe, an increase in unrepresented defendants is likely to increase "the use of court resources and costs, and decrease services and access to justice for already vulnerable and marginalised groups". In England and Wales, McConville and Marsh (2014: 224) similarly argue that this outcome is "generating enormous costs, displacing them from one part of the system to another and doubtless increasing overall expenditure".

Further to an increase in unrepresented defendants, there has been a notable increase in defendants presenting with some degree of mental impairment (and associated high levels of alcohol and drug use), pleading guilty. Understandably, concerns around resourcing the legal system and the tension between efficient outcomes and undue pressure to resolve matters are further heightened in these cases. This chapter examines the prevalence and implications of resourcing restrictions in the context of negotiated guilty pleas, with a specific focus on unrepresented defendants and defendants presenting with mental health concerns.

Pressured Guilty Pleas

Baldwin and McConville (1979: vi) have argued:

> The guilty plea system transforms criminal justice from one which seeks to determine whether the State has reliably sustained its burden of proof to another which seeks to determine whether the defendant, irrespective of guilt or innocence, is able to resist the pressure to plead.

While this statement may have been reflective of the experience in England and Wales in the late 1970s, based on the perspectives presented in this study, similar concerns are not evident in the Victorian context, at least to this degree. A number of participants did however identify the types of pressures that a defendant may experience in the negotiation process. As Judge11F maintained:

> People can be encouraged to plead guilty to a lesser charge or to a charge to get a lesser penalty to avoid going to jail [or] to avoid a conviction against their name, a non-conviction outcome, because they can't afford a defence, because they're being leant on by other people who are perhaps taking a rap for someone else. People can plead guilty for wrong reasons and their will can be overborne. The plea negotiation may operate to divert some people who have a proper

> defence and should be – or in fact not just have a proper defence but are objectively ultimately not guilty – from being able to properly exercise their rights [to a trial] because of a fear that they won't be accepted or the risk that there's not enough money or level of representation to properly defend them[selves].

Defence17F likewise claimed that there "is a pressure from the courts, pressure from magistrates and prosecutors to settle cases". Research has similarly found that defendants can face a number of potential pressures to engage in negotiations (Flynn 2011, 2016; McConville 2002). For example, Flynn (2016: 572) argues that a defendant may plead guilty to save "the cost of a trial, which is particularly burdensome when contrasted with the potential benefits of a plea-agreement that may reduce the conviction severity, and possibly the sentence imposed". In this study, Defence09F described it as "the system wearing them [the defendant] down". She commented, "I've had clients who have felt like they should plead because they've been offered a good deal. Clients who genuinely have defences and who shouldn't be pleading guilty, but they're worn down" (Defence09F). Defence02F similarly claimed, "our clients are so vulnerable … and sometimes, at the end of the day, you get this poor person who just goes, oh look, I'll plead guilty just to get rid of it. It's absolutely awful". Similar concerns were voiced in Euvrard and Leclerc's (2017: 525) Canadian study, where they found that situations like "pre-trial detention can be a source of coercion, particularly if there are lengthy procedural delays and eventual sentences can be expected to be fairly short". Judge13F also reflected on this "inherent danger" in plea negotiations:

> There's an inherent danger in plea bargaining that people who actually have a reasonable defence [and] then shouldn't have to wear a conviction, just find it all too difficult, expensive and onerous to run the defence. And so they end up, because they're offered some really light sentence [indication] that maybe doesn't involve custody, some sort of community [order] or something, they just think, oh, well, you know, I don't want to take the chance of getting a bad result in court so I'll plead guilty even though I'm not actually guilty. I think that's one of the dangers.

Judge05M identified the same issue, specifically in relation to mandatory sentencing regimes (such as those discussed in Chap. 7), where there is "the big danger that people put their hand up to stuff, for fear of going down on the bigger [charge]". This reflects the concerns raised by VLA (2016c: 7) in a submission to the SAC: "where matters resolve, the threat of a mandatory penalty may place undue pressure on a defendant to plead guilty to a lesser charge". This point was also made by Defence14FR, who claimed that, "for our clients, there can be too much pressure and too much inducement not to [plead guilty]". Defence08MR went further in describing the "drive to force people to plead guilty" as creating "unjustifiable pressures". He explained:

> The pressures are absolutely shocking, shocking! I mean it would only be, in my view, until, you know, the police minister or the Attorney-General, or a couple of judges, or until their family are in the court system for them to realise just how much pressure there is to get people to plead guilty even when they've got arguable defences.

While accepting that there are some pressures, most participants rejected the idea that defendants will plead guilty when they are not guilty (of something) as a result of such pressures. Judge07M, for example, claimed:

> In the Australian, Victorian experience, over a lengthy period of time, I don't think those criticisms are justified. I think the system and the way that things are negotiated are pretty robust. … If the people want a trial, they're getting one … they are not put under pressure. That's just not what happens.

Judge08M and Prosecutor07M similarly maintained that, in their long careers in the law, there have not been any instances where someone has pleaded guilty when they are not guilty, due to overwhelming pressure. As Judge08M observed, "I've never found that to be the case here after 30 years of running a criminal practice and now six years as a judge". And Prosecutor07M commented, "my own personal feeling is over the years, with my 40 years' experience, I don't think I've seen too many of those. There's been a few who you can sense are very reluctant about what they're doing, but that doesn't mean they're doing it [pleading guilty] because of pressures". In a similar vein, Prosecutor01F identified that "there have been some instances where people plead guilty due to some form of pressure, but they're pretty rare I think".

To date, there has been limited research into the number of defendants who pleaded guilty, only to later be acquitted, particularly in Australia. Examining the US experience, Flynn (2016: 573) draws on data from the *Innocence Project* (a public policy organisation dedicated to exonerating the wrongfully convicted), and the US *National Registry of Exonerations*, to demonstrate that there is some evidence supporting concerns that innocent people will sometimes plead guilty. She argues that in the US, 10 per cent ($n = 31$) of the 325 post-conviction DNA exonerations since 1989 involved a guilty plea, and 10 per cent ($n = 151$) of all legally acknowledged exonerated felony defendants between 1989 and 2013 ($n = 1428$) pleaded guilty (Flynn 2016:

573). Also in the US context, Gold et al. (2017: 1068) argue that the risk of an innocent person pleading guilty can occur because the "criminal system promotes settlements by empowering prosecutors to make the price of going to trial and risking conviction intolerably high for defendants". In Euvrard and Leclerc's (2017) study of 23 convicted defendants, 22 of whom had pleaded guilty to offences ranging from uttering threats and shoplifting, to dangerous driving, second-degree murder, drug production and drug trafficking, 11 of the defendants maintained that, despite their guilty plea, they were innocent of the crime with which they had been charged. As Martin—one of their participants—explained: "I pleaded guilty to something I did not do to get out. If you plead guilty, you get out immediately. Well, I wanted to get out! I was fed up, I wanted to get out!" Similar views were presented by Defence02F, who said that some defendants simply want to have "it over and done with and out of their lives" (Defence02F). Defence03F similarly commented, "people plead up to stuff all the time to just get it out of the way. That's a common catchcry". Defence14FR likewise claimed, "we've had clients where we've said, 'I will run this [trial], and they say, I don't want to keep doing it. I don't want to – I just want it over and done with, so they plead [guilty]". Judge05M similarly maintained, "I suspect that there are hundreds of people who plead guilty in the Magistrates' Court who would have beaten it if they'd fought it". Defence03F also argued that people "can be forced into [guilty] pleas where they just shouldn't be", and provided the following example of a matter in which she had been involved:

> I have an example of that. He was charged with [*drug offences*]. He was an … asylum seeker that for him being found guilty meant that he would sit in immigration detention indefinitely at [*a young age*]. And he'd been forced into a [guilty] plea. The lawyer had not been to see him. The brief that I got didn't have a mark on it. They [the defence lawyer] just said to him, no, this is overwhelming, you have to plead. And so he entered a [guilty] plea. Luckily that wasn't led at the trial I then did. It was a reasonably strong case, but for him everything was at stake, there was no detriment to him to running that trial and I guess this is why you have to understand your client's entire circumstances. Because, for him, whether he spent five years in jail and then the next ten in immigration detention or whether he missed out on his plea discount a little bit, it just didn't matter. And so [we] ran the trial and he got acquitted and … he's now making an application for a protection visa. And if he'd been found guilty there is absolutely no way that he would've ever, because you have to get invited by the minister to make the application, he would never have had that happen. So, I think that's the danger of putting too much focus and pressure on plea negotiations is there can be situations where people are really crunched into a plea that they just shouldn't be entering.

The majority of the participants who recognised that such situations do occur stressed that it was not "innocent" defendants who were pleading guilty; rather, it was defendants who had a "defensible" (Defence03F) or strong case with a high chance of "beating the charges" (Defence03F). As Defence03F observed, "there's definitely a danger of that, that things that are defensible ended up being pled to". Defence25MR similarly claimed that "someone enters a plea when they shouldn't have because it was the best that their lawyer could do for them and they just wanted it done, I expect that happens all the time, I know it probably does".

Research has generally shown that guilty people are more likely to plead guilty than innocent ones, though there is a danger that innocent defendants will plead guilty in some cases if the discount is sufficiently large (Redlich et al. 2017: 463). However, even in experimental settings, factually innocent people are less likely to plead guilty than guilty people (Redlich et al. 2017: 463). Gazal-Ayal and Tor (2012: 358) found that generally innocent people are reluctant to accept plea offers except in some very limited circumstances, such as when they recognise that conviction is very likely, when the plea concession is great and when they are facing the risk of the death penalty. Accordingly, Gazal-Ayal and Tor (2012: 339) argue that the dangers of wrongful conviction of the innocent due to plea negotiation are "less problematic than previously believed – maybe even socially beneficial". Supporting such research, several participants in this study expressed the view that defendants plead guilty due to the pressures they face in plea negotiations, but not necessarily when they are "completely innocent" (Defence02F).

Interestingly, where participants in this study did acknowledge the pressures to plead guilty, a common theme to emerge was that "sometimes the pressure's a good thing because they've got to face the reality" (Judge03M). In this vein, Defence22M maintained, "I think we're all too precious, we've got to make sure that the accused's got [a] right to a trial and we know we can't ever impede that, but sometimes they need a forceful hand". Defence21M offered a similar perspective: "look some people will plead guilty when they shouldn't. But it's not a real drawback. I mean, they are the only people that can assess their lives and weigh up the risks and benefits". Describing the pressures placed on defendants as "a forceful hand", a "good thing" and "not a real drawback" highlights some of the tensions that exist for defence practitioners in weighing up efficiency concerns and the reality of the law against their client's views. It also raises some concern for defendants coming before the law if their right to a contested trial is considered "arbitrary" by some legal stakeholders, regardless of the strength of their case.

Legal Aid Funding and the Unrepresented Defendant

Flynn (2016: 573) argues that the pressures that may be experienced by defendants in plea negotiations most extensively affect the (many) vulnerable people coming before the court. A policy advisory participant in her comparative analysis of plea negotiations in Victoria and the UK reflected on this concern, noting:

> There are [sic] such a high proportion of people who will go through the system who weren't functioning very well at the time they committed the crime and are not functioning any better by the time the case gets to court, and for that kind of client, pressure to plead is a real issue. (Policy Advisor B, Flynn 2011: 378)

This view is similarly reflected in Mack and Roach Anleu's (2000: 82) research, which found that those most likely to plead guilty in Australian summary courts were Indigenous people and defendants who would "not present well in court". A similar concern was raised by Judge11F in this study, who claimed, "the more vulnerable are more likely to be the victims of that [pressure to plead guilty]".

The pressures defendants face in plea negotiations and in the criminal justice system more generally are even more prevalent in light of continuing constraints on Legal Aid services which limit access to lawyers throughout the legal process, and leave defendants to navigate complex legal processes without adequate support (Flynn and Hodgson 2017a; Flynn et al. 2016). In this regard, a recognised safeguard for defendants in combatting pleading pressures is legal representation. This view is based on the idea that a lawyer will provide quality advice about a guilty plea which helps the defendant make a principled, informed and appropriate pleading decision. In practice, however, this safeguard is threatened given the very strict eligibility criteria for legally aided assistance, including means, merits and case assessments which have been a consequence of increasing budget restrictions and rising demand for legal services. A defendant's means assessment is based on their level of income, assets and whether the case is deemed to be appropriate. To be automatically eligible for legally aided assistance, a defendant's total income must be no more than $360 per week—$18,720 after tax per year (VLA 2016a). To be considered for eligibility, which requires that the defendant must contribute to the legal costs, they can earn between $364 and $434 per week—$18,928 to $22,568 per year (VLA 2016a). As Community Law Australia (2012: 7) argues, "due to chronic government underfunding, legal assistance services are forced to limit eligibility to people on very low incomes". In a recent report on access to justice in Australia, the Productivity Commission (2014: 30) likewise asserts that "it is not the case that people are 'too wealthy' to be eligible for legal assistance, but rather that they are not sufficiently impoverished". In other words, many people who need help, but cannot afford a lawyer, miss out. In Victoria, for example, this can be seen in policies implemented within VLA including that individuals facing summary criminal charges where imprisonment or detention order outcomes are unlikely are automatically deemed ineligible for legally aided assistance, regardless of their means (see Flynn and Hodgson 2017b).

Outside of Victoria, policy decisions regarding the timing of when a defendant is "entitled" to access legal representation have been identified as affecting the capacity for a lawyer to act as a safeguard. In the US context, Mulroy (2017: 215) claims that the Sixth Amendment right to counsel "attaches only after the initiation of criminal proceedings", the consequences of which, he claims, allows for "improper interrogations, lineups, and negotiations". In this regard, Gold et al. (2017: 1610) argue that in the US:

> Rather than facilitating settlements based on the crimes defendants committed and the strength of the evidence against them, the criminal system essentially allows prosecutors to choose the terms of settlement. Because prosecutors have so much leverage, defendants often find themselves unable to turn down even poor settlement terms and proceed to trial. As a result, the criminal system does not produce optimal outcomes.

While this degree of power imbalance was not represented in the views of the participants in this study, Defence28M commented on the guideline changes to legally aided assistance at the roundtable, noting how they have resulted in "quite serious offences that will attract a CCO" not being funded, but instead being left to duty lawyers[1] who assist only on the day. He explained:

> We will automatically get funding and assistance for someone who might've served ten jail terms already and they're looking at another short jail term on a conviction for what they're facing, but an 18-year-old with no or limited priors facing a really serious charge who's looking at a Community Correction Order may only be assisted by a duty lawyer that they've met on the day.

Concerns related to unrepresented defendants were flagged by several participants, including Defence15M, who suggested that a lack of representation often results in people "pleading guilty rather than trying to represent themselves in a summary hearing at the Magistrates' Court". He continued:

> There would be plenty of junior lawyers around who would be terrified by the concept of running a summary contested hearing, and they've got legal training and spent heaps of time in [the] Magistrates' Court. So what's an unrepresented person going to think? (Defence15M)

Defence05M similarly maintained that "unrepresented people can fall into a trap of pleading guilty". This situation was articulately summarised by Defence06MR, who claimed:

> We're in a situation where, unless someone's going to qualify for a grant of legal assistance, we're not supposed to really do anything apart from give them advice on the day, and most of the people who are appearing in court have limited skills and expertise, that's what the duty lawyer is there for. So days gone by where I could say, right okay, I'll appear for you; I'll go and speak to the prosecutor to see if I can negotiate down to this, that or the other, we don't have that opportunity anymore because of guidelines. … I think guilty plea rates are certainly going up, but I think people are pleading guilty to things that they shouldn't be pleading guilty to.

Participants pointed to the myriad of difficulties and "dangers" (Defence10FR) that arise for unrepresented defendants in attempting to engage in plea negotiations "because they are not equipped to negotiate on their own behalf" (Defence10FR). As Defence20M stated, "a defendant's ability, for example, to negotiate with a police prosecutor in a case conference would be extremely limited". Defence23M similarly maintained, "it is likely that the negotiations with the police, if they're acting by themselves, are going to be less successful". Defence13FR expanded on this:

> There is a risk of clients being pushed to negotiate matters that they don't really want to, by things like there being no Legal Aid funding to run that sort of matter and they know they can't afford a lawyer and they don't want to do it [run a hearing] themselves.

Numerous participants described problematic situations like the defendant unintentionally "giving away their defence, which is something the defendant doesn't have to disclose and it might be in their interests not to disclose, and this results in them failing to negotiate any kind of decent resolution" (Defence20M); or agreeing to plead guilty to something without fully understanding the consequences of that decision, "and attracting a conviction, for example, on something that might affect their future" (Defence05M; see also Spencer 2017).

Perhaps the most common concern identified by participants was the power imbalance that exists in any plea negotiation between an unrepresented defendant and a police prosecutor: "the [VLA] funding [changes] are all to the advantage of the prosecution and the disadvantage of the accused" (Defence01M). Judge06M similarly maintained:

> The VLA funding restrictions are a significant stain on the quality of justice that our system administers when people aren't given timely and appropriate advice and assistance and it's at the very point of negotiation where they need it most, because negotiations are only successful when the parties are on equal footing and there's no way an unrepresented accused person and a police prosecutor are anywhere near on a level footing in a Magistrates' Court.

Some participants were more cynical in their view of the police prosecutors in this instance, arguing that the prosecutors use this situation "to their advantage" (Defence08MR). Defence08MR claimed:

> A client on their own is more likely to just kind of take whatever and get it over and done with. … They're not going to be as au fait with like … they won't know – and even if they do know – they won't always have the capacity to do so in a really constructive way that they're going to do themselves huge favours. They will be very much overwhelmed by the process to be able to articulate what they really want to say.

While others were not critical of police prosecutors themselves, they stressed that having to "deal with a police prosecutor is not a good situation to be in" (Defence24M). Defence24M continued:

> You need that independent person to look after your interests because, unless you happen to be unrepresented and a lawyer, you're at a complete disadvantage. Now I accept that police prosecutors aren't lawyers, but most of them have got considerable court experience. They do get training on evidence and all this and that and all the rest of it, so an accused is in a very difficult situation, an undesirable situation, but unrepresented accused are a very big part of the system now unfortunately.

As flagged by Defence24M, recent restrictions on the types of matters that can be funded have led to increasing numbers of unrepresented defendants coming before the courts. In addition to the difficulties participants identified in relation to plea negotiations, the data suggest that another major outcome is that magistrates and prosecutors are becoming quasi-defence practitioners in order to assist unrepresented defendants. Reflecting on his own experiences in this situation, Judge02MR explained:

> If the system's to work, the defence part of it has to be equally supported by way of proper funding for Legal Aid. ... We're finding that we're dealing with more and more and more people unrepresented. With the more high-level offences and when people do not want to seek Legal Aid, I'm tending to ask them not to enter a plea and I'll give them a sentence indication to try to protect them. So now 'we' are becoming the defence practitioner and there's many cases lately where I've said, look, this is a diversion, so then I've got the police to say, yes, absolutely we're stepping in. But you're the judicial officer for that day, someone else is meant to be also protecting the interest of the accused. I would say most prosecutors act in good faith, but it is a difficult situation.

Prosecutor02FR also drew on her experiences of "having to summary case conference with self-represented accused", about which she spoke of having to be "really, really careful". She explained:

> It wouldn't surprise me that, as a result of the Legal Aid funding ... it will lead to some major issues when the accused gets to the bar table and says, oh yes but the prosecutor said I should plead guilty to this, and that's going to cause some major issues. ... It concerns me that one of my guys [prosecutors] will say or I will say something that's misconstrued and that they'll get to the bar table and say, yeah, but the prosecutor said for me to say that, and that's not what we said at all. (Prosecutor02FR)

Prosecutor09F likewise discussed these consequences of funding constraints on state-funded legal services:

> The issue is you have people with no court experience, or not a lot of court experience, and so they come for a summary case conference. ... You can't talk to them about legal issues. They don't understand the processes of the court. They don't understand the system of adjournments and getting further and better particulars from informants and adjournments for that. And they want to plead not guilty on the day and have a contested hearing on the day that they first arrive. It blows out the summary case conference in time because within our role, you can't give legal advice so you can't tell them what to do or what may happen or anything like that, so you have to be really careful in regards to the discussions that you have with them, and then the magistrates it takes a

longer time for them because they have to ensure that the accused at all times understands all of their options.

These concerns were also raised during the roundtable, with participants reflecting on the difficult situation which government changes to legal aid policies have placed prosecutors and magistrates in. Prosecutor11F observed:

It's really time consuming on a prosecutor, and they are having to be very, very careful that they're not giving legal advice, they're not legal practitioners and in the wake of the legislative changes of the Legal Profession Rules, they have to be very careful to not be giving legal advice because they're not able to and it can be really challenging when a person asks you for advice and they cannot get Legal Aid advice and they're asking the questions, what will happen if I plead guilty, what will happen if I don't? They will regularly say, what do you think I should do? And you have to tell them, that's not for me to tell you what you should do. It's really challenging for the prosecutors.

These comments raise a number of serious concerns relating to power imbalances, the potential for miscarriages of justice and the difficult position in which magistrates and particularly police prosecutors are placed in, having to ensure they do not overstep their roles or take advantage of the situation. As Defence18M maintained:

You have an under-resourced prosecuting service, you have an expectation that everyone goes to court to conduct summary case conferences, you have unrepresented accused, or under-represented accused. It's just stupid in my opinion. It is creating a product of injustice.

In the context of plea negotiations, again this raises questions about the defendant's ability to understand the implications of pleading guilty, and the potential for coerced or misunderstood guilty pleas being entered.

Participants also reflected on how restrictions on how VLA implement their policies have resulted in duty lawyers taking on representative roles for vulnerable defendants without pay to avoid a potential injustice occurring. As Defence10FR explained:

People who aren't eligible for assistance, we'll provide them with advice and then say, look, these are the issues, you go and have the chat with the prosecution yourself. Generally, I tend to make an assessment of a person and if I think they can't negotiate or they can't have that discussion, I might have the negotiation with the prosecutor, but then [I have to] send them into court on their own once it's resolved. So often, that's the approach I'll take, where if I'm on duty

> and there's complex issues that you can't expect your average person to be on top of, or the person is, you know, just not presenting particularly well, but is not eligible for formal assistance or a grant of aid, then I'll help out.

Defence19M also commented on assisting defendants with no legal grants, noting that "it's rubbish, because where's the time for that? You don't have the time for that, so it makes it much harder, but you can't just leave some of these people on their own".

The changing nature of the court process due to the increasing number of self-represented defendants was noted as adding immense delays to hearing lists and having "a massive negative effect on the whole system" (Judge05M), such as "a lot of unnecessary adjournments" (Judge04FR), which ironically reduces any of the savings the government may gain from reducing Legal Aid funding. As Flynn and Hodgson (2017b: 10–11) argue:

> Resource-driven decisions … are unlikely to result in the delivery of significant savings, because they fail to take into account the broader picture implications, such as higher levels of incarceration, fewer quality lawyers working in Legal Aid areas, increased numbers of self-represented defendants and litigants, and issues that might have been prevented by recourse to legal assistance being escalated to major problems requiring public resources.

Rebuli (2015: 20–1) likewise observes that:

> Reduction to legal assistance spending creates a false economy where the cost is transferred to other departments of government and the community. … Whilst the easily quantifiable savings achieved by cutting legal assistance funding may be attractive to governments in the short-term, a long-term and sustainable approach is required to ensure access to legal justice is not affected.

Mental Illness

The prevalence of mental illness within the criminal justice system has been the focus of much contemporary and historic research (see, e.g. Baldry et al. 2011; Flynn and Hodgson 2017a; Giddings 1998; Noone 2017; Noone and Tomsen 2006; Productivity Commission 2014; Spivakovsky 2014; Ulbrick et al. 2016). However, there has been limited discussion on these matters specifically in relation to plea negotiations. In view of the difficulties that persons who are not mentally disordered may have in understanding what a guilty plea entails, it is likely that mentally impaired persons will be less able to make a fully voluntary and comprehending decision to plead guilty (Redlich et al. 2017: 461). Indeed, studies indicate that defendants with "mental health and cognitive impairments are significantly less able and less likely to make knowing and voluntary decisions in comparison to non-disordered adults" (Redlich et al. 2017: 461). *The Queen v Pain*[2] provides an example of this, where the Court, while recognising that "certainly, it is not a case where there is no evidence upon which the applicant could have been convicted",[3] held that "the applicant's plea of guilty cannot be attributed to a genuine conscientious of guilt on his part because of his unrecognised intellectual disability".[4] The Court further stated that the defendant's "disability is a circumstance that so affects the integrity of the plea that he has entered that it would be a miscarriage of justice to hold the applicant to that plea. I am satisfied that the integrity of the applicant's plea of guilty is impugned".[5]

Perhaps not unsurprisingly, given that the empirical data in this study were based on VLA case files, a key finding was the extent of mental impairment among the offending sample, with evidence of mental impairment, including intellectual disability, in 60 per cent (n = 29) of cases in which the defendant's background was recorded (see Fig. 2.8).[6] The prevalence of mental impairment among those coming before the courts was not limited to the findings drawn from the de-identified case file data, but was also a significant issue identified by the interview participants. As Judge11F maintained, "a large, significant number of offenders have deprived upbringings, mental health problems, intellectual impairment, substance abuse problems which play a significant role in their offending behaviour". Judge10F similarly claimed, "I'm yet to see someone who doesn't get a diagnosis in a psych report, basically, that comes before this court". Defence05M described mental health as "the highest problem area", a comment supported by Defence09F, who suggested that "anywhere between 80 to 90 per cent of my clients have substantial mental health issues". A number of participants quoted different statistics to highlight the number of defendants with a mental illness. Judge01M maintained, "if we're right, if 22 to 25 per cent of people [in the general population] have got serious mental conditions … it's got to be a much higher figure amongst those who commit offences". Defence17F likewise stated, "a forensic nurse when I was first starting out told me that 99 per cent of offenders within the Magistrates' Court have got a personality disorder and I think that's probably true".

These views are supported by a recent report conducted by the Victorian Ombudsman (2014: 6), which found that 42 per cent of Victorian prisoners present with psychiatric risks, including mental health concerns. Indeed, it is now well established that there are significantly higher rates of psychiatric morbidity in Australian prison populations than exist in the wider community, a trend that is also consistent internationally (Ulbrick et al. 2016).

Participants also linked the high levels of alcohol and drug use among defendants with increased prevalence of mental illness. As Prosecutor01F observed, "the mental health issue is a real issue facing all of us. A very big issue induced sometimes by ice [and] marijuana. Marijuana is a huge factor in young, male adults". Problematically, many of the defence practitioners and judges described large numbers of defendants as "having problems" (Judge01M) and "being broken" (Judge05M):

> What's a nice way of saying they're hopeless? … They're hopeless. … And that's a lot of pressure on all of us because obviously we've got to look after these people, they're not going to make good decisions themselves, so we really are trying to act in their best interests. (Defence06MR)

Judge03M similarly maintained:

> Most accused people suffer from a trifecta of difficulties. They come from a broken family. The father has frequently left the home. The person, at an early age, has been brought up by a single mother often without any paternal support. Associated with that is poverty, homelessness or instability moving from school to school. Overlaid on that are drug, alcohol or mental health issues, or combinations of them. A third factor is chronic unemployment or under-employment. Those are the typical profile of people we see in the court.

These statements highlight a critical problem currently facing the criminal justice system in relation to how it can or should respond to the prevalence of mental illness. The extent of this issue was well summarised by Prosecutor07M, who described mental illness as a "daily diet" in the OPP:

> There's a whole spectrum of mental illness at a very low level of offending up to, you know, your Sean Prices[7] and Adrian Baileys.[8] At a very low level, I'm seeing a discussion at this table every day involving serious lack of capacity or mental illness of people who are carrying out pesky offending – you know, shoplifting … because the police don't know what to do with them. That's the problem. The Magistrates' Court currently has very limited powers. … They are indictable offences, but if you've got someone who has a mental capacity of a 12 year-old and has [some] sort of underlying mental illness and they're repeat shoplifters, pinching chocolate bars and things like that, the Magistrates' Court has got very limited ability to deal with them, so the police say, well this person, you know, we've got to control them in the public interest. … And the question for [the

DPP] is whether [it is] kick[ed] up to the County Court to get some form of supervision going. And we're quite rigorous on those. We do tend to deal with the ones that have violence. You know, if someone is escalating in their violence, you reach a point where you think. … Yeah, [it] needs some heavy-duty intervention. Another one is arson [and] … mental illness, and suddenly you're finding an escalation of conduct so that someone who has got a serious mental illness is lighting fires in the bush on a hot day and you're thinking, someone needs to be managed at something higher than Magistrates' Court level with that, but what can you do?

In line with Prosecutor07M's comment, participants similarly pointed to mental illness and impairment being a significant problem, with limited avenues available to respond within the criminal justice system. This view is supported by the findings of research conducted in the post-sentencing context which has found a lack of mental health beds in the system, a lack of appropriate programs within prison for cognitively impaired defendants, and prisons in general failing to meet the complex needs of defendants with a mental illness (Noone and Tomsen 2006; Redlich et al. 2017; Ulbrick et al. 2016).

In terms of plea negotiations specifically, many participants identified mental illness as adversely affecting negotiations, particularly when the defendant has a mental impairment (such as a cognitive impairment like intellectual disability) that is not recognised under the mental impairment defence. The strict remit of the *Crimes (Mental Impairment and Unfitness to Be Tried) Act 1997* (Vic) (CMIA) has meant that in practice, it can only be successfully relied on in very limited circumstances, approximately 1 per cent of the higher court cases processed each year (VLRC 2014: 15). This is consistent with the use of a mental impairment defence in other Australian jurisdictions (VLRC 2014: 15). This means that there may be some proportion of defendants who have a significantly reduced level of cognitive functioning, but who are not able to access a mental impairment defence. During the interviews, Defence09F provided the following example of a recent case involving a mentally impaired client who did not meet the CMIA remit:

I just finished a case this morning … a plea in the County Court for a client who is severely intellectually disabled. He's also schizophrenic and he has an acquired brain injury. His money is handled by estate trustees so he doesn't have disposable income and he'd go into restaurants, eat a meal, be unable to pay, pick up a butter knife from the table and say I want food or I want money and would be told, no, sit down, which he would do, and wait for police to come and that was classed as attempted armed robberies. … The treatment options or the sentencing options available for him are very limited and he has been in

> custody nearly a year. He's extremely institutionalised. I obviously obtained reports ... to consider whether or not you've got a defence of mental impairment or whether or not there are issues as to fitness to plead ... but to no avail.

In discussing mental illness in relation to plea negotiations, Defence03F claimed:

> I've got quite a few clients with reasonably significant intellectual disabilities at the moment, not to the point, they're not mentally impaired, they wouldn't meet a mental impairment defence [via the CMIA] ... but when it comes to any sort of complex reasoning they just don't understand and they are some of the most difficult to negotiate resolutions with, because they just go, no didn't do it. And trying to get them to that point to fully understand: (a) that the evidence is overwhelming if it is, but (b) what the implications for them are if they run a trial can be really difficult. And I think that that's something that I don't know that the courts fully comprehend, that they're not necessarily unfit to give instructions, but some of them you'd almost say you don't have a mental impairment defence, but whether you actually do really comprehend what is going on is another story.

Participants mentioned the numerous difficulties faced in trying to engage in plea negotiations when there is a mentally impaired defendant involved. Defence09F maintained that "mental health issues certainly do affect the kind of negotiations that you can undertake. It makes it difficult for them to understand what's going on and it also makes the sentencing dispositions that are available seem a lot less attractive". She continued, noting that "it's not as simple as just saying to a client, this is better for you in the long term and this is why. It's very difficult for people from backgrounds of disadvantage to understand" (Defence09F). Judge10F also spoke of such difficulties, insofar as often "there's no rationality behind decision-making" among those with a mental illness. Defence15M expanded on this, describing mentally impaired defendants as having "less capacity to engage in the [plea negotiation] process ... [and] it makes it much harder to engage in that process to get them to understand".

A common concern participants identified in this context revolved around trying to assure such defendants that the defence practitioner was independent of the prosecution and the police—something that could be difficult for them to comprehend. Defence13FR commented, "mental illness, intellectual disability, it's difficult to explain how the process works, how you talk to prosecutors and then come to an agreement". Defence09F further claimed:

> Depending on the level of disadvantage, it can be hard to try and explain to your client. A lot of the time clients think if you're speaking to the prosecution or you're speaking to the police, and particularly because they don't understand the process and that's understandable, it's confusing enough for practitioners, but there can be a misconception on their part that you're onside with the police or 'onside' with the prosecution, and you have to be at pains to explain to them, I'm not telling you to plead, I'm not on their side, but this is what I think is in your best interests. Trying to explain to them the whole way that an early plea of guilty counts as a discount, what you're likely to get further down the track if you continue on to a trial, that sort of thing, that's very difficult.

Defence17F also raised this concern, claiming that "a lot of our clients, they see us going and talking to the police, they think we're in with the police and not necessarily on their side. ... It's hard to help assuage some of that distrust [with mentally ill defendants] and [get them to] see that it's [the plea negotiation] supposed to be in their best interests".

Of course, these concerns are relevant for all defendants, but are heightened in cases involving mentally ill defendants, who may not have the capacity to understand the relationships that exist between the prosecution and defence and between counsel and the judiciary, as well as how they interact—which can often be in a jovial manner, or what McConville and Marsh (2014: 68) refer to as "the cosy relationship between barristers and judges (old-boy network)". This has been recognised in a range of research which suggests that representation may not protect a defendant against pleading pressures and that the requirement on defence practitioners to advise their clients "on the strength of the prosecution case and the dangers of pursuing a weak defence" (JUSTICE 1993: 11) may even increase such pressures, and result in them "inadvertently ... providing some inducement to the accused to plead guilty" (Freiberg and Seifman 2001: 64). In their study, Bottoms and McClean (1976) found that the most significant influence on the defendant's decision to enter a guilty plea was their lawyer's advice. McConville and Marsh (2014: 166) have observed within England and Wales that "historically, the duty of defence counsel was 'to get an acquittal if he can, whatever the merits of the case may be'", but in response to pragmatic-driven legal systems, they fear the defence has taken on a "*cooperative* role to work alongside the Prosecution towards the active 'management' and 'progression' of a case" (McConville and Marsh 2014: 198), emphasis in the original an outcome that historically may be considered "as inimical to the defence role" (McConville and Marsh 2014: 172).

There were four instances in the case file data where it appeared that the VLA solicitor started discussions with the OPP without instructions (or without final instructions) from the defendant. In each of these cases, the VLA solicitors made it clear to the prosecutor that they did not have instructions to make an offer, but were seeking an indication of what the OPP would accept so that they could take that information to their client for consideration. For example, in case 046-AL, the VLA solicitor asked the prosecution for its position on sentencing range so that they could inform their client of that in conference while taking instructions on whether to make a plea offer. These actions demonstrate how commonplace plea negotiations have become, so much so that the lawyer may commence discussions before even seeking instructions or discussing this option with their client. There are good reasons for this, for example, the practitioner may consider it appropriate in order to reduce the number of interactions for the client in circumstances where for some clients with mental health conditions, multiple interactions are counter-therapeutic. While there was only evidence of this occurring in four of the cases, it does flag some potential tensions between the defence practitioner acting as a safeguard and the pressures this type of information may put on a defendant, especially if this is the advice they receive as part of their first interaction with their representative.

The idea that the pressure placed on the defendant can be exacerbated by defence practitioners was also identified by Defence15MR, who explained that "some of our clients might be impaired because they've got an ABI or a mental illness or intellectual disability to such an extent that they have a lesser understanding of the nature of the case against them and they'll rely really heavily on our advice". Defence12FR likewise noted that, "if your client has a disability, you want to make sure that they're understanding what they're pleading guilty to and I'd be very wary of putting pressure on them in a situation to accept a negotiated outcome".

As discussed in the previous section, a major challenge for many defendants in the summary jurisdiction is an absence of representation. A number of participants identified this as even more problematic when the defendant has a mental illness and attempts to engage in plea negotiations with a police prosecutor. Judge06M maintained:

> In a negotiating environment, it's hopeless, because they [unrepresented defendants] don't know what levers they've got to exert to assert their negotiating in points. They just don't know what the law is, they don't know what the options are and if they've got a mental health issue, they're probably going to get involved in a bizarre conversation or an unhappy conversation with the cops.

Prosecutor04M likewise stated that plea negotiations are "a lot more difficult when you've got mental health concerns. There is a significant representation in the mention stream of people with some form of mental health [problem]. That makes negotiations quite difficult". In reflecting on the many serious concerns raised in the context of a person with a mental illness attempting to negotiate with a police prosecutor—such as the significant power imbalance, the potential for miscarriages of justice and the precarious position in which both the police prosecutor and magistrate are placed—Defence25MR and Judge06M summarised the issues by claiming that "any person who's not in the industry would struggle, whatever their background" (Defence25MR) and "it's very, very important that people have legal representation at that stage" (Judge06M).

The concerns addressed in this chapter are not new. Indeed, calls for increased funding for legal aid and better recognition of and responses to the prevalence of mental illness within the criminal justice system have been the focus of much contemporary and historic research (see, e.g. Baldry et al. 2011; Flynn and Hodgson 2017a; Giddings 1998; Noone 2017; Noone and Tomsen 2006; Productivity Commission 2014; Spivakovsky 2014; Ulbrick et al. 2016). However, in a similar vein to many studies of the criminal justice process, there has been limited discussion or debate on the effect of these matters in relation to plea negotiations. These findings have shed important light on several highly problematic situations that appear almost commonplace in the current economic climate, which has seen a push towards "DIY [do it yourself] justice" (Laster and Kornhauser 2017: 123). In the context of plea negotiations, such concerns are particularly heightened as there is an inherent power imbalance between a prosecutor and an unrepresented defendant (something significantly exacerbated by the presence of a mental illness) and because the outcomes of a guilty plea are potentially life changing, but not always initially obvious—for example, loss of licence, loss of employment or loss of custody (see also Spencer 2017). For these reasons, there is a need for further research to be conducted into the self-represented defendant's experiences with plea negotiations, following the model of the work conducted by Baldwin and McConville (1977, 1979) in England in the late 1970s. There is also a pressing need for research into the prevalence of mental impairment among defendants in the justice process, and how this plays out in relation to guilty pleas and plea negotiations.

Notes

1. Duty lawyers are lawyers from VLA who provide free legal information, advice and representation to clients. This includes duty lawyers working within the criminal law program, who service summary crimes in the Magistrates' Court and crimes in the Children's Court. In the 2016–17 financial year, duty lawyers provided 93,697 services (not all of these were criminal cases). As VLA (2017: 22) observe "duty lawyers do not represent everyone. We prioritise serious cases, including people who are in custody or at risk of going into custody and people who need intensive support".
2. [2016] VSC 532 (12 September 2016).
3. Ibid. [at 57].
4. Ibid.
5. Ibid.
6. VLA has an Independent Mental Health Advocacy Program funded by the Department of Health and Human Services, but this only provides support for those experiencing compulsory mental health treatment, not in criminal proceedings (VLA 2017: 20).
7. Among other offences, Sean Price murdered 17-year-old Masa Vukotic in 2015 and pleaded guilty to murder and a separate rape in 2016.
8. Among other offences, Adrian Bayley was convicted of the rape and murder of Jill Meagher in 2013.

9

Building Trust and Confidence in the Criminal Justice System

The criminal justice system aspires to be open, transparent and accountable to the public. As outlined in *Pun v The Queen*:

> Plea bargaining is peculiar to our adversarial system, unregulated by statute and wholly dependent upon prosecutorial discretion. … A negotiated outcome may, and often does, result in a plea to a less serious offence than could be established by the facts available to the prosecution. … While the *Public Prosecutions Act 1994* and *Victims' Charter Act 2006* do touch on the process, they neither define nor address it in any detailed or systematic fashion. [i]

Indeed, the courts and the key organisations involved in the criminal justice system in Victoria, including Victoria Police, VLA and the OPP, all recognise that transparency, integrity and accountability are key goals. The three criminal courts operating in Victoria state their aims as being to increase trust, to maintain or increase public confidence and to be seen to be transparent and accountable. The Supreme Court (2015: 14), for example, lists its purpose as being "to ensure equal access to justice; to ensure fairness, impartiality and independence in decision-making; to ensure processes are transparent, timely and certain; and to ensure accountability for the Court's use of public resources". The County Court (2015) likewise aims to ensure respect, integrity, fairness, timeliness and transparency, "which is achieved through open and reasoned decision-making and clear, understandable processes", and identifies "maintaining and reinforcing public trust and confidence in the court and the administration of justice" as a primary objective. VLA (2016b) declares two of its main purposes to be "encouraging a fair and transparent legal system", and striving to "make a positive difference to the community

A. Flynn, A. Freiberg, *Plea Negotiations*, Palgrave Socio-Legal Studies,
https://doi.org/10.1007/978-3-319-92630-8_9

through the justice system". The OPP (2016) aspires to act "with integrity … uphold public trust" and act "fairly … [to] promote an environment that is free from bias, favouritism and self-interest". In light of the above, it might be asked how these values fit with a system that embraces plea negotiations. As McConville and Marsh (2014: 221) observe, "while the 'general public' doubtless entertains certain misconceptions", regarding the trial being the main way in which a case resolves, they argue that "it is disconcerting to find that one of these [misconceptions] is 'wide' and on such an important matter" (McConville and Marsh 2014: 211).

In each interview, time was set aside to discuss public perceptions and understandings of plea negotiations, and how these might affect people who come into contact with the criminal justice system, whether as a victim or a defendant. The majority of participants acknowledged that there is a significant problem with public (mis)understanding of plea negotiations and how this process operates in the Australian context, which is tainted by the fictionalised versions created by US television shows:

> The way in which plea negotiations are conducted has served the community well. … But I don't think the public knows and understands enough about it. They've got American pictures in mind. The more we can educate them about that, I think the more that they will actually come to respect what takes place. … If there is a lacuna here, or gap in the process, it's not that the system is not working, it's just that we are not communicating how the system works to the public. (Judge09M)

Participants highlighted a lack of public understanding of the importance of negotiations, how they work, and their benefits: "people need to understand how these things come about and why deals are done and what the purpose of it all is" (Judge05M). Defence03F explained:

> I think when people just hear that you've been charged with X and you've pleaded to Y and they think, well that seems like a slap on the wrist. They don't understand why sometimes things fall over because a complainant doesn't want to participate or because there just isn't evidential basis or the person was completely overcharged and should never have been charged with that offence. So, I think the more the public knows about all of it can only benefit us.

Defence09F similarly described the public view as "very black and white". She observed that:

> A lot of people don't understand that the legal system isn't as black and white as someone's guilty or not guilty. They don't understand that there's an area of grey

> which is plea resolutions which is, this may have happened but did it happen this way? Is this the appropriate charge? How is it going to resolve? I think probably that's not a bad thing for people to know that it's not as black and white as when someone goes to trial. (Defence09F)

When asked specifically whether it would be beneficial for the public to better understand plea negotiations, most participants expressed support for greater education of the public about plea negotiations in general, on the proviso that it did not involve sharing the "particularities" of individual cases: "I think that they do have a right to know. We pride ourselves on being an open system and people are allowed into court, and I think they should know the general framework of what happens" (Defence05M). Judge12M expressed a similar view, maintaining that:

> I think the more the public knows about all of our justice processes, the better. … Do they need to know what's happening in particular cases? No. … But is it appropriate for the public to know that these things happen? … If you're an interested member of the public how do I find out what this is all about? I think the answer to that is they should be able to.

Prosecutor01F likewise claimed, "it would be really helpful if they knew more. The public don't generally seem to know, unfortunately, much of what we do". This view was supported by Defence10FR, who stated that "there's no knowledge of the OPP. No one knows who the DPP is. No one has any idea what the OPP do. And it's surprising". She went on:

> There's a lot of ignorance in the community about what actually goes on at court. Because I think, for the public, what it boils down to is outcomes. But I think if there was greater understanding about getting to that outcome that would be better because I think for the public it's, what did he get? That's all that matters for them, but there's really no understanding of, why the prosecution might have accepted a plea offer to manslaughter instead of murder or why things happen the way they do. … Occasionally when I have clients come in here if they haven't been involved with the legal system before, they have no understanding of how it works. … There's a common perception that what the police tell them is what will happen and that, you know, when the police guarantee a CCO that that's what they're going to get and that, in fact, you're looking at a term of imprisonment. And in fact, it's the OPP that prosecute. And in fact, it's the Director that makes the decision about whether your matter proceeds. … That real lack of knowledge makes things really difficult for us and it takes a lot of effort and discussion to explain. (Defence10FR)

Defence17F also reflected on the benefits of providing more information to help defendants better understand the process:

> I think there's a bit of suspicion and distrust of the legal profession so the more transparency about the legal process there is, the better. The more well-educated consumers of legal services there are, the better. So that we're not having to totally inform them, do Legal Studies 101 every time you sit in front of a client.

Several participants linked more information with increased confidence in the criminal justice process overall. As Judge11F maintained, "a better-informed public is always better in terms of having real confidence in the criminal justice system or an understanding of how it works". Judge06M likewise observed that providing more information would "improve the confidence that the community has in the criminal justice system". He maintained:

> For people to understand that negotiations and settlements are appropriate and save a bundle, and that it's not 'plea bargaining', it's not the American kind of negotiation where they literally do settle the sentence before it goes to the judge. I think that's grossly inappropriate and I suspect that the community may think that that's what happens here because everybody watches too much television. I think a properly crafted communications strategy around these things is sensible and would be helpful to shed some light on the dark corners of ignorance. (Judge06M)

Defence12FR also claimed that people "have this impression that criminal lawyers either get people off on a technicality, or you're running trials all the time. But the vast majority of matters settle. And I think if people knew more about the process, then they might have more confidence in the system, and outcomes being the right outcomes".

While most participants felt that the public's understanding of plea negotiations is limited, some suggested that "the community aren't all that interested" (Defence06MR) and that "people that are actually interested in the law, they already know" (Defence06MR). Taking a slightly different view, Defence11M observed that "the public know about plea negotiations. I mean I'm not an expert on this area ... [but] I think that everyone knows that it takes place". A few participants stated that sufficient information is readily available for interested parties, and therefore there is little need to increase education or public awareness. As Judge08M explained:

> They are informed about the process of how the DPP approaches it, that's all in their Act or guidelines. And I'm sure you can go on the DPP website and find out all that stuff ... that's all already publicly available.

Prosecutor06M also pointed to the "Director's policy [being] online", so "people can access information in relation to it". During the roundtable, Prosecutor14M similarly identified that, "in terms of making those processes more widely transparent, [the OPP have] published policies on early resolution and giving reasons for decisions on [their] website, the information is there".

The OPP has gone to great lengths to ensure a degree of transparency in relation to its commitment to early resolutions by providing a clear statement on its website—a publicly accessible form of information—that it is "committed to pursuing appropriate early resolution of matters, which contributes significantly to the efficiency of the criminal justice system" (OPP 2016). And, as several participants noted, the relevant Director's Policies pertaining to early resolutions and guilty pleas are also available for the public online (as part of 50 Director's Policies published on the same webpage). Further to this information, the OPP has an excellent reputation for keeping victims informed and abreast of their case in matters involving plea negotiations (Flynn 2012). Indeed, a key focus of the new OPP structure is maintaining communication with victims. Since the introduction of s 9 of the *Victims' Charter Act 2006* (Vic), prosecutors in Victoria are required by statute to inform victims of any decision to modify the charge(s) being proceeded with or to accept a guilty plea to a lesser charge(s). Flynn's (2012: 95) study found that there have been some positive outcomes emerging for victims in relation to increased information and involvement in the case as a direct result of this legislation:

> By requiring that prosecutors not only inform, but explain to victims why certain decisions were made in their case, the limitations relating to victims feeling alienated and disempowered by the plea bargaining process can be reduced. Importantly, additional explanation of the plea bargain and why the decision was made to resolve the case can address the significant limitation that impacts on victim perceptions of being sold out, or the process failing to offer just outcomes.

At the roundtable, Judge16F reflected on the positive way in which the OPP was undertaking this role, noting that, "generally, there seems to be an acceptance, certainly at County Court level, by victims of the negotiated outcome as we see it reflected, for example, in the victim impact statement". She suggested that this was "a good illustration of how, with real information and people who are prepared to engage, you can get a better outcome". In discussing this role, Prosecutor14M noted at the roundtable:

> It is the case that we've invested far more time, training and focus on consulting with victims often face to face so that they understand the process, and in many

> more cases we're giving them reasons for the decision, and again that may be by letter but it's often, and more and more often, face to face, and it does have that effect of them understanding and accepting the process.

In considering ways to better inform the public about the process of plea negotiation, there is good reason to reflect on what might be learned from the OPP's engagement with victims.

In discussing the subject of how to better inform the public, participants identified a number of difficulties. As Judge10F explained, "these are complex issues so it's not going to work in a column inch grab or a 30-second sound bite". One of the primary difficulties identified related to how to improve the public's understanding of the broader benefits of resolutions. Prosecutor02FR maintained that "most people would probably be horrified that you sit there and you negotiate with defence the result of a traumatic experience in their life. How do you explain that?" Several participants spoke of the lack of legal knowledge as making it difficult to explain the process to members of the general public. As Prosecutor04M claimed, "it's not something that can always be adequately explained to the public because the public might not have a trained legal mind and understand why we've done what we've done". Defence19M similarly maintained that "the level of education that would be required to bring the public up to a level that they could comprehend why certain things happen. … I would be concerned that it [would] create more confusion rather than resolve confusion".

Participants reflected on this difficulty being compounded by the media, who many considered do not provide accurate or sufficient information on legal matters:

> The way that cases are reported in the media is quite shocking. We've got reporters reporting only the allegations and basically none of the mitigation and so the public is then left with the allegation and then the end result which doesn't in their opinion reflect what happened. (Defence02F)

Defence13F similarly observed, "the media, a lot of the time, paint it [plea negotiations] in quite a negative way …. [so] the public are aware that the process occurs, it's just the media doesn't explain how and why, which makes it [plea negotiations] look bad". Indeed, the way in which the media depict plea negotiations is important because, without any direct involvement in the process, most people only obtain information, gain knowledge and make sense of the criminal justice process via the media. As Judge01M maintained:

> There's nothing wrong with having the public made properly aware of what takes place. If we had competent journalists who actually understood and were legally qualified and could actually write sensibly … that would help a great deal.

As alluded to by Judge01M, the media are very powerful in that they can effectively construct the reality of the plea negotiation process, as opposed to simply reflecting that reality. Defence11M observed that "negotiations, unfortunately, are misunderstood through the media, which puts, in turn, political pressure on the government to introduce ridiculous measures like baseline sentencing". Defence27M similarly noted at the roundtable that "understanding is driven by the tabloid press and when we've got to dance to the tune of the tabloid press then we're in trouble".

Defence07M recognised a need to enhance the public's understanding of plea negotiations, but explained that the public's "case law references and text books are the *Herald Sun* and *The Age*,[1] which don't do justice to the legal community at all". He continued:

> I think the public should know a lot more about all of it and efforts are being made through various organisations but most of those organisations don't reach out to the ordinary Joe Blow in the public. … I think the public should know everything and all the intellectual energy that goes into all the processes but in a much more informed way than currently [occurs] and it's an indictment on our media. (Defence07M)

In addition to flagging ideas about how to better educate the public, a number of participants were wary that providing more information to the public could negatively affect the plea negotiation process, either by "constraining" (Defence03F) the flexibility of discussions or shedding light on a practice that "doesn't reflect what the public thinks happens" (Prosecutor02F), which may generate public dissatisfaction and result in some kind of restrictions being imposed on the process. As Defence11M claimed, this could lead to "knee-jerk reactions to uninformed public outcry". Defence03F also raised this concern:

> I wonder if that [more education] would then constrain us, and anything that would possibly put further constraints on how we go about that would trouble me I think. … My concern would be that some of the slightly unconventional things that we might engage in might then not happen.

Defence09F similarly maintained that more information could lead to public outrage:

> There could be the possibility that it would be misunderstood and people would think all these awful criminals are getting these really great deals cut for them and that shouldn't be happening and it's an abuse of the process and it's an abuse of the system and they should all go to jail, because that tends to be the common perception anyway.

Defence16F likewise claimed, "with education there's always a risk that the information can be misused. … They're already going to be saying, is all this closed shop?" Defence19M offered a similar view, arguing that "you could even inflame matters almost, [for example] because she won't give evidence against him, he gets a better deal? What? I think people would start getting really concerned about it". And Judge03M felt that enlightening the public "might have the opposite effect" to that intended. He explained:

> It might simply create outrage as to how a murder charge ultimately was pleaded down to a manslaughter charge. … Police lay every charge in the book. … Now you'd never be able to explain to the public that that's the way in which charges are initially laid. That people get 30 charges and the expectation is that someone will plead to two or three. (Judge03M)

In line with these concerns, some participants suggested that it was not worth educating the public on plea negotiations, as they "are not going to be able to understand it anyway" (Defence06MR) and "probably don't need to" (Defence11M). Defence11M went on:

> Should or do they need to [understand]? … People are hypercritical of the justice system, whilst being ignorant of the justice system, and that finds its way into the papers and it finds its way across the population generally. Are you going to be able to stop that criticism by educating? Probably not. … I don't think education, in real terms, will assist. I don't think you'll find utility in education.

Several participants argued that not only was there no value in providing information on plea negotiations to the public but also that "it's not any of the public's business" (Judge08M). As Defence09F observed, "people outside the legal system don't need that much understanding of it". Defence01M went further than this, asserting that plea negotiations are "none of anyone's business"; and, despite recognising that the public may be a party to the negotiations as the body whom the state is representing—"a party to negotiations might be the state, an individual or both"—he maintained that providing information on plea negotiations to the public was "stupid … it's idiotic".

Judge08M also questioned: "what's it got to do with the public?", while Defence03F asked, "should you actually educate all of those people who have no idea about our system entirely?"

These comments raise a range of important questions about the plea negotiation process. They highlight the existence of a legal profession that views non-lawyers as outsiders. Some of the views expressed above are also in conflict with the aims of the justice system as outlined at the beginning of this chapter: to ensure transparency, integrity and accountability. Further to this, referring to the "unconventional things" (Defence03F) that can occur in negotiations, recognising that discussions are a "closed shop" (Defence16F), and suggesting that the public may get "really concerned" (Defence19M) or even "outrage[d]" (Judge03M), simply by being provided with information on the nature of plea negotiations, all imply that there is something untoward about this practice, despite its clear benefits and widespread use. These comments also touch on the issues raised in Chap. 6 in relation to family violence cases, where negotiations are considered to be at odds with the public interest and a less appropriate way to dispose of a case than a contested hearing or trial.

The views expressed by these participants also contrast with studies that suggest that, when the public are given more information, they have increased confidence in the justice system overall and that the "level of public knowledge of crime and criminal justice" is significantly improved (Freiberg 2003: 228). Indeed, much research indicates that providing more information to the public about the roles of those involved in the legal system, including "what they are doing, and why they are doing it, [will] … reduce the likelihood that people will perceive a gulf between their expectations of the criminal justice system and the reality" (SAC 2006: 23). Research also shows that providing the public with increased information reduces their levels of punitiveness (Lovegrove 2007; SAC 2006; Warner et al. 2011). For example, in examining 698 juror reactions to the sentences imposed in the trials in which they were involved, Warner et al. (2011) found that 90 per cent agreed that the sentence delivered was "very" or "fairly" appropriate, and 52 per cent chose a more lenient sentence than the one imposed by the judge. Likewise, in their study of 987 jurors from 124 criminal trials in the County Court of Victoria, Warner et al. (2016) found that the views of judges and jurors are much more closely aligned than mass public opinion surveys would suggest. While the studies on these issues to date have generally been focused on sentencing, similar arguments could apply to plea negotiations. Indeed, one of the few studies that has examined plea negotiations and public perceptions directly was conducted by Stanley Cohen and Anthony Doob in Canada in the 1980s. In their study, they found that "most Canadians disapprove of the process of plea bargaining" (Cohen and Doob 1989: 108) and that "legitimacy of court processes and outcomes as perceived by the Canadian public are affected by the nature of the plea discussions that take place between Crown and defence counsel" (Cohen and Doob 1989: 108). While recognising that plea negotiations "may lower the public's confidence in the ability of the sentencing judge to deal with the case in a fair and appropriate manner", Cohen and Doob (1989: 108) went onto claim that "much of this detrimental impression is removed if the full explanation of the process is given in open court". This supports the research on sentencing that more information and transparency can lead to increased public confidence. Barry (2017) has proposed a similar need for transparency in order to gain public confidence in plea negotiation in New Zealand. He claims:

> Public confidence in a system so heavily centred on plea bargaining depends not just on the effectiveness of the checks on prosecutors' decision making, but on the transparency of that decision making. One without the other will either lead to unbridled prosecutorial power or a robust system of checks which the public does not understand. … This is not because as lawyers and legal policymakers we expect members of the public to regularly scrutinise negotiated plea bargains, but because a series of checks which are transparent create the right incentives for prosecutors to exercise their discretion in a way which is consistent with their overriding duty as an advocate for the wider public. (Barry 2017: 178)

Thus, there is a basis to suggest that if more information is provided to the public, they may not only be capable of understanding the process, but they may also recognise the value of plea negotiations.

In line with the views of many participants, we believe that it is important that more information be made available to the public on plea negotiations, and we have identified two ways in which this could be achieved: (1) an interactive plea negotiation scenario—"You be the Lawyer"—and (2) factsheets.

Interactive Plea Negotiation Scenario

Reflecting on the positive role the SAC[2] has had in increasing public understanding of the sentencing process, some participants suggested that similar avenues could be used to explain the plea negotiation process. As Judge12M maintained, "you can have information on websites and in the public domain. … The Sentencing Advisory Council would be the best entity to do this. … It's an excellent organisation, it has a public educational role, and it does that very well". Judge04FR similarly suggested, "like the stuff on the Sentencing Advisory Council, they did that, you know, *You be the Judge* sort of thing. You could have some things that are online that are interactive: what the prosecutor does, what the defence lawyer does".[3]

The idea of introducing an interactive plea negotiation scenario to help educate the public received some support among our stakeholder participants at the roundtable. Prosecutor13F, for example, thought that this would be effective "in regional areas, where people are more likely to participate and then to talk amongst each other". However, she noted that "in the metropolitan [area], it really is about the media so it may have less input" (Prosecutor13F). Judge15M suggested that it may be "too complicated" to implement successfully. He explained that:

> *You be the Judge* is easy because that's an open process in court which has clear sentencing principles. It's much harder I think to do something similar with negotiation because it's a personality-based system which is a phone call and an email. … It's often a nuanced conversation that's not as clear as sentencing principles.

While recognising these limitations, there may be some benefits in exploring the possibility of developing a set of interactive plea negotiation scenarios to assist defendants, victims and members of the general public to understand how cases can resolve and what types of outcomes may occur. The scenarios could shed light on the common forms of negotiation identified in this report, and, importantly, highlight the rationales behind negotiations. By using a specific set of scenarios, more detailed (hypothetical) information could be provided as to why matters might resolve—such as the evidentiary considerations, the public interest and the interests of the victim and the defendant. It could also provide more detailed information on how the charging process works, to counter some of the unrealistic expectations of victims and the public that arise when charges are first laid by the police, and to shed light on how options like rolled-up and representative counts operate. The scenarios could be made available in a public forum online, and, in that regard, they could provide a useful tool for defence practitioners to bring to the attention of their clients, and assist prosecutors in explaining the process to victims in a clear, concise manner. They could also be used as an education source in police training and within law schools.

Factsheets

The other potential means of providing more information to the public and those coming before the courts is the use of online and hardcopy factsheets. Defence13FR explained that "there could be information distributed, like pamphlets or something like that, just talking about the process and how it works and the role of victims and things like that". Providing a snapshot of the plea negotiation process, potential outcomes and the rationale behind the decisions made during negotiations was considered a positive step by many participants. As Judge12M maintained, "that's a simple thing to do and it gives it a sort of hook which is the current daily articulation in courts across Victoria". In describing what could be included in the factsheet, Judge12M suggested an overview that states:

> This is what happens, this is what the public sees, this is what the public doesn't see and these are the views of judicial officers and others about these processes. ... You could say, as a matter of public education, every day in courts in Victoria, prosecutors read agreed statements of facts, what has happened to reach an agreed statement of facts, is boom, boom, boom, boom, and that'd be your public information.

Defence17F offered a similar view on factsheets, recommending that they include information stating that:

> Your lawyer and the prosecutor will discuss the case in a summary case conference. This is how and what the process will look like. Your lawyer always acts on your instructions. There can be a bit of back and forth. It doesn't always have to be a one-way street. That kind of thing.

Defence17F considered factsheets to be a very useful tool for defence practitioners, as well as duty lawyers, victims and unrepresented defendants, maintaining that "factsheets are good and should be handed out to the parties when they turn up to court".

The factsheet could adopt a similar format to that created by the South Australian (SA) Department of Public Prosecutions which is used as a basis to inform victims of the plea negotiation process and their rights within it. Entitled, *Information Factsheet: Understanding Plea Negotiations*,[4] the document prepared by the Witness Assistant Services division of the SA Department of Public Prosecutions includes the following key headings:

- What is meant by the term plea negotiation?
- Are plea negotiations a usual part of criminal proceedings?

- Why do plea negotiations occur in criminal matters?
- Are there specific rules or guidelines prosecutors must follow?
- Why do plea negotiations occur?
- How do plea negotiations occur? Is there a standard process?
- Who is involved in the plea negotiation process?
- What things are prosecutors required to consider before accepting or rejecting a plea offer?
- Do I get to have a say?
- What is meant by the term disputed facts?
- Are there any benefits to accepting a plea offer?
- What if I am unhappy or dissatisfied with a decision made by the DPP?

Each heading includes two to three brief paragraphs responding to the questions. It is presented in a conversational tone and in language that is easy for those outside the legal community to comprehend. While offering a good insight into the negotiation process in SA, the factsheet is focused on victims' interests specifically within the process, and does not include information that would be of value for defendants, and possibly, interested members of the community. This study proposes that multiple factsheets could be created to address the different, relevant stakeholders within plea negotiations (e.g. defendants, victims and witnesses), as well as providing an overview for the general community.

At the roundtable, in discussing the potential benefits of a factsheet describing the plea negotiation process, Defence28M agreed that they could make the public "understand and come to accept negotiations a little bit more readily". However, he raised some concerns about who should produce the information, suggesting that if it were produced by VLA, it might be considered by the public to represent "a vested interest – a bit biased", and that it might be "a bit more objective" coming from the OPP.

There are limitations to either VLA or the OPP being responsible for preparing the factsheet. As Defence28M flagged, there is the potential for a factsheet to appear biased to the public if prepared by VLA, insofar as there is a dominant public perception that plea negotiations mean that the defendant is "getting away with something". In addition, if the factsheet were prepared by the OPP and VLA provided this to their clients, it might compound some of the issues identified in Chap. 8, in that some clients may interpret the information as a pressure to plead guilty or as evidence of the defence and prosecution working together "against" them. This concern can be seen in relation to the SA factsheet, which would not be an appropriate document to provide to defendants (although it is noted that providing information for defendants is not the purpose of that particular factsheet). However, a factsheet could be developed by an independent third party or body (such as the SAC or the Law Foundation). The factsheet should not be a "how to" guide for unrepresented defendants; rather, it should present important information on the process so that an individual reading it, even without any legal background, would better understand what may happen, why it may happen, what the discussions may involve and what the outcomes may be. It could be made available on relevant legal organisation and stakeholder websites, such as the Department of Justice, SAC, courts, OPP and VLA, and a hardcopy version could be made available at relevant legal organisations including the courts, VLA, the OPP, Victoria Police and private legal practices, as well as forwarded to media outlets to encourage better understanding and reporting of plea negotiations.

While the usefulness of both the factsheet and the interactive plea negotiation scenarios may be reliant to some extent upon interested members of the public accessing them, ensuring that more information on the process is available is an important step in shedding light on the common, but often misunderstood practice of plea negotiation. One needs only look at the role the SAC has had in this regard in relation to sentencing. Both options would also provide valuable, transparent information to anyone who has some level of involvement in the criminal justice system—an important outcome in light of this study's finding that plea negotiations are a common occurrence in Victoria.

Notes

1. A Victorian daily newspaper that tends to take a less populist approach than its main morning rival, the *Herald Sun*, one of the titles of the Murdoch press in Australia. It has a far lower circulation than the *Herald Sun*.
2. Emeritus Professor Freiberg is the Chair of the Victorian Sentencing Advisory Council.
3. *You be the Judge* is an interactive video presentation of various sentencing scenarios which requires the viewer to move through various stages of the sentencing process: see https://www.sentencingcouncil.vic.gov.au/you-be-the-judge/virtual-judge.
4. Available from http://www.dpp.sa.gov.au/wp-content/uploads/2016/12/2016-12-20-Plea-Negots-Fact-Sheet.pdf

10

Concluding Comments

Plea negotiations are a fact of life and have been so for many years. In Victoria, these negotiations are not of the kind depicted in fictionalised American television dramas in which plea deals are done and presented as fait accompli to the court, but are part of everyday legal life in a semi-adversarial criminal justice system. Indeed, the stark reality is that the majority of convictions in Western jurisdictions are the result of a guilty plea and a majority of those pleas are the product of some form of negotiation between the prosecution and defence. This chapter presents a summary of the main findings and contributions of this book to the field, including reform recommendations and the need for further research on plea negotiations.

This book has sought to contextualise plea negotiations within a rapidly changing justice system that is experiencing an increase in legal need, changes in public demands and expectations, and shifts in government-funded service provisions. In doing so, it has built on the pivotal works on plea negotiations to date, moving beyond examinations of plea negotiations primarily in relation to the negative effects on defendants and as a challenge to due process and rule of law ideals (see, e.g. Baldwin and McConville 1977, 1979; Buckle and Buckle 1977; Mack and Roach Anleu 1995; Mather 1979; Maynard 1984; McConville and Marsh 2014; McConville et al. 1994; McCoy 1990; Pizzi 1999; Utz 1978). In addition to providing a contemporary contribution to this field, this book expands upon existing work on access to justice, criminal justice procedure and sentencing by applying a specific focus on the prevalence, nature and effects of plea negotiations within these areas, presenting rich empirical data in a comprehensive study of plea negotiations, including criminal case file analysis, legal stakeholder interviews and consultations.

A. Flynn, A. Freiberg, *Plea Negotiations*, Palgrave Socio-Legal Studies,
https://doi.org/10.1007/978-3-319-92630-8_10

Guilty pleas and the associated negotiation processes have long been recognised as essential to the effective and economic functioning of the criminal justice system. Indeed, early resolution-focused pre-trial hearings have the potential to save resources and reduce the time taken to finalise cases, with benefits for defendants and victims alike. However, as this book has shown, there are a number of impediments that can hinder the occurrence of plea negotiations at an early stage. Perhaps most pertinent to this is the allocation of funding within government-funded legal services, such as VLA and Victoria Police, which continue to prioritise the trial, as opposed to properly resourcing pre-trial proceedings where plea negotiations can occur. As Flynn et al. (2016: 211–12) contend:

> For the majority of people arrested and facing possible criminal charges, the pre-trial process is thus likely to be the most significant, and possibly the only stage in their case. … [As such] an accused person's right to a fair trial should go beyond the trial, to include the pre-trial process and police custody, in line with established jurisprudence under art 6 of the *ECHR* [*European Convention on Human Rights*].

Using examples from the European Court of Human Rights, Flynn et al. (2016: 212–13) show how:

> Early access to legal aid standards has … been adopted in international instruments and bodies to recognise that the fairness of the trial will be affected by the fairness of the pre-trial. In this way, the *ECHR* provision goes beyond the narrow definitions of fair trial applied by the Australian courts.

For an effective plea negotiation process to operate, it is important that the funding structure of government-funded legal services, such as VLA, be reviewed and consideration be given to placing greater importance on the pre-trial process, thereby ensuring that adequate resources are available to staff to engage in these processes, particularly, in the Victorian context, the summary case conference. Similar consideration should be given to prosecuting bodies to ensure that additional funding and resources are allocated in order to provide a clear contact point for defence practitioners attempting to engage in early negotiations.

Linked to funding is the development of effective pre-trial processes that work to encourage early guilty pleas. One such mechanism utilised in some Australian jurisdictions, across New Zealand and in England and Wales are sentence indication schemes (ALRC 2006; New Zealand Law Reform

Commission 2005).[1] While sentence indication schemes appear to be operating effectively in summary jurisdictions, they remain under-utilised in the higher courts, even where available. One reason for this in Victoria is that judges are unable to provide an indication as to the range or quantum of the sentence that is likely to be imposed in addition to the type of sentence. In order to redress this, a pilot trial could be undertaken of an expanded version of the Victorian scheme to determine whether more, or earlier, guilty pleas are produced. If effective, this could become the norm across all Australian (and possibly international) jurisdictions.

Another clear impediment to plea negotiations and appropriate guilty pleas in the case study jurisdiction is the mandatory placement of defendants found guilty of a wide range of sex offences on the sex offenders' register, which is a possible (partial) explanation for the low rate of guilty pleas in sex offence cases. In light of research raising doubt about the effectiveness of sex offenders' registers, particularly that they fail to affect recidivism rates (Law Institute of Victoria [LIV] 2011a; Powell et al. 2014; Ombudsman Victoria 2011; Vess et al. 2011; VLRC 2012: 55; Freiberg et al. 2015: 212), there may be scope for consideration to be given to increasing judicial discretion as to who is to be placed on the registry, which may result in an increase in guilty pleas in sex offence matters, an outcome that is likely to offer benefits to victims by sparing them from the well-recognised traumatic and often re-victimising experience of a rape trial (Daly 2011; Flynn 2015; Henry et al. 2015).

As US research has shown, popular mandatory and presumptive sentencing regimes adversely affect plea negotiations by decreasing the number of guilty pleas to charges that carry a mandatory penalty and consequently increase the number of trials (Harris and Jesilow 2006; Rakoff 2014). They also place more power in the hands of prosecutors and move discretion from the courts to prosecution and defence counsel, usually in the shadow of the trial (McCoy 1990; Rakoff 2014; Simon 2007; see also Aas 2005; Flynn 2016; Soloenc 2015 for research outside the US). The use of these types of restrictive sentencing policies, while appealing to a law and order view of justice, is likely to have significantly negative outcomes for achieving justice in the courts. They are also likely to increase the (possibly unnecessary) investment in court time, in government-funded legal services and in prosecution resources. For these reasons, and in line with the arguments of US scholars, caution should be taken when considering the expansion of the use of such regimes, particularly in a system that values and requires plea negotiations to function.

Plea negotiations take many forms—far more than is generally understood. They include not only the withdrawal or substitution of charges but also negotiations over the use of rolled-up charges and representative counts where there are multiple possible charges, the facts that will be put before the courts, the appropriate jurisdiction in which the case should be determined, further investigations relating to the defendant or other defendants (or even those known to the defendant), the payment of costs and the relevance of time served in custody. Although negotiations around sentence outcomes in the Australian context are constrained by High Court decisions as to the appropriate role of the prosecution,[2] there is still scope for negotiation about submissions relating to the nature of the sanction that might be suitable. The High Court's decision in *Barbaro*[3] limited the Crown's ability to make submissions on sentencing. Prior to this case, negotiations relating to sentencing submissions were considered valuable by defence counsel, though less so by prosecuting authorities. As discussed in Chap. 7, the Queensland State Government has legislated to remove the restrictions on prosecutors making submissions by providing that a "sentencing submission, made by a party, means a submission stating the sentence, or range of sentences, the party considers appropriate for the court to impose".[4] It would be useful to monitor the effects of this legal change, as it could result in more effective plea negotiations across Australia, should the relevant state governments and DPPs accept the usefulness and practicality of such a change.

As well as the economic benefits of plea negotiations and guilty pleas to the criminal justice system, there are benefits to defendants and victims. However, these benefits must be weighed against the implicit dangers of permitting, or encouraging, defendants to forego their right to a trial and to challenge possibly arguable charges. They must also be weighed against potential disadvantages to victims, who may consider that their rights, interests or feelings have been overlooked or disregarded. One clear area where there is room to address both victim and defendant concerns in relation to plea negotiations is police charging practices, in particular, the practice of charging a defendant with multiple alternative offences. As discussed in Chap. 5, this is problematic because it may place prosecutors in a position of power over the defendant, while simultaneously creating false hope for victims, who may feel that their victimisation experience has been downgraded when charges are withdrawn. This is partly the product of the number of possibly overlapping or related offences that can be charged, and partly reflects "defensive" charging practices intended to ensure that no relevant offence is inadvertently omitted. This problem may be addressed by reforms to the structure of the criminal law and/or changes to the charging process. In England and Wales, the CPS is consulted by police before charging decisions are made in the first instance (in serious and complex cases) to ensure that only the most appropriate charges likely to proceed are listed on the indictment. There is scope for other jurisdictions, such as Victoria, to consider how a similar process may work in the Australian context.

In late 2016, the VLRC (2016: xxii, recommendation 9) recommended that the DPP be required to provide victims with written reasons for any decision to modify charges, not to proceed with some or all charges, or to accept a guilty plea to a lesser charge (in other words, when a plea negotiation occurs), unless the victim has expressed a wish not to be so informed. They also recommended (VLRC 2016: xxii, recommendation 10) that the *Victims' Charter Act 2006* (Vic) should be amended to:

(a) establish a right for victims to seek internal review of a decision by the DPP to discontinue a prosecution or to proceed with a guilty plea to lesser charges;
(b) require the DPP when informing the victim of these decisions and the reasons for these decisions to notify the victim of their right to seek internal review and the procedure for doing so.

A similar scheme, the *Victims' Right to Review* (VRR), operates in England and Wales.[5] This scheme enables victims to request a review of a prosecutor's decision not to proceed with charges, the outcome of which can include a reversal of that decision. However, it does not permit victims to request a review in cases where:

(i) A single charge or charges are discontinued, but another charge or charges relating to that victim continue (this includes where the matter is resolved through plea negotiation); and
(ii) A single charge or charges are substantially altered, but proceedings involving that victim continue (this similarly involves where a case resolves through plea negotiation) (Iliadis and Flynn forthcoming).

A number of concerns have been expressed in relation to the VRR, specifically regarding the independence of the review, the lack of readily available information about its operation and the eligibility limits of the scheme which prevent its use where the case has resolved through a plea negotiation (Iliadis and Flynn forthcoming; Kirchengast 2016; Shaw 2014).

The recommendation of the VLRC to introduce a victim's statutory right to request an independent review has some merit; however, it remains to be determined who would conduct the internal review and what the outcome of the review would be if the decision were deemed to be in error. For example, would the initial decision be overturned (as is possible in England and Wales), and/or would the victim be entitled to some form of compensation? There may be similar concerns to those identified by Iliadis and Flynn (forthcoming) in the context of the VRR scheme whereby "the absence of data surrounding pre-charge decision-making and the lack of perceived independence in the review process itself means the provision of transparent information about the decisions made in a case may still be problematic for some victims, even post the VRR's implementation". They continue:

> Having the review conducted 'in-house' reduces the level of accountability associated with the VRR, and not recording data on the prosecutor's pre-trial decision-making means we cannot fully understand whether out-dated stereotypes and problematic patterns still exist in relation to prosecutorial decision-making. (Iliadis and Flynn forthcoming)

Further recommendations were made by the Royal Commission into Institutional Responses to Child Sexual Abuse (2017a), whereby it was proposed that each Australian Department of Public Prosecutions or Office of the Director of Public Prosecutions (ODPP) should adopt a formalised internal complaints mechanism which would allow victims to seek an internal merits review of key decisions, particularly decisions that would result in a prosecution not being brought or being discontinued in relation to charges for alleged offending against that victim. The form of this internal merits review would be quite different from that applying in England and Wales under the VRR scheme—in particular, given the difference in size of the CPS compared with Australian ODPPs, and because decision-making in Australian ODPPs already occurs at a higher level of seniority than in the CPS.

While recognising some potential for these reforms to assist victims, a formalised complaints mechanism should not in any way reduce the priority given to consulting with victims in the course of preparing a prosecution, including obtaining their view in advance of making any recommendations on key decisions. Prioritisation should be given to early and ongoing open, honest and effective communications between victims and prosecutors, as opposed to relying primarily upon a later procedure to address or rectify any limitations.

Negotiations must also take into account the interests of the public at large, who may be sceptical, if not suspicious, of events that take place out of their sight, albeit that their gaze might only be directed at these processes when unusual cases are drawn to their attention by the media. The depiction of these cases by the media usually invites the conclusion that deals have been done that result in a defendant being dealt with far less severely than they deserve. It is evident that the operation of the criminal justice system is not well understood by the general public. Sentencing is the subject of many myths and misconceptions, and the plea negotiation process even more so. Providing the community with more information is one means of dispelling misconceptions held by the public. This book has proposed creating a better-informed community by the publishing of a factsheet about the plea negotiation process (somewhat similar to the *Information Factsheet: Understanding Plea Negotiations* (SA) available for victim in SA), produced by an independent body, such as the Law Foundation or SAC in the Victorian context, and creating a set of interactive plea negotiation scenarios, possibly along the lines of the SAC's *You be the Judge* online video presentation, to assist defendants, victims and members of the public to understand how cases can resolve and what types of outcomes may be produced. The benefits of increased public understanding and awareness of plea negotiations may also allow for the value of plea negotiations to be recognised and for greater preparedness for this type of outcome among victims and defendants who come before the court.

Due to budgetary and other resource considerations, this study did not interview defendants and victims. Across the study, however, it became evident that changes to the level of service provision by VLA have left a significant number of defendants without access to a legal representative. Similar concerns have been identified in international research (see, e.g. Flynn and Hodgson 2017a; McConville 2002; Redlich et al. 2016). Accordingly, there is a need for further research to be conducted into the self-represented defendant's experiences with plea negotiations and pleading guilty, as well as defendant experiences more generally, in line with the approach used in the ground-breaking research conducted by Baldwin and McConville (1977, 1979). The findings in this book also show that the need to address and respond to defendants with a mental illness and mental impairments is one of the most critical issues facing the criminal justice system at the present time. Further research is needed into the prevalence of mental impairment among defendants involved in the justice process, with a specific focus on defendants with mental illness who plead guilty and engage in plea negotiations (with or without legal representation). Qualitative interviews directly with such defendants would offer an important and rich source of data for this type of study. There is also scope to undertake interviews with victims—both primary and secondary—whose cases have resolved by plea negotiation. Such qualitative in-depth interview data would provide a mechanism to fully understand the lived experiences of victims within this process, something currently missing from the literature in this field.

This book has provided an empirical account of current plea negotiation practices in the case study jurisdiction of Victoria (Australia). It has documented the frequency of plea negotiations, identifying the different forms and outcomes of negotiation, discussing the varying processes involved in reaching an agreement and presenting observations about the process. The study found that the plea negotiation system is operated by dedicated professionals working within the context of significant financial constraint, which places them under considerable pressure to deal with large workloads quickly and efficiently. All parties—courts, prosecution, defence and police—work within legal, administrative and ethical guidelines. There are benefits and limitations of this method of case finalisation, all of which are made much more complex by the limited data, research and evidence of the process to those outside the legal community. Plea negotiations do not operate in a lawless silo. They play a valuable role in the legal realm. However, they ultimately remain a pragmatic form of somewhat mysterious justice in a largely unknown and imperfect criminal justice system.

Notes

1. See also *R v Goodyear* [2005] EWCA 888.
2. See, for example, *Barbaro v The Queen; Zirilli v The Queen* [2014] HCA 2.
3. [2014] HCA 2.
4. *Criminal Law (Domestic Violence) Amendment Act 2016* (Qld) amending s 15(3) of the *Penalties and Sentences Act 1992* (Qld).
5. *R v Christopher Killick* [2011] EWCA Crim 1608.

Appendix 1

Policy of the Director of Public Prosecutions for Victoria: Chapter 4—Resolution

Introduction

1. This chapter states the DPP's policy on resolution. It sets out:

- why resolution is important
- when resolution may occur
- when the solicitor must try to reach resolution
- when the solicitor must seek the views of the victim and informant about resolution
- that resolution requires CP or DPP approval
- that a consent mental impairment hearing requires CP or DPP approval
- that CP's and solicitors must not discuss resolution with an accused's legal representative unless conducting the prosecution
- that resolution must be reduced to writing
- principles concerning resolution with unrepresented accused

Why Is Resolution Important?

2. Resolution is necessary for the effective and efficient conduct of prosecutions. It relieves victims and witnesses of the burden of having to give evidence and may help victims put their experience behind them. It provides certainty of outcome and saves the community the cost of trials.

A. Flynn, A. Freiberg, *Plea Negotiations*, Palgrave Socio-Legal Studies,
https://doi.org/10.1007/978-3-319-92630-8

When May Resolution Occur?

3. Resolution may only occur if it is in the public interest. In determining whether a proposed resolution is in the public interest, regard must be had to:

   (a) whether there is a reasonable prospect of a conviction on each charge. If there is no reasonable prospect of a conviction on a charge, then that charge must not proceed. It is improper for such a charge to proceed to committal with a view to the prospects of conviction being reassessed after the committal
   (b) the strength of the evidence on each charge
   (c) any defences
   (d) the likelihood of an acquittal on any of the charges
   (e) whether the charge or charges to which the accused will plead guilty:

      (i) adequately reflect the accused's criminality
      (ii) allow for the imposition of an appropriate sentence
      (iii) allow for the making of all appropriate ancillary orders.

   (f) the views of the victims and the informant
   (g) the need to minimise inconvenience and stress to witnesses, particularly those who may find it onerous to give evidence
   (h) the likely length of a trial
   (i) any proceeds of crime implications. If a restraining order is in force, the solicitor must consult the POC solicitor prior to resolving the matter. Trade-offs between criminal charges and forfeiture of assets should not occur, because criminal and confiscation proceedings involve different considerations and standards of proof.

When Must the Solicitor Try to Reach Resolution?

4. The solicitor must try to reach resolution through discussion with the accused's solicitors at all stages of proceedings, namely:

   - prior to the committal mention;
   - prior to the committal;
   - prior to the initial directions hearing;
   - prior to the final directions hearing; and
   - prior to and during the trial.

When Must the Solicitor Seek the Views of the Victims and Informant About Resolution?

5. The solicitor must seek the victims' views prior to a resolution, unless the victim:

   - does not want to be contacted about the prosecution; or
   - cannot be contacted after reasonable attempts.

6. The solicitor must seek the informant's views prior to resolution.
7. The victims' and the informant's views must be taken into account in determining whether the resolution is in the public interest. However, the decision to resolve the prosecution ultimately rests with the CP or the DPP (as the case may be) and must be made in accordance with Paragraph 3 of this Chapter.
8. The solicitor must inform the victims and the informant of a resolution prior to the resolution being announced in court.

Resolution Requires CP or DPP Approval

9. Resolution requires a CP's or the DPP's approval, unless the resolution simply involves the withdrawal of lesser alternative charges. Prior to seeking a CP's or the DPP's approval, the solicitor should seek guidance from their Team Leader, a Legal Prosecution Specialist or the File Reviewer, as the solicitor considers appropriate. The identity of the CP who approves a resolution must not be revealed to the accused, the accused's legal representatives or any victims.
10. In any case involving a death, a resolution requires approval of the DPP, or in his absence, the CCP. In any other case, the solicitor may seek the DPP's approval of a resolution if the solicitor considers it appropriate. In any case in which the DPP is asked to approve a resolution, written advice must first be obtained from a CP.

Consent Mental Impairment Requires CP or DPP Approval

11. A matter may not proceed as a consent mental impairment hearing without a CP's approval. If the matter involves a death, the matter may not proceed as a consent mental impairment without the DPP's or the CCP's approval. Prior to seeking the DPP's approval, written advice must be obtained from a CP.

CPs and Solicitors Must Not Discuss Resolution with an Accused's Legal Representative Unless Conducting the Prosecution

12. A CP must not discuss resolution with an accused's legal representative unless the CP is briefed to appear in the prosecution. An OPP solicitor must not discuss resolution with an accused's legal representative unless the OPP solicitor has conduct of the prosecution.

Resolution Must Be Reduced to Writing

13. The solicitor must record any resolution in writing (letter or email) and ensure that the accused's legal representatives have a copy of that document before the resolution is acted upon. The document should confirm:

    - the charges to which the accused will plead guilty;
    - any agreed facts;
    - any agreement about sentencing submissions;
    - any agreement about ancillary orders; and
    - any other matter relevant to the accused's decision to plead guilty.

14. Plea offers made by the accused's legal representatives should be in writing. However, if the accused's legal representative makes a verbal plea offer, the solicitor must respond to it in writing.

Unrepresented Accused

15. Written plea offers made by an unrepresented accused may be considered and responded to in writing. However, the solicitor must not initiate resolution discussions with an unrepresented accused without the DPP's instructions.

Appendix 2

Methodology

The study builds on the small body of Australian- and Victorian-based research, with the key aims of increasing understanding of plea negotiations and the processes involved in reaching a plea agreement. Significantly, the study sought to provide an empirical account of, and document, the plea negotiation process and identify the key issues relating to this process.

The study was informed by a mixed qualitative and quantitative methodology, the aim of which was to ensure that the findings were reflective of the needs of those who are most affected by the outcomes of plea negotiations. The project had three research phases:

Phase 1	Phase 2	Phase 3
Documenting plea negotiation processes	Perspectives on plea negotiation processes	Policy consultations with key legal stakeholders

Phase One

One of the most significant contributions of this study was the ability to access and analyse de-identified case files which no Australian-based research has managed to do for this purpose. The files were collated from VLA's indictable and sexual offence divisions for cases resolved between 1 July 2012 and

A. Flynn, A. Freiberg, *Plea Negotiations*, Palgrave Socio-Legal Studies,
https://doi.org/10.1007/978-3-319-92630-8

30 June 2014. Files were randomly selected from the VLA list of case files that had been finalised by a guilty plea within this time period. This task was completed by the research coordinator at VLA. A major advantage of using only VLA de-identified case files over a designated timeframe is that the danger of file corruption or controlled data, whether by intention, self-case selection or because of the researcher effect, was avoided.

As would be expected of the clients of VLA, given the stringent means tests and qualification criteria, vulnerable and marginalised groups represent a significant proportion of defendants assisted by the organisation. Of the individuals granted Legal Aid assistance in the 2012–13 financial year:

- 30 per cent were from rural/regional Victoria.
- 22 per cent were from a culturally and linguistically diverse background (including 21 per cent of criminal law clients being born in non-English-speaking countries).
- 3 per cent identified as having an Aboriginal or Torres Strait Islander background.
- 19 per cent had a disability or mental illness.
- 13 per cent were under 19 years of age.
- 2 per cent identified as homeless.
- 55 per cent were receiving some type of government benefit or pension (VLA 2014a).

For the equivalent figures from 2013 to 2014:

- 30 per cent were from rural/regional Victoria.
- 22 per cent were from a culturally and linguistically diverse background (including 21 per cent of criminal law clients being born in non-English speaking countries).
- 3 per cent identified as having an Aboriginal or Torres Strait Islander background.
- 22 per cent had a disability or mental illness.
- 12 per cent were under 19 years of age.
- 3 per cent identified as homeless.
- 55 per cent were receiving some type of government benefit or pension (VLA 2015).

While these figures represent a significant portion of disadvantage, because VLA provides assistance in around 80 per cent of all criminal matters in Victoria (Flynn 2010b; PricewaterhouseCoopers 2008), it is likely that the case file data are representative of the main body of defendants who come before the courts in the case study jurisdiction.

The research was conducted under s 6(2)(b)[1] and s 7(1)(j) of the *Legal Aid Act 1978* (Vic).[2] Due to the obligations on VLA to maintain client confidentiality, the project necessitated that ways be found to ensure that confidentiality be protected while still allowing access to the information required. Before accessing the files for analysis purposes, each file needed to be de-identified of all identifying characteristics and personal information relating to the defendant and victim, such as names, addresses and contact information. The de-identification process was undertaken by three Monash law students—Monica Lee, Jake Collom and Jacob Uren—under the supervision of VLA staff. The students accessed the original files on-site at VLA, and after de-identifying photocopied versions of the files, the process of analysis was able to commence.

Upon accessing the de-identified files, the files were analysed using a *Case File Analysis Schedule*, prepared in consultation with VLA staff. Each file was assigned a pseudonym comprising three numbers and two letters—for example, 005-BD, and are referred to as such throughout this book. The analysis process involved extracting data on a systematic basis, searching the de-identified case files and recording relevant responses to each issue/question listed in the schedule. This enabled the collection of both quantitative and qualitative datasets with the assistance of NVivo 10 and Statistical Package for the Social Sciences (SPSS) software. The type of data collected included:

- the nature and number of the original charges and resolved charges, such as:
  - type/s (indictable offences: sexual, violence, drugs, property, homicide-related, fraud/deception, theft and related offences).
  - number of offences.
  - location of offence/s (rural, urban, regional).
  - victim characteristics—where known and not breaching confidentiality concerns (identification as Aboriginal and Torres Strait Islander, age, gender).
- timing as to:
  - when negotiations began.
  - when decisions were made.
  - when a guilty plea was entered.

- procedures:
  - who initiated negotiations.
  - how much "bargaining" was involved before an agreement was reached.
  - who was involved.
  - what factors informed the plea agreement.
  - how these factors were agreed upon.
- defendants' characteristics (where known and not breaching confidentiality concerns):
  - identification as Aboriginal and Torres Strait Islander.
  - immigration status.
  - age range.
  - prior convictions.
  - gender.
  - remand/bail status.
- defendants' involvement:
  - what level of involvement the defendant had in the negotiation process.
  - how s/he was kept informed throughout.
  - what discussions took place between the legal representative and the defendant regarding the benefits/implications of pleading guilty (where documented).
- whether a sentence indication was given.
- what sentence was imposed.
- what discount amount was applied as a result of the guilty plea.
- whether an appeal was lodged by the prosecution or defence and, if so, on what basis and what the outcome was.
- whether the overall outcome of the case was reflective of the negotiations.
- whether the outcome deviated (favourably/unfavourably) in any way from that intended (e.g. the judge imposed a sentence outside the estimated range discussed).

One disadvantage of relying only on VLA material is that the files were prepared for other purposes and, accordingly, the data relevant to the study were not always included or systematically recorded. The study was therefore reliant upon the information that the lawyers chose to record, and some content may have been subject to misinterpretation, given the potentially discretionary nature of note-taking. These potential limitations were able to be redressed in three key ways:

1. The establishment of an advisory group of two VLA staff members who provided guidance on the data collection process and answered any queries that arose during the analysis stage. Accordingly, any misunderstandings were able to be clarified with the advisory group.
2. Only de-identified case files prepared by in-house VLA lawyers were accessed. VLA has protocols in place that require particular materials to be recorded, including an "indictable offence process checklist", which advises VLA lawyers on what information should be recorded and which processes should be followed. This meant that there was less scope for discretionary note-taking and this ensured greater consistency in the content of the de-identified case files.
3. Interviews with VLA in-house lawyers were conducted as part of Phase Two, during which the researchers were able to identify and resolve queries regarding the way information was recorded in the de-identified case files.

It is recognised that having access to information related to only one side of a negotiation does not provide a complete picture of the processes involved. To gain a balanced understanding of the negotiation process, the Victorian DPP was approached for access to a selection of de-identified case files covering the same time period. Unfortunately, consent was not forthcoming. However, the DPP did consent to several of the OPP's employees and Crown prosecutors being interviewed. Ultimately five representatives of the OPP and/or Crown prosecutors, including the DPP himself, were interviewed.[3] Also interviewed were five judicial officers with a background in prosecutions, five police prosecutors, and, as discussed below, representatives of the OPP attended the stakeholder roundtable as part of Phase Three of the research. Feedback was also sought and received on a draft of the study's findings from the DPP and two senior OPP employees. Accordingly, the researchers were able to discuss the findings from the case file analysis and test their accuracy in relation to the views of a range of individuals with prosecutorial backgrounds, thereby compensating for limitations in obtaining data from only one side of the negotiation process.

Phase Two

A central element of the research design was consultation and engagement with those involved in plea negotiations. This approach provided the opportunity to present findings that are practical and sensitive to the constraints in which police and OPP prosecutors, defence practitioners and judicial officers operate, and which reflect the "real" processes involved in resolving a case by guilty plea.

In order to achieve this, 48 in-depth interviews were conducted with defence practitioners from VLA ($n = 12$) and private practice ($n = 13$), police prosecutors ($n = 5$), OPP solicitors and Crown prosecutors ($n = 5$) and judicial officers ($n = 13$) located in six locations in Victoria—the capital city, Melbourne, and regional and/or rural centres, Geelong, Shepparton, Gippsland, Ballarat and Dandenong. These locations were selected to capture a variety of experiences with plea negotiations across city, rural and regional environments. In doing so, it was possible to capture the nuances specific to different areas, and identify common approaches and themes across varying prosecution offices and defence practices.

The interviews were conducted between September 2015 and January 2016. They had an average duration of 65 minutes. The interviews were general in nature and not case specific. Participants were initially selected according to their location, availability and level of seniority and experience, in order to gather perspectives from a broader, more representative range of the participant groups. To conform with the ethical guidelines that governed this research, the participants were assigned pseudonyms which comprise the occupation (prosecutor, defence, judge), a randomly assigned sequential number based on the number of participants interviewed in their occupational group, the participant's gender (M/F) and whether they were from a rural or regional location (R). For example, a male prosecutor based in Melbourne might be assigned Prosecutor04M. A female magistrate from a rural or regional location might be assigned Judge09FR.

The interviews focused on the participants' experiences with early resolution processes. In addition, participants were presented with snapshot findings from the interim case file analysis to assess whether the patterns identified were reflective of participants' experiences with plea negotiations more generally. The interviews were broken into categories, exploring four key areas:

1. The different forms of negotiation
   - These open-ended questions asked participants to provide examples of their experiences with the forms of plea negotiation that had been identified in the de-identified case file analysis and to discuss other forms of plea negotiation not present in the de-identified case file data.
2. Defining and describing negotiated guilty pleas
   - These questions focused on understanding the processes involved in negotiations, such as how often negotiations occur, any obstacles to negotiations, the types of defendants involved in negotiations and which cases more or less readily resolve.

3. Early resolution processes
   - These questions focused on processes aimed at encouraging early guilty pleas (such as the contest mention and summary case conference processes, sentence indications and the vocalising of sentence discounts by the judge when imposing the sentence) and how they are operating; what, if any, affect these processes have on negotiations and/or outcomes; and how they could be improved, if at all. These questions were also intended to explore sentencing issues, such as mandatory and presumptive sentencing regimes and the plea negotiation process post the High Court's decision in *Barbaro*.[4]
4. Informing public understanding
   - These questions focused on how the participants felt plea negotiations were perceived outside the legal community (such as by the public, victims and defendants), whether the public need more information on negotiation processes, and negotiations are needed.

All interviews were audiotaped and transcribed verbatim. The transcripts were then systemically coded to allow for thematic analysis of the data. Once the key themes had been identified, it was possible to undertake a comparative analysis of the interview data according to factors such as occupation of the participant; rural-, regional- or city-based participant; and level of experience of participant in their current role. Importantly, it was also possible to examine the emerging themes in the interview data against the de-identified case file analysis to compare and contrast the findings.

Phase Three

The final phase involved holding a roundtable workshop with key legal and policy stakeholders to discuss the interim research findings from the case file and interview data.

The two-hour workshop was held at the Monash Law Chambers in Melbourne in May 2016 and was attended by 15 stakeholders, 8 of whom had been interview participants. At the workshop, 15 key themes that had emerged from the interview and case file data were identified, including:

1. Most common forms of negotiation.
2. Most common offences negotiated.
3. Offences more difficult to negotiate.
4. Obstacles to negotiations.

5. Frequency of negotiations.
6. Personalities.
7. Early resolution culture.
8. Educating the public.
9. *Barbaro*.[5]
10. Family violence.
11. Sentence discounts.[6]
12. Mental health.
13. Legal Aid.
14. Sentence indications.
15. Mandatory and presumptive sentencing regimes.

Participants were asked to respond to specific questions related to these themes and the interim findings, and to identify any flaws or issues of importance that did not appear in the findings—for example, whether the de-identified case files were representative of the types of offences most commonly negotiated. This allowed the accuracy of the findings to be tested against the views of those directly involved in plea negotiation processes.

The roundtable event was audiotaped and transcribed. This transcript was systemically coded to allow for thematic and comparative analysis of the data against the findings from Phases One and Two. Roundtable participants were assigned pseudonyms which include the participant's occupation, a randomly assigned sequential number (based on the number of participants in their occupational group, including interview and stakeholder participants) and gender (M/F). For example, a male defence practitioner attending the roundtable might be assigned Defence28M.

The roundtable provided the opportunity to test the interim findings and to address any inconsistencies across the data. For example, divergent views were expressed by defence practitioners and prosecutors on sentence recommendations forming part of negotiations. This enabled a comparison of these differences in opinion against the findings from the case file data and an exploration of these differences with members of the stakeholder group.

Finally, in February 2017, a draft copy of the findings was presented to VLA, Victoria Police and the OPP for feedback. This offered all parties an opportunity to discuss and reflect upon the key findings.

Phase Three provided a comprehensive framework to analyse the plea negotiation process in the case study jurisdiction, capturing insider perspectives to ensure that the data are truly representative of what happens in practice.

Glossary

Accused A person charged with a criminal offence.

Agreed summary of facts The facts describing the circumstances of the offending conduct which will inform the court's sentencing decision.

De-identified case files Details of 50 cases resolved by guilty plea (obtained from Victoria Legal Aid).

Combined or combination sentence A sentence order that includes a period of imprisonment and a Community Correction Order.

Committal hearing A pre-trial hearing in the Magistrates' Court (either an oral hearing or it proceeds on paper) for indictable offences to test whether the Crown's evidence is strong enough to support a conviction.

Committal mention A pre-trial hearing in the Magistrates' Court for indictable offences that provides a forum for parties to identify the key issues for resolution, as well as those matters not in dispute.

Community Correction Order (CCO) A sentencing order served in the community that may require the defendant to undertake a series of activities such as unpaid community work, rehabilitation or treatment and supervision. CCOs can also include curfews and various restrictions.

Crown prosecutors Crown prosecutors are responsible for conducting trials and advising on plea negotiations in serious offences heard in Victoria's County and Supreme Courts, and conducting criminal appeals in the County Court, the Court of Appeal and the High Court of Australia. Crown prosecutors are appointed by the Director of Public Prosecutions but are not direct employees of the Office of Public Prosecutions.

Director of Public Prosecutions (DPP) The head of Victoria's public prosecutions service, responsible for instituting, preparing and conducting serious criminal matters in the High Court, Supreme Court and the County Court on behalf of the Crown.

A. Flynn, A. Freiberg, *Plea Negotiations*, Palgrave Socio-Legal Studies,
https://doi.org/10.1007/978-3-319-92630-8

Guilty plea A guilty plea is an admission of the essential ingredients of the offence charged. When a defendant pleads guilty, they forego their right to a trial.

Higher courts For the purposes of this book, the higher courts refer to the County and Supreme Courts of Victoria.

Indictable offences Serious offences prosecuted in Victoria's higher courts before a judge and jury.

Indictable offences triable summarily Certain serious offences that can be prosecuted in the summary stream (the Magistrates' Court) subject to the consent of the defendant and agreement by the court.

Indictable stream For the purposes of this book, the indictable stream refers to cases proceeding in the County and Supreme Courts of Victoria.

Mandatory sentencing When Parliament sets a requirement that the courts sentence in a particular way, usually by specifying a fixed period of imprisonment or other sanctions that must be imposed if a defendant is found guilty (by trial or verdict) of specified offences.

Office of Public Prosecutions (OPP) The OPP is responsible for prosecuting serious offences in Victoria's County and Supreme Courts, and conducting criminal appeals in the County Court, the Court of Appeal and the High Court of Australia.

OPP solicitors Employees of the Office of Public Prosecutions responsible for instructing and preparing serious offences heard in Victoria's County and Supreme Courts, and assisting in criminal appeals conducted in the County Court, the Court of Appeal and the High Court of Australia.

Plea hearing A hearing conducted following a guilty finding (trial or plea) in which relevant material is presented to the judge or magistrate to inform the sentence.

Plea negotiations A discussion between the prosecution and defence regarding the possibility of negotiating the charge(s) (number, severity and structure), case facts and/or the Crown's sentencing submission in exchange for the defendant entering a guilty plea.

Police prosecutors Employees of Victoria Police responsible for prosecuting offences heard in the Magistrates' Court.

Presumptive sentencing When Parliament sets a requirement that the courts sentence in a particular way, usually by specifying a fixed period of imprisonment or other sanctions that must be imposed if a defendant is found guilty (by trial or verdict) of specified offences but which may be departed from in exceptional or special circumstances.

Representative counts A way of presenting a course of conduct on an indictment. It allows a defendant to plead guilty to one (or more) offence(s) that is representative of several offences against the same individual committed over a period of time.

Rolled-up counts A way of presenting offences against the same statutory provision that occurred on different occasions as one charge.

Section 6AAA A statement made by the court in sentencing—required under s 6AAA of the *Sentencing Act 1991* (Vic)—which outlines the sentence and non-parole period, if any, that it would have imposed on the defendant, but for their guilty plea.

Sentence indication An indication given by the court of the likely sentence a defendant would receive if they were to enter a guilty plea.

Sentencing Advisory Council (SAC) An independent statutory body created by the *Sentencing Act 1991* (Vic) in 2004 that provides information on sentencing, conducts research, disseminates information and advises the Attorney-General on sentencing issues.

Summary case conference A required out-of-court communication that occurs before a contested hearing in the Magistrates' Court between the prosecution and the defence, with the aim of managing the progression of the case smoothly, including resolving matters at an early stage.

Summary offences Offences prosecuted in the Magistrates' Court.

Summary stream For the purposes of this book, the summary stream refers to cases proceeding in the Magistrates' Court.

Suspended sentences A term of imprisonment that is suspended (i.e. not activated) wholly or in part for a specified period.

Victoria Legal Aid (VLA) An independent statutory body governed by the *Legal Aid Act 1978* (Vic) which provides free legal information and education to all Victorians, and provides legal advice and representation to people who meet certain eligibility criteria.

References

Cases

Barbaro v The Queen; Zirilli v The Queen [2014] HCA 2 (12 February 2014)
Boulton v The Queen [2014] VSCA 342 (22 December 2014)
Cameron v R (2002) 209 CLR 339
Director, Fair Work Building Industry Inspectorate v Construction, Forestry, Mining and Energy Union [2015] 229 FCR 331 (1 May 2015)
DPP v Carleton [2014] VSCA 19
DPP v Meulenbrock [2010] VSC 113
DPP v Perry; Perry v The Queen [2016] VSCA 152 (1 July 2016)
DPP v Walters (a pseudonym) [2015] VSCA 303
Dux v The Queen [2012] VSCA 118
Guariglia v The Queen [2010] VSCA 343 (16 December 2010)
Malvaso v R [1989] HCA 58
Matthews v The Queen; Vu v The Queen; Hashmi v The Queen [2014] VSCA 291
Pun v The Queen [2017] VSCA 219 (30 August 2017)
R v Andrew Foster Brown (1989) 17 NSWLR 472
R v Anthony-Cook 2016 SCC 43, [2016] 2 S.C.R. 204
R v Davis [2010] VSC 274 (17 June 2010)
R v Di Simoni [1981] HCA 31
R v Gallagher (1991) NSWLR 220
R v GAS; R v SJK (2004) 217 CLR 198
R v GAS & SJK [2004] HCA 22
R v Goodyear [2005] EWCA 888
R v Christopher Killick [2011] EWCA Crim 1608
R v MacNeil-Brown [2008] VSCA 190 (24 September 2008)
R v Nguyen [2011] VSC 73 (9 March 2011)

A. Flynn, A. Freiberg, *Plea Negotiations*, Palgrave Socio-Legal Studies,
https://doi.org/10.1007/978-3-319-92630-8

R v Spark [2009] VSC 374 (11 September 2009)
R v Thomson (2000) 49 NSWLR 383
R v Trezise [2009] VSC 520 (31 August 2009)
R v Verdins (2007) 16 VR 269
R v Watson [2009] VSC 403 (22 September 2009)
R v Williams [2007] VSC 490 (15 November 2007)
Talbot v The Queen; Dux v The Queen [2012] VSCA 118
The Queen v Bacak [2015] VSC 474 (4 September 2015)
The Queen v Deing [2014] VSC 270 (11 June 2014)
The Queen v Pain [2016] VSC 532 (12 September 2016)
The Queen v Prately [2013] VSC 298 (7 June 2013)
The Queen v JO [2009] NTCCA 129

Legislation and Policy

Cameron v R (2002) 209 CLR 339
Code for Crown Prosecutors 2013 (UK)
Confiscation Act 1997 (Vic)
Crimes Act 1914 (Cth)
Crimes Act 1958 (Vic)
Crimes Amendment (Gross Violence Offences) Act 2013 (Vic)
Crimes (Mental Impairment and Unfitness to Be Tried) Act 1997 (Vic)
Crimes (Sentencing Procedure) Act 1999 (NSW)
Criminal Law (Domestic Violence) Amendment Act 2016 (Qld)
Criminal Procedure Act 2009 (Vic)
Criminal Procedure (Sentence Indication) Amendment Act 1992 (NSW)
Crimes (Sentencing) Act 2005 (ACT)
Director's Guidance on Charging 2013 (UK)
Department of Public Prosecutions Director's Guidelines (Qld)
Department of Public Prosecutions Guidelines Charge Negotiations (NT)
Department of Public Prosecutions Prosecution Policy (ACT)
Director's Policy: Prosecutorial Discretion (Vic)
Director's Policy: Resolution (Vic)
Director's Policy: The Crown's Role on Plea and Sentence Hearings (Vic)
Federal Rules of Criminal Procedure (US)
Information Factsheet: Understanding Plea Negotiations (SA)
Legal Aid Act 1978 (Vic)
Magistrates' Court Act 1989 (Vic)
Magistrates' Court Practice Direction No. 7 of 2013 (Vic)
Office of the Director of Public Prosecutions Guideline 6 (NSW)
Office of the Director of Public Prosecutions Guideline 20, Charge Negotiation and Agreement: Agreed Statement of Facts: Form 1 (NSW)

Office of the Director of Public Prosecutions Prosecution Policy and Guidelines (Tas)
Penalties and Sentences Act 1992 (Qld)
Practice Note 1 of 1999 (Vic)
Practice Note 1 of 2004 (Vic)
Practice Note 5 of 2006 (Vic)
Prosecution Policy of the Commonwealth (Cth)
Prosecution Policy Guideline Number Two – Charge Bargaining (SA)
Public Prosecutions Act 1994 (Vic)
Sentencing Act 1991 (Vic)
Sentencing Amendment (Abolition of Suspended Sentences and Other Matters) Act 2013 (Vic)
Sentencing Amendment (Baseline Sentences) Act 2014 (Vic)
Sentencing Amendment (Community Corrections Reform) Act 2011 (Vic)
Sentencing Amendment (Sentencing Standards) Act 2017 (Vic)
Serious Sex Offenders (Detention and Supervision) Act 2009 (Vic)
Sex Offenders Registration Act 2004 (Vic)
Statement of Prosecution Policy and Guidelines (WA)
Summary Offences Act 1966 (Vic)
Supreme Court (Criminal Procedure) Rules 1998 (Vic)
Victims' Charter Act 2006 (Vic)
Victims' Right to Review (UK)
Victoria Police Summary Case Conference Service Charter

References

Aas, K F 2005, *Sentencing in the age of information: from Faust to Macintosh*, Routledge, London.

ABC 2010, 'Carl Williams bashed and killed in jail', *ABC*, 20 April. Available from: http://www.abc.net.au/news/2010-04-19/carl-williams-bashed-and-killed-in-jail/402028 [accessed 18 January 2016].

ABC 2015, 'Luke Batty inquest: perpetrators of family violence must be accountable says Rosie Batty', *ABC*, 28 September. Available from: http://www.abc.net.au/news/2015-09-28/rosie-batty-on-inquest-findings/6809906 [accessed 18 January 2016].

Access to Justice Advisory Committee 1994, *Access to justice: an action plan* (Sackville Report), National Library of Australia, Canberra.

Acker, J & Brody, D 2004, *Criminal procedure: a contemporary perspective* (2nd edn), Jones and Bartlett Publishers, Massachusetts.

Alschuler, A 1995, 'Plea bargaining and its history', in R Abel (ed.), *The law and society reader*, pp. 138–61, New York University Press, New York.

Ananian-Walsh, R & Gover, K (2015), 'Before the High Court – Commonwealth v Director, Fair Work Building Industry Inspectorate: the end of penalty agreements in civil pecuniary penalty schemes?', *Sydney Law Review*, vol. 37, pp. 417–35.

Ashworth, A 1994, *The criminal process: an evaluative study*, Clarendon Press, Oxford.

Ashworth, A 2010, *Sentencing and criminal justice* (5th edn), Cambridge University Press, New York.

Atkins, B & Pogrebin, M 1982, 'Discretionary decision-making in the administration of justice', in B Atkins & M Pogrebin (eds), *The invisible justice system: discretion and the law* (2nd edn), pp. 3–16, Anderson Publishing Co., Ohio.

Australian Bureau of Statistics [ABS] 2005, *Year book Australia, 2005*, ABS, Canberra. Available from: http://www.abs.gov.au/ausstats/abs@.nsf/0/190F18FC4E767C01CA256F7200832FA2?opendocument [accessed 18 January 2016].

Australian Law Reform Commission [ALRC] 2006, *Same crime, same time: sentencing of federal offenders* (Report #103, 2006).

Bagaric, M 2014, 'The need for legislative action to negate the impact of *Barbaro v The Queen*', *Criminal Law Journal*, vol. 38, no. 3, pp. 133–5.

Baldry, E, Dowse, L & Clarence, M 2011, 'People with mental and cognitive disabilities: pathways into prison', Background paper for the National Legal Aid conference, Darwin 2011, School of Social Sciences and International Studies, UNSW. Available from: https://www.mhdcd.unsw.edu.au/sites/www.mhdcd.unsw.edu.au/files/u18/pdf/MHDCDbackgroundOutlaws%20Conf1.pdf [accessed 18 January 2016].

Baldwin, J & McConville, M 1977, *Negotiated justice: pressures to plead guilty*, Martin Robertson, London.

Baldwin, J & McConville, M 1979, 'Plea bargaining and the research dilemma', *Law and Policy Quarterly*, vol. 1, pp. 223–33.

Barry, J 2017, 'Prosecutors – should we trust them? A cross-jurisdictional analysis of the effectiveness and transparency of limits on prosecutorial discretion during plea bargaining', *Te Wharenga – New Zealand Criminal Law Review*, vol. 152–313, pp. 154–179.

Bibas, S 2003, 'Bringing moral values into a flawed plea bargaining system', *Cornell Law Review*, vol. 88, pp. 1–11.

Bibas, S 2012, 'Incompetent plea bargaining and extrajudicial reforms', *Harvard Law Review*, vol. 126, p. 150.

Bishop, J 1989, *Prosecution without trial*, Butterworths, Sydney.

Blumberg, A 1967, *Criminal justice*, Quadrangle Books, Chicago.

Booth, T & Carrington, K 2007, 'A comparative analysis of the victim policies across the Anglo-speaking world', in S Walklate (ed.), *Handbook on victims and victimology*, pp. 280–415, Willan Publishing, Cullompton.

Bottoms, A & McClean, J 1976, *Defendants in the Criminal Process*, Routledge, London.

Boyd, W 1979, *The myth of plea bargaining, bureaucratic justice: police prosecutors and plea bargaining*, Sage Publications, Beverly Hills.

Breitel, C D 1960, 'Controls in criminal law enforcement', *University of Chicago Law Review*, vol. 27, no. 3, pp. 427–35.

Brereton, D & Willis, J 1990, *The committal in Australia*, Australian Institute of Judicial Administration, Canberra.

Brown, D 2014, 'The perverse effects of efficiency in criminal process', *Virginia Law Review*, vol. 100, pp. 183–223.

Buckle, S & Buckle, L 1977, *Bargaining for justice: case disposition and reform in the criminal courts*, Praeger Publishers, New York.

Buckman, R, Mohaghegh, T, Savage, H, Lim, A & Reynolds, H 2016, *Equal Justice Project: Plea Bargaining in our Justice System*. Available from: http://equaljusticeproject.co.nz/wp-content/uploads/2016/10/symposiumpaper.pdf [accessed 26 January 2018].

Bushway, S D, Redlich A D & Norris, R 2014, 'An explicit test of plea bargaining in the "shadow of the trial"', *Criminology*, vol. 52, no. 4, pp. 723–54.

Caldwell, H M 2011, 'Coercive plea bargaining: the unrecognized scourge of the justice system', *Catholic University Law Review*, vol. 61, no. 829.

Canadian Law Reform Commission 1989, *Plea discussions and agreements* (Working paper #60), Canadian Law Reform Commission, Canada.

Carol, A, Brook, B F, Harvey, D, Marcus, P, McEwan, J & Pomerance, R 2016, 'A comparative look at plea bargaining in Australia, Canada, England, New Zealand, and the United States', *William and Mary Law Review*, vol. 57, p. 1147.

Champion, J 2012, 'Plea offers and discontinuances: DPP speech', paper presented at the Law Institute of Victoria Annual Criminal Law Conference, Melbourne, 27 July. Available from: http://www.opp.vic.gov.au/getattachment/4391b56c-dfce-4569-ba7f-571999aa0388/DPP-speech-to-LIV-annual-criminal-law-conference.aspx [accessed 18 January 2016].

Champion, J 2014, 'The importance of plea agreements: our approach and accountability', paper presented at the 14th International Criminal Law Congress, Melbourne, 12 October. Available from: http://www.opp.vic.gov.au/getattachment/8eed0322-7d85-40b0-b593-d8ef97aaf41a/The-Importance-of-Plea-Agreements-Our-Approach-and.aspx [18 January 2016].

Chan, J & Barnes, L 1995, *The price of justice: lengthy criminal trials in Australia*, Hawkins Press, Sydney.

Chen, K 2013, 'Pressures to plead guilty. Factors affecting plea decisions in Hong Kong's magistrates' courts', *British Journal of Criminology*, vol. 53, no. 2, pp. 257–275.

Clark, P 1986, 'The public prosecutor and plea bargaining', *Australian Law Journal*, vol. 60, no. 4, pp. 199–214.

Cohen, S & Doob, A 1989, 'Public attitudes to plea bargaining', *Criminal Law Quarterly*, vol. 32, pp. 85–109.

College of Policing 2015, *Prosecution and case management: charging and case preparation*, Authorised Professional Practice, College of Policing. Available from: http://

www.app.college.police.uk/app-content/prosecution-and-case-management/charging-and-case-preparation/ [accessed 18 January 2016].

Community Law Australia 2012, 'Unaffordable and out of reach: the problem of access to the Australian legal system', Community Law Australia, report.

Cook, B, David, F & Grant, A 1999, *Victims' needs, victims' rights: policies and programs for victims of crime in Australia* (Research and Public Policy Series #19). Australian Institute of Criminology, Canberra.

Coopers & Lybrand 1989, *Review of the New South Wales Court System* (Coopers Lybrand Report, May 1989), Parliament of New South Wales, Sydney.

Corns, C 1997, *Anatomy of long criminal trials*, Australian Institute of Judicial Administration, Melbourne.

Corrections Victoria 2017, *Annual Prisoner Statistical Profile 2006-07-2015-16*, Corrections Victoria. Available from: http://www.corrections.vic.gov.au/utility/publications+manuals+and+statistics/annual+prisoner+statistical+profile+2006-07+to+2015-16 [accessed 8 February 2018].

County Court of Victoria 2015, *2014–15 annual report*, County Court, Victoria. Available from: https://www.countycourt.vic.gov.au/sites/default/files/County_Court_2014-2015_AR_web_02.pdf [accessed 18 January 2016].

County Court Victoria 2016, *Vision and values*, County Court, Victoria. Available from: https://www.countycourt.vic.gov.au/vision-and-values [accessed 18 January 2016].

Daly, K 2011, *Conventional and Innovative Responses to Sexual Violence*, ACSSA Issues, no. 12 Australian Centre for the Study of Sexual Assault, Melbourne.

Daudistel, H 1980, 'On the elimination of plea bargaining: the El Paso experiment', in W McDonald & J Cramer (eds), *Plea bargaining*, pp. 55–77, Lexington Books, Massachusetts.

Dixon, J 1996, 'Rights of victims', paper presented at Prosecuting Justice. Melbourne, Australia, 18–19 April, Australian Institute of Criminology, Canberra.

Douglass, J 1988, *Ethical issues in prosecution*, National College of Dallas, Houston University Law Centre, Texas.

Dubber, M D 1997, 'American plea bargains, German lay judges & the crisis of criminal procedure', *Stanford Law Review*, vol. 49, p. 547.

Dumont, H 1987, 'The need for sentencing reform in Canada', in H Dumont (ed.), *Sentencing*, pp. 175–213, Les' Editions Yvon Blair, Canada.

Euvrard, E & Leclerc, C 2017, 'Pre-trial detention and guilty pleas: Inducement or coercion', *Punishment and Society*, vol. 19, no. 5, pp. 525–542.

Feeley, M M 1979, *The process is the punishment: Handling cases in a lower criminal court*, Russell Sage Foundation, New York, NY.

Fionda, J 1995, *Public prosecutors and discretion: a comparative study*, Clarendon Press, Oxford.

Fitzgerald, O 1990, *The guilty plea and summary justice*, Carswell Publishing, Toronto, Canada.

Flatman, G & Bagaric, M 2001, 'The victim and the prosecutor', *Deakin University Law Review*, vol. 6, no. 1, pp. 238–54.

Flynn, A 2009, 'Sentence indications for indictable offences: increasing court efficiency at the expense of justice – a response to the Victorian legislation', *Australian and New Zealand Journal of Criminology*, vol. 42, no. 2, pp. 244–68.

Flynn, A 2010a, 'An indication of injustice: an analysis of the problems inherent to maintaining the sentence indication scheme in Victoria's Higher Courts', *Flinders Law Journal*, vol. 12, no. 2, pp. 41–78.

Flynn, A 2010b, 'Victoria's Legal Aid funding structure: hindering the ideals inherent to the pre-trial process', *Criminal Law Journal*, vol. 34, no. 1, pp. 48–63.

Flynn, A 2011, '"Fortunately we in Victoria are not in that UK situation": Australian and United Kingdom perspectives on plea bargaining reform', *Deakin Law Review*, vol. 16, no. 2, pp. 361–404.

Flynn, A 2012, 'Bargaining with justice: victims, plea bargaining and the Victims' Charter Act 2006 (Vic)', *Monash University Law Review*, vol. 37, no. 3, pp. 73–96.

Flynn, A 2015, 'Sexual violence and innovative responses to justice: Interrupting the recognisable narrative', in N Henry, A Powell & A Flynn (eds), *Rape Justice: Beyond the Criminal Law*, pp. 92–111, Palgrave Macmillan, Basingstoke.

Flynn, A 2016, 'Plea negotiations, prosecutors and discretion: an argument for legal reform', *Australian and New Zealand Journal of Criminology*, vol. 49, no. 4, pp. 564–82.

Flynn, A & Fitz-Gibbon, K 2011, 'Bargaining with defensive homicide: examining Victoria's secretive plea bargaining system post law reform', *Melbourne University Law Review*, vol. 35, no. 3, p. 905.

Flynn, A & Hodgson, J 2017a (eds) *Access to justice & legal aid: comparative perspectives on unmet legal needs*, Hart Publishing, Oxford.

Flynn, A & Hodgson, J 2017b, 'Access to justice and legal aid cuts: A mismatch of concepts in the contemporary Australian and British legal landscapes', in A Flynn & J Hodgson (eds), *Access to justice & legal aid: comparative perspectives on unmet legal needs*, pp. 1–22, Hart Publishing, Oxford.

Flynn, A, Hodgson, J, McCulloch, J & Naylor, B 2016, 'Legal aid and access to legal representation: redefining the right to a fair trial', *Melbourne University Law Review*, vol. 40, no. 1, pp. 207–39.

Fountain, E N & Woolard, J L 2017, 'How defense attorneys consult with juvenile clients about plea bargains', *Psychology, Public Policy, and Law*, doi: https://doi.org/10.1037/law0000158.

Fox, R & Deltondo, N 2015, *Victorian criminal procedure*, The Federation Press, New South Wales.

Frankel, M E 1982, 'Criminal sentences: law without order', in B Atkins & M Pogrebin (eds), *The invisible justice system: discretion and the law* (2nd edn), pp. 104–15, Anderson Publishing, Ohio.

Freedman, M. H 1975, *Lawyers' ethics in an adversary system*, Bobbs-Merrill, Indianapolis.

Freiberg, A 2003, 'The four pillars of justice: a review essay', *Australian and New Zealand Journal of Criminology*, vol. 36, no. 2, pp. 223–30.

Freiberg, A 2005, 'Managerialism in Australian criminal justice: RIP for KPIs?' *Monash University Law Review*, vol. 31, no. 1, pp. 12–36.

Freiberg, A 2014, *Fox and Freiberg's sentencing: state and federal law in Victoria* (3rd edn), Thomson Reuters, Sydney.

Freiberg, A, Donnelly, H & Gelb, K 2015, *Sentencing for child sexual abuse in institutional contexts*, Royal Commission into Institutional Responses to Child Sexual Abuse, Sydney.

Freiberg, A & Fox, R G 1987, 'Silence is not golden: the functions of prosecutors at sentencing in Victoria', *Law Institute Journal*, vol. 61, p. 554.

Freiberg, A & Murray, S 2012, 'Constitutional perspectives on sentencing: some challenging issues', *Criminal Law Journal*, vol. 36, no. 6, pp. 335–55.

Freiberg, A & Seifman, R 2001, 'Plea bargaining in Victoria: the role of counsel', *Criminal Law Journal*, vol. 25, no. 2, pp. 64–74.

Freiberg, A & Willis, J 2003, 'Sentence indication', *Criminal Law Journal*, vol. 27, pp. 246–59.

Freidman, L 1982, 'Discretion and public prosecution', in B Atkins, & M Pogrebin (eds), *The invisible justice system: discretion and the law* (2nd edn), pp. 69–74, Anderson Publishing, Ohio.

Gabbay, E 1973, *Discretion in criminal justice*, White Eagle Press, London.

Gazal-Ayal, O & Tor, A 2012, 'The innocence effect', *Duke Law Journal*, vol. 62, pp. 339–401.

Gerber, P 2003, 'Current issues: when is plea bargaining justified?', *Queensland University of Technology Law and Justice Journal*, vol. 13, pp. 1–9.

Gerstein, R 1981, 'Plea bargaining: an overview', in M Edwards & K Meyer (eds), *Settlement and plea bargaining: published for the association of trial lawyers America*, pp. 276–86, Association of Trial Lawyers America, National College of Advocacy, Washington.

Giddings, J 1998, *Legal aid in Victoria: at the crossroads again*, Fitzroy Legal Service, Melbourne.

Gold, R M, Hessick, C B & Hessick, F A 2017, 'Civilizing Criminal Settlements', *Boston University Law Review*, vol. 97, pp. 1607–1660.

Goldstein, A 1981, *The passive judiciary: prosecutorial discretion and the guilty plea*, Louisiana State University Press, Louisiana.

Graham, K 2014, 'Overcharging', *Ohio State Journal of Criminal Law*, vol. 11, pp. 701–24.

Hansard Parliamentary Debates 2007, 'Criminal Procedure Legislation Amendment Bill, Legislative Assembly', 6 December 2007, pp. 4348–50. Available from: https://www.parliament.nsw.gov.au/hansard/Pages/home.aspx?s=1 [accessed 18 January 2016].

Harris, J & Jesilow, P 2006, 'It's not the old ball game: three strikes and the courtroom workgroup', *Justice Quarterly*, vol. 17, pp. 185–203.

Harris, K 2003, 'Moving into the new millennium: towards a feminist vision of justice', in E McLaughlin, R Fergusson, G Hughes & L Westmarland (eds), *Restorative justice: critical issues*, pp. 31–49, Sage, London.

Henham, R 2001, *Sentence discounts and the criminal process*, Ashgate, London.

Henry, D 1992, 'Serious fraud, long trials and criminal justice', *Denning Law Journal*, vol. 7, pp. 75–92.

Henry, N, Powell, A & Flynn, A 2015 (eds) *Rape Justice: Beyond the Criminal Law*, Palgrave Macmillan, Basingstoke.

Heumann, M 1978, *Plea bargaining: the experiences of prosecutors, judges and defence attorneys*, University of Chicago Press, Chicago.

Heumann, M & Loftin, C 1995, 'Mandatory sentencing and the abolition of plea bargaining: the Michigan Felony Firearm Statute', in R Abel (ed.), *The law and society reader*, pp. 185–213, New York University Press, New York.

Hidden, P J 1990, 'The benefits of committal proceedings', *Current Issues in Criminal Justice*, vol. 2, no. 2, pp. 19–25.

Hill, I 1999, 'The Crimes (Criminal Trials) Act 1999', in Leo Cussen Institute (ed.), *Changes to criminal law*, pp. 2.1–2.12, Leo Cussen Institute, Melbourne.

Hodgson, J 2010, 'The future of adversarial criminal justice in 21st century Britain', *North Carolina Journal of International Law and Commercial Regulation*, vol. 35, no. 2, pp. 101–141.

Hogarth, J 1971, *Sentencing as a human process*, University of Toronto Press, Toronto.

House of Commons Justice Committee 2009, *The Crown Prosecution Service: gatekeeper of the criminal justice system – government response to the Committee's Ninth Report of Session 2008–09, Second Special Report of Session 2009–10*, House of Commons, The Stationary Office Limited, London.

Iliadis, M & Flynn, A, 'Providing a check on prosecutorial decision-making: an analysis of the Victims' Right to Review', article in progress.

Jamieson, P 2009, 'Sentence indication in the Supreme Court: a Victorian initiative', *Journal of Judicial Administration*, vol. 18, pp. 169–77.

Johns, R 2002, *Victims and plea bargaining: victims of crime – plea bargains, compensation, victim impact statements and support services briefing paper*. Available from: https://www.parliament.nsw.gov.au/researchpapers/Documents/victims-of-crime-plea-bargains-compensation-vict/10-02.pdf [accessed 18 January 2016].

Johnson, G & Edwards, A 2013, *Encouraging appropriate early guilty pleas: models for discussion*, Preliminary Submission, Consultation Paper 15, New South Wales Law Reform Commission, Sydney. Available from: http://www.lawreform.justice.nsw.gov.au/Documents/Completed-projects/2010-onwards/Early-gulity-pleas/Consultation-paper/cp15_2.pdf [accessed 28 February 2017].

JUSTICE 1993, *Negotiated justice: a closer look at the implications of plea bargains*, JUSTICE Publications, London.

Kellough, G & Wortley, S 2002, 'Remand for plea: Bail decisions and plea bargaining as commensurate decision', *British Journal of Criminology*, vol. 42, no. 1, pp. 186–210.

Kerstetter, W & Heinz, A 1979, *Pre-trial settlement conference: an evaluation*, United States Department of Justice, National Institute of Law Enforcement and Criminal Justice, Washington.

King, M, Freiberg, A, Batagol, B & Hyams, R 2014, *Non-adversarial justice*, The Federation Press, Sydney.

King, N & Wright, R 2016, 'The invisible revolution in plea bargaining: Managerial judging and judicial participation in negotiations', *Texas Law Review*, vol. 95, pp. 325–397.

Kirchengast, T 2016, 'Victims' rights and the right to review: a corollary of the victim's pre-trial rights to justice', *International Journal for Crime, Justice and Social Democracy*, vol. 5, no. 4, pp. 103–15.

Kirkwood, D, McKenzie, M & Tyson D 2013, 'Justice or judgment: the impact of Victorian homicide law reforms on responses to women who kill intimate partners', Domestic Violence Resource Centre Victoria (DVRCV)/Monash University, Discussion Paper 9.

Krauss, R 2009, 'The theory of prosecutorial discretion in federal law: origins and development', *Seton Hall Circuit Review*, vol. 6, no. 1, pp. 1–8.

Kutateladze, B L, Lawson, V Z & Andiloro, N R 2015, 'Does evidence really matter? An exploratory analysis of the role of evidence in plea bargaining in felony drug cases', *Law and Human Behaviour*, vol. 39, no. 5, pp. 431–442.

Laster, K & Kornhauser, R 2017, 'The rise of "DIY" law: implications for legal aid', in A Flynn & J Hodgson (eds), *Access to justice and legal aid: comparative perspectives on unmet legal need*, pp. 123–40, Hart Publishing, Oxford.

Law Council of Australia 2014, *Mandatory sentencing*, Policy Discussion Paper, Law Council of Australia, Canberra.

Law Institute of Victoria [LIV] 2011a, 'Sex Offenders Act needs review', *LIJ*, CEO's LIJ Articles. Available from: http://www.liv.asn.au/Practice-Resources/News-Centre/Ceo-s-Page/Sex-Offenders-Act-needs-review [accessed 18 January 2016].

Law Institute of Victoria [LIV] 2011b, *Mandatory minimum sentencing*, Submission to the Attorney-General, June 2011, LIV. Available from: https://www.liv.asn.au/getattachment/22c3c2c9-45a5-45c4-96e6-f0affdfe2ff8/mandatory-minimum-sentencing.aspx [accessed 18 January 2016].

Law Reform Commission of Western Australia 1999, *Review of the criminal and civil justice system in Western Australia: final report*. Available from: http://www.lrc.justice.wa.gov.au/P/project_92.aspx [accessed 18 January 2016].

Leivore, D 2004, *Prosecutorial decisions in adult sexual assault cases: An Australian study*, Office of the Status of Women, Canberra.

Louthan, W C 1985, 'The politics of discretionary justice among criminal justice agencies', in C F Pinkele & W C Louthan (eds), *Discretion, justice and democracy*, pp. 13–19, Iowa State University Press, Iowa.

Lovegrove, A 1997, *The framework of judicial sentencing*, Cambridge University Press, Cambridge.

Lovegrove, A 2007, 'Public opinion, sentencing and lenience: an empirical study involving judges consulting the community', *Criminal Law Review*, pp. 769–81.

Mack, K & Roach Anleu, S 1995, *Pleading guilty: issues and practices*, Australian Institute of Judicial Administration, Victoria.

Mack, K & Roach Anleu, S 2000, 'Choice, consent and autonomy in a guilty plea system', *Law in Context*, vol. 17, no. 1, pp. 75–92.

Mackenzie, G, Vincent, A & Zeleznikow, J 2015, 'Negotiating about charges and pleas: balancing interests and justice', *Group Decision and Negotiation*, vol. 24, no. 4, pp. 577–94.

Magistrates' Court of Victoria 2018, *CISP program*, Magistrates' Court of Victoria. Available from: https://www.magistratescourt.vic.gov.au/court-support-services/court-integrated-services-program-cisp [accessed 22 January 2018].

Mallet, S 2015, 'Judicial discretion in sentencing: a justice system that is no longer just?', Victoria University of Wellington Legal Research Paper, Student/Alumni Paper, no. 37, pp. 533–71.

Manikis, M 2012, 'Recognizing victims' role and rights during plea bargaining: a fair deal for victims of crime', *Criminal Law Quarterly*, vol. 58, no. 3–4, p. 411.

Mather, L 1979, *Plea bargaining or trial? The process of criminal case disposition*, Lexington Books, United States.

Maynard, D 1984, *Inside plea bargaining: the language of negotiation*, Plenum Press, New York.

McConville, M 1998, 'Plea bargaining: ethics and politics', *Journal of Law and Society*, vol. 23, pp. 562–87.

McConville, M 2002, 'Plea bargaining', in M McConville & G Wilson (eds), *The handbook of the criminal justice process*, pp. 353–79, Oxford University Press.

McConville, M 2007, 'Development of empirical research techniques and theory', in M McConville & W Hong Chui (eds), *Research Methods for Law*, pp. 207–29, Edinburgh University Press, Edinburgh.

McConville, M, Hodgson, J, Lee, B & Pavlovic, A 1994, *Standing Accused: The Organisation and Practices of Criminal Defence Lawyers in Britain*, Clarendon Press, Oxford.

McConville, M & Marsh, L 2014, *Criminal judges: legitimacy, courts and state-induced guilty pleas in Britain*, Edward Elgar Publishing, Cheltenham.

McConville, M & Mirsky, C 2005, *Jury trials and plea bargaining: a true history*, Hart Publishing, Oxford.

McConville, M, Sanders, A & Leng, R 1991, *The case for the prosecution: police suspects and the construction of criminality*, Routledge, London.

McCoy, C 1990, *Politics and plea bargaining: victims' rights in California*, University of Pennsylvania Press, Philadelphia.

McDonald, W 1985, *Plea bargaining: critical issues and common practices*, United States Department of Justice, National Institute of Justice, Washington.

McEwan, J 2011, 'From adversarialism to managerialism: criminal justice in transition', *Legal Studies*, vol. 31, no. 4, pp. 519–546.

Miller, S 2005, *Victims as offenders: the paradox of women's violence in relationships*, Rutgers University Press, United States.

Ministry of Justice 2013, 'An overview of sexual offending in England and Wales – Statistics bulletin', *Ministry of Justice, Home Office & the Office for National Statistics*. Available from: https://www.gov.uk/government/statistics/an-overview-of-sexual-offending-in-england-and-wales [accessed 24 January 2018].

Morris, N 1977, 'Sentencing and parole', *Australian Law Journal*, vol. 51, no. 3, pp. 523–31.

Moxon, D 1988, *Sentencing practice in the Crown Courts* (Home Office Research Study #103), Her Majesty's Stationary Office, London.

Mulroy, S 2017, 'The bright line's dark side: pre-charge attachment of the sixth amendment right to counsel', *Washington Law Review*, vol. 92, no. 1, pp. 214–252.

Newman, D 2013, *Legal aid Lawyers and the quest for justice*, Bloomsbury Publishing, London.

New South Wales Legislative Council 2013, *The partial defence of provocation*, Select Committee on the Partial Defence of Provocation, Standing Order 231, 23 April 2013, Legislative Council, NSW.

New Zealand Law Reform Commission 2005, *Criminal pre-trial processes: justice through efficiency* (Report #89 2005).

Noone, M A 2017, 'Challenges facing the Australian legal aid system', in A Flynn & J Hodgson (eds), *Legal aid and access to justice: comparative perspectives of unmet legal need*, p. 23e42, Hart Publishing, Oxford.

Noone, M A & Tomsen, S 2006, *Lawyers in conflict: Australian lawyers and legal aid*, Federation Press, New South Wales.

Office of Public Prosecutions Victoria [OPP] 2016, *Our vision and values*. Available from: http://www.opp.vic.gov.au/About-Us/Our-Vision-and-Values [accessed 18 January 2016].

Olding, R & Saulwick, J 2015, 'Domestic violence register could lead to increased not guilty pleas, privacy experts warn', *Sydney Morning Herald*, 6 March. Available from: http://www.smh.com.au/nsw/nsw-state-election-2015/domestic-violence-register-could-lead-to-increased-not-guilty-pleas-privacy-experts-warn-20150306-13wzwp.html [accessed 18 January 2016].

Ombudsman Victoria 2011, *Whistleblowers Protection Act 2001: investigation into the failure of agencies to manage registered sex offenders*, Ombudsman Victoria. Available from: https://www.ombudsman.vic.gov.au/getattachment/8ba099dd-0b7d-46f1-8bc4-5932db9c2c01//publications/parliamentary-reports/whistleblowers-protection-act-2001-investigation-i.aspx [accessed 18 January 2016].

Payne, J 2007, *Criminal trial delays in Australia: trial listing outcomes* (Research and Public Policy Series #74), Australian Institute of Criminology, Canberra.

Pedley, M 1998, 'The problems with court rules and procedures in criminal cases: a prosecution perspective', paper presented at Reform of Court Rules and Procedures in Criminal Cases Conference, Australian Institute of Judicial Administration,

Brisbane, Australia, 3–4 July. Australian Institute of Judicial Administration, Victoria.

Pegasus Taskforce 1992, *Reducing delays in criminal cases*, Pegasus Taskforce Report, September 1992, Victoria.

Pizzi, W 1999, *Trials without truth: why our system of criminal trials has become an expensive failure and what we need to do to rebuild it*, New York University Press, New York.

Police Association of NSW 2013, *Encouraging appropriate early guilty pleas: models for discussion*, Parliamentary Submission, Consultation Paper 15, New South Wales Law Reform Commission, Sydney. Available from: http://www.lawreform.justice.nsw.gov.au/Pages/lrc/lrc_completed_projects/lrc_encouragingearlyappropriate-guiltypleas/lrc_encouragingearlyappropriateguiltypleas.aspx [accessed 8 February 2018].

Powell, A, Henry, N, Flynn, A & Henderson, E 2013, 'The meanings of sex and consent: the persistence of rape myths in Victorian rape law', *Griffith Law Review*, vol. 22, no. 2, pp. 456–80.

Powell, M, Day, A, Benson, M, Vess, J & Graffam, J 2014, 'Police officers' perceptions of interviewing offenders on sex offender registries', *International Journal of Police Science & Management*, vol. 16, no. 4, pp. 255–66.

PricewaterhouseCoopers 2008, *Review of fees paid by Victoria Legal Aid barristers in criminal cases*, Victorian Bar. Available from: https://webcache.googleusercontent.com/search?q=cache:DpiEwVW29YQJ:https://www.aph.gov.au/DocumentStore.ashx%3Fid%3Dd7260048-61e2-4d53-88e4-15f7e7a53af3+&cd=1&hl=en&ct=clnk&gl=au&client=safari [accessed 18 January 2016].

Productivity Commission 2014, *Access to justice arrangements inquiry*, Report No. 72, 5 September, Productivity Commission, Canberra.

Queensland Government 2016, *Media statements*, The Queensland Cabinet and Ministerial Directory. Available from: http://statements.qld.gov.au/Statement/2016/4/19/barbaro-amendments-herald-important-changes-for-legal-profession [accessed 18 January 2016].

Rahman, S, Poynton, S & Weatherburn, D 2017, *The NSW rolling list court evaluation: Final report*, Contemporary Issues in Crime and Justice, no. 208. Available from: http://www.bocsar.nsw.gov.au/Documents/CJB/2018-Report-The-NSW-Rolling-List-Court-Evaluation-Fianl-Report.pdf [accessed 26 January 2018].

Rakoff, J S 2014, 'Why innocent people plead guilty', *NY Books*, November 20 issue. Available from: http://www.nybooks.com/articles/2014/11/20/why-innocent-people-plead-guilty [accessed 18 January 2016].

Rapke J 2010, 'Looking to the future', in *The pursuit of justice: 25 years of the DPP in Victoria*, pp. 40–45. Available from: http://www.opp.vic.gov.au/Home/Resources/The-Pursuit-of-Justice-25-years-of-the-DPP-in-Vict [accessed 18 January 2016].

Rebuli, A 2015, 'The cost of cutting legal assistance funding', *Access to Justice Bulletin: Law Society of South Australia*, vol. 37, no. 9, pp. 20–1.

Redlich, A D, Wilford, M M & Bushway S 2017, 'Understanding guilty pleas through the lens of social science', *Psychology, Public Policy and Law*, vol. 23, pp. 458–471.

Redlich, A D, Bushway, S D & Norris, R J 2016, 'Plea decision-making by attorneys and judges', *Journal of Experimental Criminology*, vol. 12, no. 4, pp. 537–561.

Remington, F J 1993, 'The decision to charge, the decision to convict', in L E Ohlin & F J Remington (eds), *Discretion in criminal justice: the tension between individualization and uniformity*, pp. 73–135, State University of New York Press, Albany.

Royal Commission into Institutional Responses to Child Sexual Abuse 2017a, *Criminal Justice Report: Executive Summary and Parts 1–II*, Royal Commission, Sydney.

Royal Commission into Institutional Responses to Child Sexual Abuse 2017b, *Criminal Justice Parts III–VI*, Royal Commission, Sydney.

Rubenstein, M & White, T 1980, 'Alaska's ban on plea bargaining', in W McDonald & J Cramer (eds), *Plea bargaining*, pp. 25–57, Lexington Books, Massachusetts.

Russell, J & Hollander, N 2017, 'The disappearing trial – the global spread of incentives to encourage suspects to waive their right to a trial and plead guilty', *New Journal of European Criminal Law*, vol. 8, no. 3, pp. 309–322.

Sebba, L 1996, *Third parties: victims and the criminal justice system*, Ohio State University Press, Ohio.

Seifman, R 1982, 'Plea bargaining in Victoria: getting the judges' views', *Criminal Law Journal*, vol. 6, no. 2, pp. 69–88.

Shaw, D 2014, 'Victims' Right of Review Scheme sees 146 charged', *BBC News*, 19 July. Available from: http://www.bbc.com/news/uk-28377445 [accessed 18 January 2016].

Sheehy, E, Stubbs, J & Tolmie, J 2014, 'Securing fair outcomes for battered women charged with homicide: analysing defence lawyering in *R v Falls*', *Melbourne University Law Review*, vol. 38, pp. 666–708.

Simon, J 2007, *Governing through crime: how the war on crime transformed American democracy and created a culture of fear*, Oxford University Press, New York.

Smith, T & Cape, E 2017, 'The rise and decline of criminal legal aid in England and Wales', in A Flynn & J Hodgson (eds), *Access to justice & legal aid: comparative perspectives on unmet legal needs*, pp. 63–86, Hart Publishing, Oxford.

Solomon, P 1983, *Criminal justice policy: from research to reform*, Butterworths, Toronto.

Solonec, T 2015, '"Tough on crime": discrimination by another name – the legacy of mandatory sentencing in Western Australia', *Indigenous Law Bulletin*, vol. 8, no. 18, pp. 7–11.

Spears, D, Poletti, P & MacKinnell, I 1994, *Sentencing indication hearings pilot scheme*, Judicial Commission New South Wales.

Spencer, P 2017, 'A View from the Bench: A Judicial Perspective on Legal Representation, Court Excellence and Therapeutic Jurisprudence', in A Flynn &

J Hodgson (eds), *Access to justice & legal aid: comparative perspectives on unmet legal needs*, pp. 87–102, Hart Publishing, Oxford.

Spivakovsky, C 2014, 'Making risk and dangerousness intelligible in intellectual disability', *Griffith Law Review*, vol. 23, no. 3, pp. 389–404.

Standing Committee of Attorneys-General 1999, *Criminal trial procedure report* (Martin Report), Commonwealth Department of Attorney-General, Canberra.

Standing Committee of Attorneys-General 2000, *Deliberate forum on criminal trial reform report*, Commonwealth Department of Attorney General, Canberra.

State of Victoria, Royal Commission into Family Violence [RCFV] 2016, *Final report*, Parliament Paper No. 132 (2014–16).

Stenning, P 2010, 'Prosecutions, politics and the public interest: some recent developments in the United Kingdom, Canada and elsewhere', *Criminal Law Quarterly*, vol. 55, no. 4, pp. 449–78.

Stubbs, J & Tolmie, J 2008, 'Battered women charged with homicide: advancing the interests of Indigenous women', *Australian and New Zealand Journal of Criminology*, vol. 41, pp. 138–61.

Sulan, J R 2000, 'Defence co-operation in the trial process', paper presented at Australian Institute of Judicial Administration: Criminal Trial Reform Conference, Melbourne, Australia, 24–25 March 2000.

Supreme Court of Victoria 2015, *2013–2014 annual report*. Available from: http://assets.justice.vic.gov.au//supreme/resources/bb6d5ba7-99af-48df-9b23-8cfea8af9c8a/scv_2013-14annualreport.pdf [accessed 18 January 2016].

Tague, P W 2008, 'Guilty pleas or trials: which does the barrister prefer?', *Melbourne University Law Review*, vol. 32, no. 1, pp. 242–74.

Ulbrick, M, Flynn, A & Tyson, D 2016, 'The abolition of defensive homicide: a step towards populist punitivism at the expense of mentally impaired offenders', *Melbourne University Law Review*, vol. 40, no. 1, pp. 324–70.

United Kingdom Office of the Attorney-General 2007, *Fraud review: final report*, Office of the Attorney-General's Department, London.

Utz, P 1978, *Settling the facts*, Lexington Books, Canada.

Verdun-Jones, S 2011, 'Plea bargaining', in J Roberts & M Grossman (eds), *Criminal justice in Canada*, (4th edn), pp. 168–84, Nelson Education, Canada.

Verdun-Jones, S & Hatch, A 1987, 'An overview of plea bargaining in Canada: cautionary notes for sentencing reform', in H Dumont (ed.), *Sentencing*, pp. 71–107, Les Editions Yvon Blair, Canada.

Vess, J, Langskaill, B, Day, A, Powell, M & Graffam, J 2011, 'A comparative analysis of Australian sex offender legislation for sex offender registries', *Australian and New Zealand Journal of Criminology*, vol. 44, no. 3, pp. 404–24.

Victoria Legal Aid [VLA] 2014a, *Nineteenth statutory annual report 2013–14*, VLA, Melbourne. Available from: https://www.legalaid.vic.gov.au/sites/www.legalaid.vic.gov.au/files/vla-annual-report-2014.pdf [accessed 18 January 2016].

Victoria Legal Aid [VLA] 2014b, *Delivering high quality criminal trials: consultation and options paper*, VLA, Melbourne.

Victoria Legal Aid [VLA] 2015, *Twentieth statutory annual report 2014–15*, VLA, Melbourne. Available from: https://www.legalaid.vic.gov.au/sites/www.legalaid.vic.gov.au/files/vla-annual-report-2014-2015.pdf [accessed 18 January 2016].

Victoria Legal Aid [VLA] 2016a, *Means test changes to financial eligibility thresholds*, VLA. Available from: http://www.legalaid.vic.gov.au/information-for-lawyers/how-we-are-improving-our-services/means-test-review [accessed 18 January 2017].

Victoria Legal Aid [VLA] 2016b, *Our vision, purpose and values*. Available from: https://www.legalaid.vic.gov.au/about-us/our-organisation/our-vision-purpose-and-values [accessed 18 January 2016].

Victoria Legal Aid [VLA] 2016c, *Sentencing guidance reference*, Submission to the Victorian Sentencing Advisory Council, 12 February, VLA.

Victoria Legal Aid [VLA] 2017, *Annual report 2016–17*, VLA, Melbourne. Available from: https://www.legalaid.vic.gov.au/sites/www.legalaid.vic.gov.au/files/VLA-annual-report-2016-17.pdf [accessed 30 January 2018].

Victorian Aboriginal Legal Service [VALS] 2015, *Annual report 2014–2015*, VALS. Available from: http://vals.org.au/assets/2016/08/AnnualReport14-15_FINAL.pdf [accessed 18 January 2016].

Victorian Department of Justice 2004, *New directions for the Victorian justice system 2004–2014* (27 May 2004).

Victorian Government Solicitor's Office 2014, 'Double or nothing: the rule against duplicity charging in criminal offences', *Victorian Government Solicitor's Office*, 28 April. Available from: http://blog.vgso.vic.gov.au/2014/04/double-or-nothing-rule-against.html?m=1 [accessed 18 January 2016].

Victorian Law Reform Commission [VLRC] 2003, *Defences to homicide options paper*, VLRC, Melbourne.

Victorian Law Reform Commission [VLRC] 2007, *Victorian Law Reform Commission civil justice inquiry: draft recommendations*, VLRC, Victoria.

Victorian Law Reform Commission [VLRC] 2012, *Sex offenders registration: final report*, VLRC, Melbourne. Available from: http://www.lawreform.vic.gov.au/content/sex-offenders-registration-final-report-html-version [accessed 18 January 2016].

Victorian Law Reform Commission [VLRC] 2014, *Review of the Crimes (Mental Impairment and Unfitness to be Tried) Act 1997*, June 2014, Available from: http://www.lawreform.vic.gov.au/sites/default/files/Review_of_the_Crimes_Mental_Impairment_and_Unfitness_to_be_Tried_Act_0.pdf [accessed 8 February 2018].

Victorian Law Reform Commission [VLRC] 2016, *Victims of crime in the criminal trial process: final report*, VLRC, Victoria.

Victorian Ombudsman 2014, *Investigation into deaths and harm in custody*, Victorian Ombudsman.

Victorian Office of Public Prosecutions Victoria [OPP] 2007, *Annual report*. Available from: http://www.opp.vic.gov.au/Resources/Publications/Annual-reports [accessed 28 February 2017].

Victorian Sentencing Advisory Council [SAC] 2006, *Myths and misconceptions: public opinion versus public judgement about sentencing research paper*, SAC. Available from: https://www.sentencingcouncil.vic.gov.au/publications/myths-and-misconceptions-public-opinion-versus-public-judgment-about-sentencing [accessed 18 January 2016].

Victorian Sentencing Advisory Council [SAC] 2007, *Sentence indications and specified sentence discounts: final report*, SAC, Melbourne.

Victorian Sentencing Advisory Council [SAC] 2008, *Criminal justice diversion program in Victoria: a statistical profile*, SAC, Melbourne. Available from: https://www.sentencingcouncil.vic.gov.au/sites/default/files/publication-documents/Criminal%20Justice%20Diversion%20Program%20in%20Victoria%20Statistical%20Profile.pdf [accessed 18 January 2016].

Victorian Sentencing Advisory Council [SAC] 2010, *Sentence indication: a report on the pilot scheme*, SAC. Available from: https://www.sentencingcouncil.vic.gov.au/sites/default/files/publication-documents/Sentence%20Indication%20A%20Report%20on %20the%20Pilot%20Scheme.pdf [accessed 18 January 2016].

Victorian Sentencing Advisory Council [SAC] 2011, *Statutory minimum sentences for gross violence offences – report*, SAC. Available from: https://www.sentencingcouncil.vic.gov.au/publications/statutory-minimum-sentences-for-gross-violence-offences-report [accessed 28 February 2017].

Victorian Sentencing Advisory Council [SAC] 2012, *Baseline sentencing – report*, SAC. Available from: https://www.sentencingcouncil.vic.gov.au/sites/default/files/publicati ion-documents/Baseline%20Sentencing%20Report.pdf [accessed 28 February 2017].

Victorian Sentencing Advisory Council [SAC] 2015, *Guilty pleas in the higher courts: rates, timing, and discounts*, Sentencing Advisory Council, Melbourne.

Victorian Sentencing Advisory Council [SAC] 2016a, *Sentencing Trends 2016*, VSAC, Melbourne. Available from: https://www.sentencingcouncil.vic.gov.au/statistics/sentencing-statistics [accessed 18 January 2016].

Victorian Sentencing Advisory Council [SAC] 2016b, *Community Correction Orders third monitoring report (post-guideline judgment)*, June 2016, VSAC, Melbourne. Available from: https://www.sentencingcouncil.vic.gov.au/sites/default/files/publication-documents/Community%20Correction%20Orders%20Third%20Monitoring%20Report.pdf [accessed 18 January 2016].

Victorian Sentencing Advisory Council [SAC] 2016c, Victoria's Prison Population 2005–2016, November 2016, VSAC, Melbourne. Available from: https://www.sentencingcouncil.vic.gov.au/sites/default/files/publication-documents/Victorias_Prison_Population_2005_to_2016.pdf [accessed 29 December 2017].

Victorian Sentencing Advisory Council [SAC] 2016d, *Cases Sentenced in the Magistrates' Court*, Available from: https://www.sentencingcouncil.vic.gov.au/statistics/sentencing-statistics/people-sentenced-magistrates-court [accessed 20 January 2018].

Victorian Shorter Trials Committee 1985, *Report on criminal trials*, Australian Institute of Judicial Administration Incorporated, Canberra.

Vogel, M 2007, *Coercion to Compromise: Plea Bargaining, the Courts and the Making of Political Authority*, Oxford University Press, Oxford.

Warner, K, Davis, J, Spiranovic, C & Freiberg, A 2016, 'Measuring jurors' views on sentencing: Results from the second Australian jury sentencing study' *Punishment and Society*, vol. 19, no. 2, pp. 180–202.

Warner, K, Davis, J, Walter, M, Bradfield, R & Vermey, R 2011, 'Public judgement on sentencing: final results from the Tasmanian jury sentencing study', *Trends & Issues in Crime and Criminal Justice*, no. 407, Australian Institute of Criminology, Canberra.

Weatherburn, D & Baker, J 2000, *Managing trial court delay: an analysis of trial court processing in the NSW District Criminal Court*, New South Wales Bureau of Crime Statistics and Research, Attorney-General's Department, Sydney.

Weatherburn, D & Lind, B 1995, 'The impact of the New South Wales sentence indication scheme on plea rates and case delay', *UNSW Law Journal*, vol. 18, no. 2, pp. 211–31.

Westling, W 1976, 'Plea bargaining: a forecast for the future', *Sydney Law Review*, vol. 7, no. 3, pp. 424–432.

Winick, B J 1999, 'Redefining the role of the criminal defence lawyer at plea bargaining and sentencing: A therapeutic jurisprudence/preventive law model', *Psychology, Public Policy, and law*, vol. 5, pp. 1034–1083.

Wood, J AO QC 2013, 'Promoting a more efficient use of the criminal justice system', *NSWLRC*, 3–5 October, New South Wales Law Reform Commission.

Woolard, J L, Henning, K & Fountain, E 2016, 'Power, process, and protection: juveniles as defendants in the justice system', *Advances in Child Development and Behaviour*, vol. 51, pp. 171–201.

Wren, E & Bartels, L 2014, '"Guilty, Your Honour": recent legislative developments on the guilty plea discount and an Australian Capital Territory case study on its operation', *Adelaide Law Review*, vol. 35, pp. 361–84.

Wright, R F & Levine, K L 2014, 'The cure for young prosecutors' syndrome', *Arizona Law Review*, vol. 56, pp. 1065–1128.

Yang, K 2013, 'Public accountability of public prosecutions', *Murdoch University Law Review*, vol. 20, no. 1, pp. 28–75.

Notes

1. Section 6(2)(b) of the *Legal Aid Act 1978* (Vic) states that VLA may:

   (b) enter into arrangements from time to time with a body or person with respect to any investigation, study or research that, in the opinion of VLA, is necessary or desirable for the purposes of this Act.

2. Section 7(1)(j) of the *Legal Aid Act 1978* (Vic) states that in performing its duties, VLA must:

   (j) encourage and permit law students to participate, so far as VLA considers it practicable and proper to do so, on a voluntary basis and under professional supervision in the provision of legal aid.

3. The then Victorian DPP, Mr John Champion SC, consented to being named as a participant in this research project. However, his comments have been anonymised throughout this report in line with the treatment of other interviewees.
4. [2014] HCA 2, which effectively barred the prosecution from providing the court with a submission about the bounds of the available range of sentences. See Chaps. 3 and 7 for a discussion of this case.
5. *Barbaro v The Queen; Zirilli v The Queen* [2014] HCA 2.
6. *Sentencing Act 1991* (Vic) so 6AAA.

Index

A. Flynn, A. Freiberg, *Plea Negotiations*, Palgrave Socio-Legal Studies,
https://doi.org/10.1007/978-3-319-92630-8

The manufacturer's authorised representative in the EU is Springer Nature Customer Service Centre GmbH, Europaplatz 3, 69115 Heidelberg, Germany. If you have any concerns regarding our products, please contact ProductSafety@springernature.com

Printed and bound by CPI Group (UK) Ltd, Croydon, CR0 4YY
05/10/2026
02228138-0013